The HILLS OF SIDON

The

HILLS OF SIDON

Journal from South Lebanon
1983—85

Leila Richards, M.D.

ADAMA BOOKS

ADAM1--02--20--1988--12:26:52

Library of Congress Cataloging-in-Publication Data

Richards, Leila.
   The hills of Sidon/Leila Richards.
   p. cm.
   Bibliography: p.
   ISBN 1-557-74015-1   :$17.95
   1. Richards, Leila—Diaries. 2. Physicians—United States—
Biography. 3. Palestinian Arabs—Medical care—Lebanon—Sidon.
4. Lebanon—History—Israeli intervention, 1982—Personal
narratives, American. I. Title
R154.R388A3   1987
362.1'1'0924—dc19
[B]
87-35123
CIP

Printed in Israel
Design by Irwin Rosenhouse

Adama Books, 306 West 38 Street, New York, New York 10018

For my friends in Lebanon

بدك تكون أكبر من المصيبة

You need to be greater than the disaster

and for Carel—disgruntled advocate, reluctant ally

Contents

Part Four

Introduction

The account that follows is a description of my experiences as a member of an American medical team that worked in south Lebanon from October 1983 to June 1985. It is based on diaries I kept at the time; in describing certain well-publicized events I have also included information from Lebanese, Israeli and American newspapers.

Most of this book describes our work in setting up and operating a small hospital near the Ein el-Hilweh refugee camp on the outskirts of Sidon. During most of the time I was in Lebanon, Sidon was under Israeli military occupation, and the city was later shelled for a month by a Lebanese militia. I have described these and other political events in some detail, because they had a direct bearing on our everyday lives. I am not attempting to chronicle the complicated history of South Lebanon during the time that I was there, but only to give a sense of how some events affected the communities where we lived and worked.

The people who appear on these pages are colleagues, friends and patients. I have no intention of portraying them as "typical" of any nationality, religion or political group. Since we lived in a Druze house in a Christian neighborhood and worked in a Moslem part of Sidon, we ended up with an unusual assortment of friends. Most of our time, however, was spent among Palestinians in Ein el-Hilweh, and so most of this book is about them.

Some sections are intended as humorous pieces, in an attempt to convey how ridiculous and absurd our circumstances often were. One cannot last long in Lebanon without a sense of humor. Conversations were full of jokes and wry comments, but that did not mean that people made light of the suffering and violence around them; rather they used humor as a way of coping with it, one day at a time. Humor is a small way of helping one live with events over which one has no control, but often it is the only way.

The names of most of the people in this book have been changed. I have not changed the names of those who died, disappeared or left Sidon. The thoughts expressed in these pages are my own; they are not meant to represent those of the International Rescue Committee.

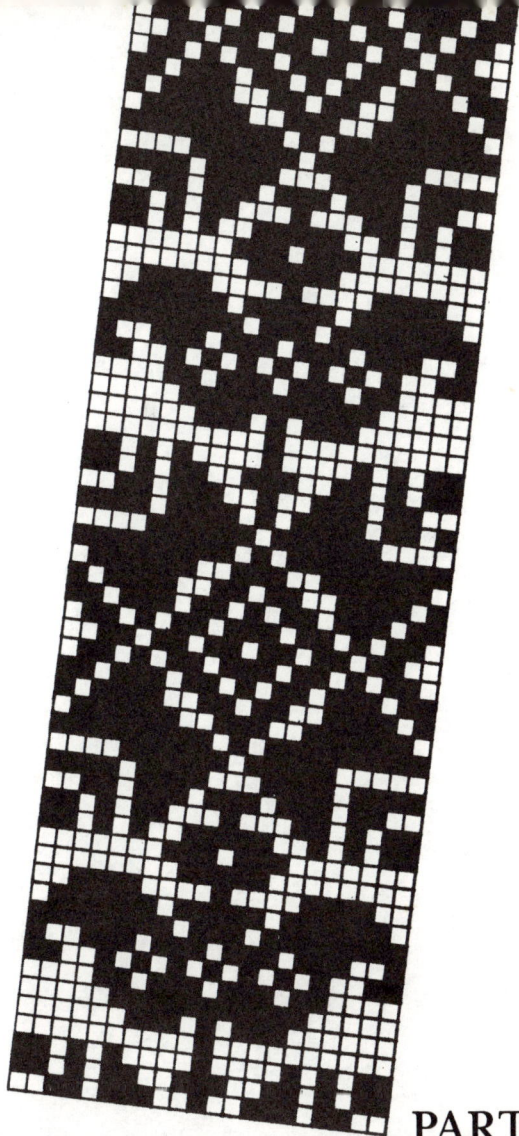

PART ONE:
OCTOBER—DECEMBER 1983

Briefing

I went to Lebanon in the fall of 1983 as part of a five-member medical team, to set up and operate a small hospital on the outskirts of the Ein el-Hilweh Palestinian camp, near the city of Sidon. Our hospital would offer treatment and short-term hospitalization to Palestinians and displaced Lebanese. The International Rescue Committee, the American organization that sent us, was operating the program with funds furnished by the United States State Department.

When we arrived in Sidon, we found that our hospital was only half built, so we spent our first weeks studying Arabic and getting to know representatives of other humanitarian agencies working in South Lebanon. Thousands of Lebanese families had fled to Sidon in the fall of 1983 to escape the fighting between Christian and Druze militias in the nearby Shouf Mountains, and were living in schools and churches all over the city. The US Marines, who had been in Lebanon for over a year as part of a four nation peacekeeping force, had gotten caught up in the country's sectarian battles, and were facing growing hostility from Lebanese militias in West Beirut. Less than a month after we arrived, car bombs demolished the Marines' headquarters and the barracks of the French multinational force in Beirut, killing 241 Marines and 58 French soldiers. But there had been no threats directed at Americans and other foreigners doing relief work in Sidon.

Sidon had been under Israeli occupation for over a year when we arrived. The Israeli occupation of South Lebanon isolated our area from the rest of the country, and caused economic hardship and widespread resentment which fueled growing acts of resistance.

Overture

I used to live in an old Druze villa on a hill above Sidon overlooking terraced groves of orange and olive trees and the sea. There were five of us living there: an administrator, two doctors, and two nurses, all American. Lebanon's civil war had been going on for eight years when we came, and the Israelis had been in South Lebanon for over a year.

The villa was old and drafty, cool in the summer and cold in the winter. There was always a breeze from the sea. The windows leaked when it rained, and some of the shutters blew off their hinges. At night when the winter wind howled the house answered with a strange hum that filled every room, rising and falling with the wind.

There was a telephone in the house that worked for a while. When you dialed the operator, he sometimes answered. At other times when the ringing stopped you found yourself instead in a space filled with voices like your own, all repeating, more or less desperately, *"Allo, Marhaba, Hello!"*

Every Sunday I worked at a desk by the window. The breeze from the sea sent a papery rustle through the date palms, and gnats and mosquitoes floated into the room. I looked over medical reports that I was writing for my patients. They all started the same way: "This patient is suffering from . . . ," "This patient is unable to . . . ," "This patient has lost his . . . "

Complaints had come back about the wording in some of the reports. I was told that I shouldn't say, "This patient was injured in an explosion," because the reader would immediately conclude that the patient was involved in *planning* the explosion. The same was true for patients with bullet injuries of any kind; if a person was shot, it must have been for a good reason. The reader might then take a military interest

in the matter, and an investigation would begin. Intelli
gence agents might come to the patient's house at night to
question him, or he might be taken away to a detention
center. It was better, therefore, to say, "This patient was
injured in an accident."

Sometimes, I was told, it was better not to say *when* the
patient's problem started, either. For example, "This patient
was injured during the Israeli invasion," had an accusatory
ring to it, did it not? It was better to say, "This patient was
injured two years ago," or even, "This patient was injured in
June 1982."

A person's appearance could make a difference, too. Two
photographs of the patient were submitted along with the
medical reports. Most people brought in decent pictures
from the local photography studio, but one photo, shot at
the same studio, showed a teenage boy with an empty eye
socket who stared straight at the camera with his good eye
and smoked a cigarette with studied nonchalance. "This
patient is in need of an artificial eye, as you can see," the the
report began. Surely we could get a better picture—one that
made him look more deserving—if we asked his mother for
one.

As I worked at my desk, from time to time I looked out
the window at one of the neighbors. He was standing behind a tree, watching our house through binoculars, as he
did every Sunday. He knew that I could see him clearly from
where I sat, but he always chose the same spot. He looked
embarrassed, standing out there among the foliage, but
when we met on social occasions, the embarrassment was
gone. He smiled at us and said nothing.

One night a group of soldiers drove up to the house to
take a look. We could hear their voices as they walked
around outside. We waited for a knock on the door. Were
they going to steal our new van? They walked back and
forth outside the window. Perhaps they were going to set off
a bomb; there had been a lot of bombings downtown lately.
They went behind the house. A few yards from where they
stood was a network of caves and foxholes that the PLO had
once used, but one couldn't find them in the middle of the

night. After a while the soldiers left. We never found out what they wanted.

When I left that old villa for the last time, it was badly battered, and I did not think that anyone would ever live in it again. But a few months later I had a chance to see it from a distance, and it seemed as if the owners had decided to repair the damage after all.

To Beirut and Sidon

"*Lebanon?*" The receptionist paused for a moment and glanced over her shoulder to make sure the door behind her was closed. "Why would you want to go *there?*"

It was late September 1983, and I had just arrived in Washington, D.C., for a briefing with the International Rescue Committee, the agency that was sending us to work in Lebanon the very next day. Like most people I had talked to, the receptionist was baffled, and a little upset, to hear that I would think of going to such a place. Hadn't we done enough over there already? We had sent the Marines to Beirut to help the Lebanese, but things had not gotten any better, and now the Marines were being shot at like everybody else. Why had we gotten mixed up in it anyway?

Since the start of Lebanon's civil war in 1975, an estimated 100,000 of the country's 3.4 million people had been killed. Another 500,000—those with money or good connections—had emigrated. Control of the country had shifted from the Beirut government to local militias and their political affiliates. Rival groups formed alliances which could shift every few weeks. Battles could erupt at any time for no immediately apparent reason, and might last for days or even weeks. As soon as heavy fighting began the roads would close, and people caught in open areas ran the risk of being kidnapped or hit by sniper fire. Recurrent fighting had left some areas of the country uninhabitable, and tens of thousands of displaced families took shelter with friends or relatives in parts of the country which for the time being seemed safe.

Leader's of Lebanon's factions had appealed to other countries, but were not happy with the help they got, for each country had its own idea of the role it should play in Lebanon's political affairs. By late 1983 there were troops from over a half-dozen nations in Lebanon, a country about the size of Connecticut. Syrian soldiers occupied the northern part of the country; Lebanon's Christian leaders had asked Syria to intervene in the civil war in 1976, and its troops had been there ever since. The Israeli Defense Force occupied southern Lebanon; Israel had invaded the country in 1978 and 1982. In October 1983 it controlled South Lebanon up to the Awali River, north of Sidon. The UN Peacekeeping Force, composed of American, British, French and Italian troops, had been sent to Lebanon after the massacre at the Sabra and Shatila Palestinian refugee camps in September 1982. They were stationed in West Beirut. UNIFIL (the United Nations Interim Force in Lebanon), another UN peacekeeping force, was sent to South Lebanon at the request of President Jimmy Carter after Israel's 1978 invasion of Lebanon. UNIFIL troops patrolled a wedge of land within Israeli-occupied South Lebanon. The PLO ran its Lebanon operations from the northern Lebanese city of Tripoli after leaving West Beirut in August 1982, while troops from the Iranian Revolutionary Guard, who had come to Lebanon after Israel's 1982 invasion, operated out of the Bekaa valley in eastern Lebanon.

Faced with this oversupply of armed elements, the Lebanese claimed that they could solve their own problems if it were not for "outside interference." But since the Lebanese Cabinet was not able to agree on a program of political reforms, and the Lebanese Army could not contain the local militias, the government was in no position to make anyone leave, and the stalemate continued.

The war in Lebanon seemed endless and pointless, the politics too complicated, and the brutality of the combatants frightening. I had friends active in antiwar and human rights work, but Lebanon was not on their agenda. Some nurses at the emergency room where I worked seemed interested in my plans to work in Lebanon, but they thought I meant Lebanon, Pennsylvania. My parents, conservative Republicans, had no use for Lebanon either. At first my father said nothing about my decision to go there, but after I left he wrote to warn me that the Arab mind was bent on death and martyrdom, and that it was time I came to my senses and returned home. He would have been surprised to learn that my first name, which I inherited from my mother's side of the family, is common among women in Lebanon (it means "night" in Arabic and Hebrew), and had led many people to assume that I came from an Arab family.

My interest in Lebanon began after I heard news reports of the Israeli invasion of the country in June of 1982—a move which culminated in the six-week siege of West Beirut, the departure of the PLO from Beirut, and the Sabra and Shatila massacres. I was appalled by eyewitness accounts of the destruction, and by the apparent lack of concern on the part of Israeli and American government spokesmen for the large number of civilian casualties—many of them victims of American-made weapons, including cluster and phosphorous bombs.

A few months later I learned that the International Rescue Committee was planning a medical program in Lebanon. I had worked with the IRC once before, when I took a leave from my internal medicine residency to join an American medical team at Khao-i-Dang, a large Cambodian refugee camp in eastern Thailand. The IRC had been operating relief and resettlement services for refugees since 1933, when it was formed to help political opponents of the Nazi regime escape from Europe. It carried on its programs with a modest budget and without fanfare; its approach was always practical, geared to the political realities of the countries it worked in and to the needs of the refugee population it served.

IRC planned to build and operate a clinic and inpatient unit in Sidon, at Ein El-Hilweh, the Palestinian camp hardest hit by the Israeli invasion. The unit would be funded by the United States State Department, and would operate in conjunction with the United Nations Relief and Works Agency for Palestine Refugees in the Middle East (UNRWA).

UNRWA provides basic health care, education and welfare services to Palestinian refugees in Jordan, the Israeli-occupied West Bank and Gaza strip, Lebanon and Syria. About one-third of UNRWA's budget comes from the United States.

I told IRC that I definitely wanted to go. But before funding for the project came through so that construction on the hospital could begin, another six months went by, and we didn't leave for Lebanon until September 1983.

"So you're going to Lebanon," said the bank manager who was helping me get travellers cheques. "Well, I've got a question for the people over there: why are you killing each other? You used to be so good at making money!"

Businessmen and tourists who travelled to Beirut during the 1960s and early 70s remembered its nightclubs and beachfront hotels, its boutiques and old *souks*. Lebanon was the banking and commercial center of the Middle East and its artistic and cultural capital, a place where artists and intellectuals from Arab and western countries lived and worked together and spoke freely without fear of government censorship.

But the wealth on display in Beirut was enjoyed by very few, and the tolerance seen on college campuses was deceptive. Thousands of Lebanese living in shanty towns around Beirut or in rural areas of the south got little in the way of government services. Their loyalties extended mainly to the heads of a few powerful families and to religious leaders who, through a series of agreements and compromises among themselves, kept the government functioning. Many of Lebanon's seventeen officially-recognized religious sects had come to the region to escape from religious persecution elsewhere. Some lived in close-knit communities; others settled in towns and villages inhabited by members of other sects. But generations of quiet coexistence could not erase memories of past battles and massacres in the minds of many, and the trust that had grown up between members of different sects was not strong enough to withstand a prolonged assault.

Complicating matters was the presence in Lebanon of some 400,000 Palestinians. In 1982 they made up about twelve percent of the country's population, but only a few of them had Lebanese citizenship. This sizeable Palestinian minority upset the balance between Lebanon's Christian and Moslem populations. The entry of the Palestine Liberation Organization into Lebanon's civil war may have been inevitable, but it widened the scope of the conflict and caused many Lebanese to blame the Palestinians for their troubles.

The PLO had made Lebanon its headquarters after it was expelled from Jordan in 1970. In addition to its political and military activities, the PLO operated a network of economic, medical and social welfare programs, including factories, cooperatives, hospitals and clinics, kindergartens and day camps. The jobs and subsidies provided by the PLO had improved the standard of living and had raised the political expectations of Lebanon's Palestinians, particularly those still in refugee camps around large towns and cities. But the guerilla raids and rocket attacks on Israel which the PLO launched from South Lebanon during the 1970s had led to retaliatory bombing raids which drove thousands of Lebanese and Palestinians from their homes. Now Israel, which had invaded Lebanon in 1978 and again in 1982 to try to crush the PLO, was unwilling to leave South Lebanon without assurances from the Lebanese government that the PLO's military operations would cease.

In IRC's Washington office I met Kay, a physician from La Junta, Colorado, who was also going to Lebanon. Kay too had worked with IRC in Khao-i-Dang, though not at the time I was there; but she had never been to the Middle East before. Neither of us knew what to expect, but Kay had not had time to worry: having been wholly absorbed by her board examinations in pediatrics and anesthesiology, she had left the packing to her mother and started her travels without knowing what was packed in her suitcase.

During our briefing we met a member of the IRC staff recently returned from a trip to Lebanon. He said that the area where we would be working looked like a bombed-out section of the south Bronx. As we went through photographs taken during his trip, I felt that he was studying our reactions. The hospital was not quite ready, he said, due to unavoidable delays; the road to Beirut was often closed because of nearby fighting, the local cement factory had been bombed, and the landlord of our building had just been kidnapped. Fortunately, David and Sylvia, the administrator and nurse on our team, were there on the scene. Sidon was quiet, they reported, but if they sat on their balcony in the evening they could see a fireworks display over the Shouf Mountains, where battles were being fought between Christians and Druze. IRC's other projects in Lebanon—a planned shock-trauma unit at the American University Hospital (a donation from an American company), a children's playground on the outskirts of Beirut, and the supplying of a bulldozer-backhoe for a reconstruction project—were coming along as well as could be expected.

Kay and I walked out of IRC's office, carrying a duffel bag full of blood-pressure cuffs and endotracheal tubes (plastic tubes inserted in the airway of an unconscious person to help administer oxygen). I was wondering how I should use my last free hours in New York the following day: if I planned my time carefully, I thought I might still be able to buy the bulletproof vest that I had seen in a Soho boutique. But the day was spent instead in long taxi rides, hasty meetings, and missed appointments. When it was over I was glad that there was no time left to brood about protective clothing.

The Beirut airport was closed when we left New York in late September, so Kay and I flew to Cyprus and took a boat to Beirut from there. Lebanese families often went to Cyprus when fighting started in Beirut and returned during a cease-fire. However, there were few people on the boat that day—just a couple of Lebanese families and an American television news team.

"How often do you think these families make the trip?" I asked the newsman, who had worked in Lebanon before.

"As often as they can afford to," he said.

We arrived in Beirut as the sun was setting. The skyline looked deceptively intact from the boat, but heading for West Beirut in a taxi, we crossed the "Green Line," the devastated no-man's land between West Beirut, the city's commercial center which was now predominantly Moslem, and Christian East Beirut. Roads were closed off with rows of tires, sandbags and barbed wire, and shells of buildings stood empty and overgrown with weeds and vines. There was an eerie quiet everywhere as darkness fell. Our driver was very nervous; he didn't know his way around West Beirut, and left in a hurry after dropping us off. We stayed at the Mayflower Hotel, which in those days housed mostly journalists and visiting officials from relief organizations. As we registered by the light of a gas lantern—electricity had to be rationed in West Beirut—I could see that there were still plenty of empty rooms.

The next day Kay and I walked over to the American University Hospital to visit two doctors I knew. We passed burnt-out cars parked on the corners, but there was no sign of recent fighting. A cease-fire had been in effect for about a week. Jeeps patrolled the street carrying soldiers from the UN Multinational Peacekeeping Force (including the U.S. Marines), which guarded the American University of Beirut, the embassies, and the Palestinian camps in West Beirut. Stores were open, selling not only basic commodities, but chocolates and pastries, cut flowers, crystal, china and antiques. A sporting goods store sold T-shirts that read "Press: Don't Shoot" in three languages, or "I Survived Operation Peace in Galilee" (Israel's name for its 1982 invasion of the country).

The hospital was next to the campus of the American University. Both were founded by Presbyterian missionaries over 100 years ago. The university was accredited in the United States, and many Lebanese graduates of the medical school had gone to the U.S. for further medical training. The hospital was the finest medical center in Lebanon, and one of the best in the Middle East. Though many of the staff doctors had left the country since the start of the civil war, its services continued uninterrupted during all the battles fought in the neighborhood.

The doctors I knew were Lebanese cardiologists I had worked with in New York. They were very busy: there were thirty cardiac catheterizations scheduled every week, and ten patients a week had open-heart surgery, such as heart valve replacement and bypass surgery. One of the cardiologists invited Kay and me to the medical grand rounds and cardiology rounds that were held every week at the hospital. I wondered how the war had affected Lebanese doctors and their patients. Were there serious shortages of drugs? Were there enough hospital beds for wounded patients? How did displaced Lebanese families get medical care? But he didn't seem interested in the work other hospitals were doing. When I told him that I wanted to visit Berbir Hospital, a hospital on the Green Line which handled a large number of casualties even though it had been almost destroyed many times, he said, "It wouldn't interest you; that hospital is third-rate."

As we got up to leave, the other cardiologist said, "Never discuss politics with anyone. We don't bring it up even with our friends."

A few hours later David and Sylvia picked us up at the Mayflower and drove us down to Sidon. David and Sylvia had met in a refugee camp in Somalia, and had been together ever since. They had arrived in Lebanon a few weeks before and found us a place to live. Our landlord had just been released by his kidnappers, and we were invited to his place for coffee and whiskey.

We arrived at our house to see the sun setting over the Mediterranean. A two-story villa of white stucco, set back from the road in a grove of pine trees, the house had big old rooms with heavy carved furniture shabby from neglect. There were five bedrooms, a large kitchen, and hallways upstairs and downstairs which led to terraces overlooking the sea. Shelled during a Syrian attack on Sidon in 1976, the house had been empty ever since. Some of the upstairs walls were still pitted with shrapnel, but most of the damage had been repaired.

The ceiling in my room was twelve feet high, and the windows looked out on date palms and a grove of olive trees next door. Sylvia and David had put a vase of roses by the bed. We had hot water and plenty of blankets, and the electricity worked most of the time. It seemed just fine to me.

"So! First you bomb us, and now you want to help us!"
The arrival of an American medical team in Sidon was
greeted with skepticism in some quarters. Just two weeks
earlier, American warships anchored off the coast had
shelled a Druze-held area north of Sidon at the request of
the Lebanese Army, and the battleship *New Jersey* had been
sent to join them. The United States was trying to play the
role of neutral peacekeeper in Beirut, while the same time
backing Israel's military occupation of South Lebanon. Still,
there was a grudging affection for America; it was the home
of Clint Eastwood, John Travolta and the Marlboro Man,
and the place where many longed to study or work.

I had planned to work in Lebanon for about six months,
but after the first few weeks I stopped thinking about when
I would leave. I saw that a commitment to stay and help was
just as important as the medical skills I could offer. During
the ensuing months, bombings and kidnappings would vir-
tually empty West Beirut of foreigners, and demonstrate
how vulnerable we were, if anyone wanted to hunt us down.
Yet to our Lebanese and Palestinian colleagues in Sidon we
were a strong and solid presence, a sort of humanitarian
peacekeeping force. Cash and material aid could tide them
over for a time, but the presence of foreign relief workers
was a sign that the outside world had not abandoned them.
Building a sense of trust and keeping alive a hope for better
days were crucial in helping people start over. I stayed on
because I realized how difficult all that would be.

Sidon

Sidon, Lebanon's third largest city, lies thirty-five miles
south of Beirut. About 70 percent of its 200,000 inhabitants
are Sunni Moslems (this includes about 55,000 Palestinians
who live in and around the city). Of the remainder, about 20
percent are Shiite Moslems and 10 percent are Christians.

The Jewish historian Josephus, who lived during the first
century A.D., traces the city's origins to Sidon, the oldest

son of Canaan, and the book of Genesis speaks of Sidon as the northern border of the land of Canaan. In Greek my-thology Europa, daughter of the King of Sidon, so capti-vated Zeus with her beauty that he came to earth in the form of a white bull with golden horns and carried her away to the island of Crete.

Sidon enjoyed palmy days as a Phoenician port renowned for its glassware and its purple dye, but during subsequent waves of conquest it was destroyed and rebuilt many times. The Crusaders held the city for a time in the twelfth and thirteenth centuries, and the castle they left behind at the entrance to the harbor is Sidon's most famous landmark. In the seventeenth century, Sidon's harbor was partially filled in to keep out the Turkish fleet and since that time Beirut has taken over most of Sidon's port traffic.

Lebanon was part of the Ottoman empire for almost 400 years. After World War I the empire was divided up, and Lebanon and Syria were ruled by the French until 1943, when Lebanon gained its independence.

As seen from the hills above, modern Sidon is a strip of white office and apartment buildings stretched out along the coastline, surrounded by a green belt of citrus groves. The old part of the city, which lies next to the port, is hard to see until one plunges into Sidon's market street. The Old City houses the *souk*, a covered maze of small shops wedged between apartments, mosques, churches and schools.

Sidon was heavily damaged by Israeli shelling and bomb-ing in June 1982, and part of the downtown area was still in ruins when we arrived. The impetus and the funds for re-building the city came from a single individual: Rafik Hariri, a wealthy industrialist and philanthropist from Si-don who had become a citizen of Saudi Arabia, where he had made his fortune. Hariri, who also took an active role as a mediator in Lebanon's political disputes, had invested in large-scale cleanup and reconstruction projects in Sidon and Beirut and had financed the construction of a dazzling new university and medical center outside Sidon. But his dreams of rebuilding Lebanon were often hampered by local militias, who threatened his staff and stole their con-struction equipment.

Most of the villas along Sidon's major roads had been sprayed by machine gun and rocket fire, and the top floors of some of the apartment buildings were bombed out and sagging. But the habitable floors were occupied by the owners or by squatters—displaced families from other parts of the country. There were several generations of squatters living in Sidon. Some were Moslems who had been driven out of East Beirut when the civil war started in 1976. Others fled from villages in South Lebanon during the Israeli invasion of 1978. The newest group came to escape the war in the Shouf Mountains, which had been going on for a month before we came. Some families lived in corrugated metal shacks near the railroad tracks. Others had taken over a seaside hotel. The Lebanese displaced by the Shouf war were staying in schools and churches around the city.

The Mayor's office and local voluntary agencies had become adept at handling the needs of these newcomers. Schools housing displaced families were visited regularly by Lebanese doctors, whose prescriptions were picked up by a representative from the Mayor's office and filled by pharmacies in Sidon at no cost. According to a Lebanese doctor we spoke to, the medical problems of the newest group of displaced Lebanese were about the same as everyone else's: digestive disorders, upper respiratory infections, and minor skin infections. Fortunately, there had not been any outbreak of infectious diseases. Relief groups in Sidon had donated funds for food, bedding and portable heaters. It seemed that the city was already saturated with displaced families, but thousands more would come in the months that followed.

The stores were all open in Sidon, but there weren't many customers. You could sit at a sidewalk café and order Turkish coffee and a sweet pastry, or go shopping and buy clothes from Paris or shoes from Italy. The local cinema had a new spaghetti war film every week or so. The supermarkets stocked French cheese, Danish butter, Swiss chocolate and German beer. An examination of the labels would show that a lot of these products had reached the end of their shelf life several months ago, but still there was the appearance of plenty, and you could always come up with the makings of a good meal.

Vendors' carts in Sidon's market street were piled high with fresh fruits and vegetables. Sides of beef and lamb hung from hooks in the butcher shops, and sometimes there was a live calf tied up outside. Stores along the street sold T-shirts, toys, tapes and videos, usually for less than in the U.S. Some products had been brought into the country from Israel. You could sometimes glimpse boxes and bags with Hebrew writing in the back rooms of the stores, but any label that said "Made in Israel" was removed before the item was put out for sale. Nobody who knew that a product was from Israel would buy it; the Lebanese were snobs about the quality of their country's products, and always claimed, chauvinistically, that Israeli goods were inferior. In March of 1983, according to several news accounts, a group of Sidon merchants tried to publish a list of stores selling Israeli merchandise, but the Israelis found out about it and seized the list at the printer's.

On most days you could find Lebanese newspapers for sale in Arabic and French, and American and British magazines came down from Beirut every week or so—*Time, Newsweek, The Economist. Playboy* was for sale in a brown paper wrapper.

The products that caught the eye of the Westerner were, of course, beyond the means of the thousands of jobless Lebanese and Palestinians in Sidon, but thanks to the efforts of religious and humanitarian groups from a number of western and Arab countries the poor people of Sidon at least had access to food, shelter and basic medical care.

Sidon had been under Israeli military occupation for over a year when we arrived. There were signs in Hebrew at ever major intersection. Grim-faced, dusty Israeli soldiers patrolled the streets holding their guns at the ready. Israeli military trucks and armored vehicles drove through the streets day and night. Their gunboats patrolled the port, and their jets and helicopters flew overhead. Other military groups in Sidon played the roles assigned to them by the Israelis. The soldiers who had uniforms but no guns were from the Lebanese Police and were not allowed to do any-

thing of consequence. The men who had guns but no uniforms, whose leaders always traveled with bodyguards, were
from the Israeli-supported National Guard, a collection of
Lebanese and Palestinian informers recruited among the
deserters from the PLO and Lebanese militias during the
first weeks after the Israeli invasion. The Israelis gave them
guns but no pay, so they supported themselves by extorting
money and merchandise from local stores and businesses
and by performing favors for people who bribed them.
They did not meet with much resistance, because most of
the thousands of men they had helped to arrest were still in
prison.

Hussein Akr, who liked to drive around Sidon in a shiny
red 1984 Toyota Celica, was the leader of the National
Guard in Ein el-Hilweh. He was a Lebanese who used to
work for Fateh, the mainstream branch of the PLO. He was
a young man, slightly built, with dark, curly hair and a
beard, who would not have looked out of place in
Greenwich Village. He owned two houses in Sidon and had
acquired several cars. It was said that one of his houses was
built entirely from cement that Israel had donated to UN-
RWA. He and his men took a cut from UNRWA's food and
flour rations for the poor, and Hussein Akr also had UN-
RWA pay him a salary for being a 'school guard.' We were to
have many encounters with Hussein Akr and his men during the first months after our hospital opened, which were
also the last months of his life.

Finally, the soldiers with guns and uniforms who sat at
checkpoints at key intersections in town were members of
the South Lebanon Army of Major Saad Haddad (later succeeded by Major General Antoine Lahad). They were
trained, paid and outfitted by the Israelis, who used them
however only as policemen.

Major Saad Haddad himself was a Greek Catholic from a
village near the Israeli border. While serving in the Lebanese Army in 1976, he was given the job of regaining territory in South Lebanon that had come under the control of
the PLO. The Israelis were impressed by his performance.
In June 1978 Israel invaded and briefly occupied a portion
of South Lebanon in retaliation for a PLO raid in Israel

which had killed 35 people, mostly civilians. This invasion (as described in President Carter's book *Keeping Faith: Memoirs of a President*) left more than 1000 civilians dead and 100,000 homeless. Responding to this excessive use of force, President Carter called for a UN peacekeeping force to police South Lebanon and oversee an Israeli withdrawal, and his initiative resulted in the creation of UNIFIL (the United Nations Interim Force in Lebanon). But the Israelis chose to turn the territory over instead to Major Haddad and his troops, so that the area covered by UNIFIL was much smaller than originally intended. Major Haddad, who claimed his territory as the "Independent Republic of Free Lebanon," frequently clashed with UNIFIL troops, and he had succeeded in blocking all attempts by the regular Lebanese Army to join forces with UNIFIL in the south. When the Israelis invaded Lebanon again in 1982, they brought Major Haddad's troops north to patrol Sidon for the first time.

I was invited to spend some time with Major Haddad's soldiers one day after I had taken pictures of some old buildings along the main streets of the city. After watching me photograph a house across from their checkpoint, a soldier from the South Lebanon Army came up and tapped me on the shoulder. He did not speak any English, but he indicated that I was to follow him across the square and wait for the captain to appear. At the checkpoint, two young soldiers gave me a friendly welcome and asked me to take their pictures, but they were reprimanded by their superior, who was perched on a tank. One of the younger soldiers brought out a lawn chair, and, placing it in the middle of the vacant lot that was theirs, indicated that I was to sit down. Then they checked in by radio with their captain, who said that he would come by to talk to me in a few minutes.

I took out my handbook of colloquial Arabic and went through half the phrases in it with one of the soldiers. "Pleased to meet you. May I introduce myself? What can I do for you? How are your children? Thank you very much for your hospitality. I'm late; I must go. Take me to the American Embassy." The soldier seemed very pleased by my efforts. He corrected my pronunciation, and answered all the questions he could understand. But my cheerfulness and my stock of greetings were both running out by the time the captain finally arrived. He had a lighter complex-ion than the other soldiers, and he spoke French, which meant that he was probably Christian. Most of the lower ranks of Haddad's army were filled by poor Shiite Moslems recruited from the villages of South Lebanon, while the officers were usually Maronite Christians.

After hearing the soldier's account of my activities, the captain asked for the film in my camera. I protested that I was only taking pictures of buildings, and had not taken photographs near the checkpoint. He asked again for my film. I said that I was a doctor who worked in Sidon; I wasn't a spy. I showed him my passport. He studied my passport picture, and wrote my name down in Arabic on a piece of paper. "Go," he said. I didn't look back.

First Days

A few weeks after Kay and I got to Lebanon, Mark, an ICU nurse from New Hampshire, joined us in Sidon. He was the last member of our group to have been recruited. The five of us lived and worked together for the next several months. We had little in common except for our backgrounds in overseas medical work—an experience which tends, unfor-tunately, to highlight one's idiosyncrasies rather than soften them.

David and Sylvia were both children of Presbyterian mis-sionaries who had visited Lebanon in the past, but none of us had ever lived in the Middle East. David came from Decatur, Georgia, and worked as a steamboat captain on the Mississippi before he went to Africa. Sylvia was born in Egypt and had worked as a nurse in refugee camps in the Sudan, Somalia and Thailand. Every night after dinner she and David told us thrilling, gruesome tales of bush and jungle life: encounters with leeches, snakes, witch doctors, and patients of all kinds, including a man, rescued from the jaws of an alligator, who had his testicles sewn back together with a hair from a woman's head.

Most of us were not accustomed to group living, and at first the management of the household was left to chance. Then we tried to take turns cooking dinner, but our system broke down after a couple of weeks; during the day each of us went off to do something different, and dinner was usually forgotten. David and Mark knew how to make only one dish apiece, anyway, and Kay said she couldn't cook unless she had a cookbook with pictures. Each of us tried to contribute something to keep the house in order, and our talents complemented each other to some extent: Sylvia and I did most of the cooking, Kay washed the dishes, and David and Mark took on janitorial and troubleshooting tasks, like chasing rats around the kitchen with brooms and shovels. Finally, we arranged for a widow in Ein el-Hilweh to cook hot meals that we could take home.

The day after Kay and I arrived, David sat us down with catalogues and price lists and asked us what drugs and supplies we would need for the hospital. We ordered hospital beds and surgical lights, instrument tables, footstools, emesis basins, an EKG machine, crutches, stretchers, wheelchairs, thermometers, test tubes, feeding tubes, gauze, tape and suture materials. We decided which lab tests we wanted to have and found out how to get them done. We designed our own hospital forms, and by pooling the books we had brought made a small medical library. To find out which medicines to stock, we visited local clinics and spent mornings sitting with UNRWA doctors to see what kinds of patients came in. We met members of other voluntary agencies in Sidon, and they introduced us to local Lebanese and Palestinian officials.

Soon after our arrival David took us over to meet Abu Ahmad, the man in charge of our hospital's construction and also our landlord. Abu Ahmad was a former amateur boxer; when questioned or challenged in any way, he would throw back his shoulders and adopt a fighting stance. His experience in captivity, which left him with a bad back and a few broken ribs, had done nothing to humble him. He was a stubborn, sleazy fellow, and he and his men worked slowly when they worked at all. In early October the hospital, which was supposed to have been finished by August, was still a windowless concrete shell with wires sticking out of the walls.

A couple of weeks later David developed a high fever with a headache and abdominal pain. When he failed to improve, we ran some lab tests. One of them, a Widal test, came back strongly positive; David had typhoid fever. We could not say how he got it—none of the rest of us came down with it—but David blamed it on the soft ice cream from a stand that he alone frequented. He took chloramphenicol and stayed in bed for several days. When he recovered, he rolled up his sleeves and joined the construction crew at the hospital. Inspired by this gesture, or by the news that David had started legal proceedings against him, our landlord began working a little faster.

On October 23, three weeks after our arrival, two suicide attacks destroyed the U.S. Marine headquarters and the barracks of the French Multinational Force in West Beirut. The explosions killed 241 Marines and 58 French paratroopers. A group called the "Free Islamic Revolutionary Movement" claimed responsibility for the blast. As soon as we heard about the bombings, David called the U.S. Embassy in Beirut and the International Committee of the Red Cross to offer our services as physicians, but there was already a large medical team at the scene. The injured troops were airlifted to U.S. military hospitals in the Mediterranean and Western Europe.

The bombing, and our inability to help, made us sad and discouraged; what could we hope to do in the face of such destruction? But it did not change our views about our own safety. There were representatives from over a dozen international voluntary agencies in Lebanon, and half of them employed Americans. Most agencies were engaged in relief and reconstruction work, and their projects were broadly-based, not designed to benefit only a single faction or group. The agencies had been around for some time, and their members were attuned to the subtleties of local politics. No voluntary organization had received any political threats, and none had been prevented from carrying out its work.

Our staff gained one more American when we persuaded Marcia, a nurse from Seattle, to join us. Marcia had spent her junior year abroad in Beirut and later worked as a teacher in South Lebanon. She returned to the States to go to nursing school, and lived in Seattle for a while, but had come back to Lebanon that summer to work at a hospital funded by a French group in the nearby town of Nabatieh. Marcia spoke French and Arabic, and knew her way around Lebanon very well.

In November, a month after we arrived, Sylvia and Mark started interviewing local applicants for positions in the hospital. We decided that we would open by the end of the year, even if the hospital was not finished by then.

Learning Arabic

We started to study Arabic almost as soon as we got to Lebanon. For a while we took lessons at a junior college in the neighborhood, but each of us tried to pick up more of the language with his or her own method: Kay bought a book called *Arabic Today* (later renamed *Arabic Tomorrow*) and studied it in her room with the door closed. Mark spent hours sitting with the men who gathered in the coffee-houses of the Old City to talk and smoke water pipes together. Sylvia learned most of her new words from the nurses she got to know while she was interviewing applicants for the hospital. David picked up a lot of colorful expressions when he joined the construction crew to speed up work on the hospital.

My first Arabic teacher was a huge, fierce-looking nurse in the UNRWA clinic named Abu Hussam. Though stern and gruff with patients in the clinic, Abu Hussam was very patient with me. Perhaps having seven daughters and only one son had left him with a soft spot. He had not had much formal schooling as a boy, but over the years he had worked very hard on his English, which he learned while working with British soldiers stationed in Palestine. The last thing a British officer had taught him, as the troops were leaving for home, was "T.T.F.N.," which means "ta ta for now."

For an hour or so in the morning I sat at a card table in the waiting room of the UNRWA clinic and had an im-promptu Arabic class with Abu Hussam. He was supposed to care for patients with common eye problems and to take vital signs on others, but he seemed to spend most of his time keeping order among the hundred or so patients who sat on benches waiting to see a doctor. If the talk in the waiting room got too loud, or if people started crowding around the door of a doctor's office, a scowl and a shouted warning from Abu Hussam restored order immediately.

I was not Abu Hussam's only pupil; a very retarded teen-age boy liked to stay with him and draw pictures when he was not selling stale pastries or left-over newspapers outside the clinic. During my lesson I tried to read the headlines in Abu Hussam's newspaper aloud to him, or asked him to go over medical words and parts of the body in Arabic. The retarded boy joined us for this part of the lesson, no doubt pleased to see how much better his Arabic was than mine. Then we studied some grammar, or Abu Hussam might say, "Take dictation!" and I wrote down the words he dictated from a first grade UNRWA schoolbook. The patents who passed our table in the waiting room stopped to watch and teased Abu Hussam about his two pupils.

Late in the morning children arrived from the UNRWA schools wearing blue or brown smocks and carrying card-board bookbags. Little girls came up to me and recited the things they knew how to say in English: "Good morning, Mr. Brown. How are you today? Very well, thank you. . . . " One girl offered me a Chiclet and showed me her English reader. The stories in her book were not very different from what you would find in an American elementary school text. A couple of girls took out their notebooks and showed me the new English words they had learned, and one day one of them copied in my notebook some words she had assem-bled in a little homemade dictionary: funny, knee, people, pocket, family, Mr. Brown. Oh, to have learned Arabic at her age, I thought. She made it all look so easy. I wished I could give her the money to go to Barnard. I was sure that she would do quite well.

One day I noticed that Abu Hussam was sullen and angry. He shouted at patients with almost no provocation. "You must excuse me," he said. "My brother is an officer in the Palestine Army, and I have just heard that he was captured by the Syrians." Then he added, "Write this in Arabic: *Souria, aswa' balad fil aalam.*' ('Syria, the worst country in the world')."

I learned more Arabic as I drank coffee with the doctors and nurses at the UNRWA clinic. In answer to the question, "How is the situation?" the correct answer was *"Zift,"* meaning "very bad." The husbands and older sons of most of the women had been in prison for over a year. They were still rebuilding their homes, and some of their children were going to school in tents. It seemed as if the Israelis would never leave South Lebanon, and then in October 1983, Palestinians began fighting each other in the northern Lebanese city of Tripoli, where a breakaway PLO faction, backed by Syria, battled soldiers loyal to Yasser Arafat for control of the Palestinian camps in the area.

At the UNRWA clinic I met Hanan, a seasoned staff nurse tougher and more outspoken than most men. Her father and her brothers had been killed by the Phalangists during the siege of Tal Zaatar, a Palestinian camp in East Beirut that fell to the Christians early in Lebanon's civil war. She had heard nothing from her husband since the Israeli invasion, and did not know if he was still alive. She lived in a small apartment with her two children, one of whom was chronically ill from kidney disease. She said, "Do you want to learn Arabic? Learn this:

Shu badna namil?	What can we do?
Hadi hiya al hiyat?	This is the life?
Allah yisaidna.	God help us."

As we learned Arabic for our work, some people in town were learning English for theirs. One Sunday we went to a restaurant in the hills south of Sidon for lunch. After the meal, we looked at the art work of the owner's son: framed designs outlined in metallic thread on a black velvet background. The son also asked me to look at a rash behind his knees, and I had pulled out my pad to write a prescription for hydrocortisone cream when the owner handed me another one that he thought was mine. Inside was a handmade Arab-English dictionary, with words of another kind: Jew, plague, leech. I quickly closed it and left it on the table for somebody else to claim.

The Situation

Our neighborhood was dominated by an impressive row of old Druze villas, most of which had been empty for years. Our other neighbors, Maronite Christians of modest means, lived in smaller houses near the Maronite Church. Next door to us was the house of the Kawajis, a collection of five unmarried adults who lived with their mother. Nadim, the oldest, became a good friend of ours. He used to live in Tyre, but had moved in with his mother after his house was leveled in the Israeli invasion. Nadim worked as an *animateur sociale,* a kind of government social planner, in nearby Lebanese villages. He was trying to reintroduce traditional handicrafts to village women as a cultural and income-generating project. He also worked at the local family-planning clinic and as a *secouriste,* a first-aid volunteer. Nadim's three brothers were employed at an aluminum factory in town.

Nadim was respected by his neighbors, but his leftist views were not popular with local Phalangists. When his youngest brother was arrested for failing to put in the required number of hours each week with the local Phalangist militia, Nadim got him released, but told the Phalangists that he and his brothers would still not agree to military service. When soldiers from Saad Haddad's South Lebanon Army came to the neighborhood selling calendars door-to-door, we declined to buy one, and were relieved to learn that the Kawajis did not buy one either.

Next door to the Kawajis lived George, a musician who played with a band at nightclubs in nearby Christian towns. He lived with his parents, as did Jean, an unmarried school-teacher in the next house. Jean's family kept color photographs of President Amin Gemayel and his brother Bashir on their living room table. Jean was a shy and nervous fellow; when he was arrested with Nadim's brother for failing to pursue his military training, he meekly agreed to put in the time as he was told.

The hub of our neighborhood was a one-room shoebox of a store run by a Christian Palestinian woman named Georgette. She was a short, broad woman in her fifties, friendly but tough. There was always a card game going on in front of Georgette's store, and passers-by could pull up a chair and sit for a while to watch. At Georgette's you could buy powdered milk, bottled gas, Chiclets, stale chocolate bars and imported beer by the case.

The local Maronite Church was on the corner about one hundred yards from our house. Sunday morning services were well-attended, and the music was broadcast at top volume from a scratchy loudspeaker. The Maronite priest, Père Helou, lived in the parish house down the street from the Church with a dozen Christian refugees from the mountain war.

Our neighborhood was always a quiet and peaceful place to come home to. The streets were lined with shady trees, and the houses and walkways were surrounded by well-tended flower gardens. An olive grove sloped down the hills between the largest Druze villas, and behind a high stone wall on the other side of the street was a large grove of orange trees belonging to the Jumblatts.

When we walked through the neighborhood in midafternoon on our way to an Arabic class at a local college, the streets were empty, but sometimes we passed boys playing war games in a nearby field. One day we watched as a boy, crouched behind a cardboard box flying a paper Lebanese flag, told his friends to be the Israelis. They shot stick rifles at each other and lobbed imaginary hand grenades back and forth. They were seven or eight years old.

As we returned from our class just before dusk, an important social ritual had already begun. Our neighbors got all
dressed up and in the cool of the evening came out to
promenade along the streets until darkness fell. Groups of
men and women of all ages walked slowly past each other
on opposite sides of the street. Some walked with their eyes
lowered, seemingly absorbed in conversation with their
companions, but from time to time they raised their heads
and looked at the groups across the street. As we passed,
representatives from both sides smiled and murmured their
greetings.

Our neighbors had no objections to the work we had
come to do, but at the same time they expected us to show
some allegiance to the neighborhood. A store owner re-
proached Sylvia when he saw her one day carrying bags of
vegetables that she had bought in Sidon. "You are Christian
and we are Christian," he said. "Our prices are as low as
they are in any other store. You should do all of your shopping with us."

We had some long, leisurely dinners with our neighbors
and with Lebanese friends in town. Our most memorable
meal was certainly a Thanksgiving dinner with all the trim-
mings prepared by our friend Ghassan, a Shiite architect
who had spent several happy years living among the Indians
in Missoula, Montana. Unfortunately, our new friends did
not have many dinners with us. We knew that we could not
match the lavish and elegant meals that we were served, and
it was no secret that most Lebanese do not like American
food. We invited people for tea or coffee instead. The neighbors dropped in just for a chat or to ask Kay or me to make
a house call on one of their sick relatives. Our Druze land-
lady, Mrs. Hamdan, stopped by unpredictably and lingered
over her cup of tea to chatter about her family business and
her sinus condition as her husband, a man of few words,
walked around outside peering through the downstairs windows, no doubt trying to ascertain if we were using any of
the rugs and furniture that had been locked away in the
guest room.

When paying a visit to an Arab friend or colleague in
Lebanon, you always stayed long enough to drink some

Turkish coffee with your host. It would be brought out, thick and steaming, along with a plate of sweets or a platter of perfectly ripe fruit, and as you sipped your coffee, the conversation would eventually turn to a discussion of "The Situation." The Situation was the state of no war-no peace which affected every part of your life and made planning impossible. It was the despair of the ambitious man, and the excuse of the lazy one. It could be invoked to explain why you were two hours late for dinner (the road was closed, your car was stolen), why your business was failing (the pound had fallen, you partner was kidnapped), or why you finally decided to leave the country, but then came back again (the schools reopened, you couldn't find work anywhere else). The conversation might center on the newest obstacle you had encountered that week because of The Situation, and how to overcome it; whether you should have complained to the IDF, for example, when you went outside one morning and found your car riddled with bullets; how to send letters out of the country with the airport closed; or the best way to keep your windows from shattering when a bomb went off. A discussion of The Situation usually did not go beyond a consideration of what lay ahead in the next few weeks: Which group would come out ahead when the latest outbreak of fighting stopped? Would the next round of peace and reconciliation talks really make any difference? After exhausting this sad and limited topic, you would sigh and shrug your shoulders and put yourself in God's hands. *Inshallah*, "if God wills it," was the word that ended every polite conversation, every business transaction. If you asked the produce man when he would be getting more zucchini, he would say, "Tomorrow, *inshallah*." When you told a patient to come back for a followup visit next week, he or she would answer, "*Inshallah*."

It took Westerners a while to get used to this way of thinking. Our neighbor, Nadim, worked with a Finn employed by the ICRC during the early years of the civil war. As Nadim helped unload relief supplies from ships at the docks of Tyre one day, the Finn talked about what they would unload the next day. "Tell the men to come again at eight o'clock tomorrow," he said, and Nadim translated the message to the men in Arabic. *"Inshallah,"* they said. "Not tomorrow *inshallah,"* said the exasperated Finn, "tomorrow for sure!" When Nadim translated this, one man turned to him with surprise and said, "Is this man Christian? Doesn't he believe in God?"

When I came to Lebanon, I thought that *Inshallah* was a little verbal flourish that one used to be polite. But after a few months it became such an important part of my vocabulary that I used it even when I was talking to myself.

Ein el-Hilweh

The Ein el-Hilweh refugee camp lies on a plain at the southern edge of Sidon, surrounded by hills on the south and east. About 40,000 Palestinians live there. (Up in the hills, about ten minutes from Ein el-Hilweh by car, is a smaller Palestinian camp; Mieh Mieh, located near a Christian village with the same name, contains about 1500 people.)

Our hospital was at the northern edge of Ein el-Hilweh, where the camp blended in with the Lebanese neighborhood of Tamir. The hospital was being built on the upper floors of a building which already housed a nursery school run by a Swiss organization called Terre des Hommes, and a physical therapy center operated by the Middle East Council of Churches. Across the street was the Government Hospital, which had been heavily shelled during the Israeli invasion. Nothing was left of its upper floors but torn mattresses and twisted iron beds. A few rooms on the ground floor were still used as offices, and the building also had a simple morgue, which we got to know very well.

According to UNRWA Ein el-Hilweh was almost completely destroyed during two weeks of bombardment by land, sea and air in June 1982. By the end of 1983 much of it had been rebuilt, but it was still a sad sight—an expanse of grey cinderblock buildings with corrugated metal roofs, separated by unpaved streets and rubble-strewn fields. There were few trees left. At the lower edge of the camp, where there had once been an orange grove, children were going to classes in shifts in a tent school. (Later in the year, after the rainy season began, the school moved into some prefabricated buildings donated by an Israeli peace group.) Families with relatives who sent home money from oil-rich Persian Gulf countries could afford to rebuild their houses, but others, especially households headed by women, could not do the same using the cement alloted to them by UNRWA. Almost everyone in the camp was unemployed, and the PLO paychecks smuggled in from northern Lebanon and the Bekaa valley were slow in arriving. (The PLO continued to pay the salaries of employees of its medical, education and social welfare programs, as well as to the wives of imprisoned PLO fighters. It also provided for the families of "martyrs," a category that included both combatants and civilians who were killed in a military action.)

From our hospital window we could look out over the whole camp. The buildings seemed spread out with no discernible pattern, and were not separated from the Lebanese communities nearby. But like all Palestinian camps, Ein el-Hilweh was made up of neighborhoods corresponding to the villages in Palestine where the families came from. Every Palestinian knew the people from his or her own village. Most parents preferred to have their children marry within the family (marriage to one's first cousin was common), or to at least have them marry someone from their own village. This network was so intricate and far-reaching that you could easily locate someone from any part of Ein el-Hilweh by knowing the name of his village, or sometimes just his family name.

Ein el-Hilweh was built on land leased from the Lebanese government and from private owners by UNRWA, the UN agency which provides education, relief and health services to Palestinian refugees in the areas it serves. UNRWA is an anomalous institution: it was created as a temporary agency to help Palestinian refugees who fled from their homes to nearby Arab countries during the fighting that accompanied the creation of the state of Israel in 1948. Now, almost forty years later, it has grown into a quasi-governmental agency for some two million Palestinians living in Jordan, the Israeli-occupied West Bank and Gaza, Lebanon and Syria, and had become the largest single employer in the Middle East. Though UNRWA was serving the children and grandchildren of the original refugees, it was still regarded as a temporary agency, dependent on voluntary contributions from other countries. UNRWA would cease to exist when the Palestinians in its care had found a home. But no home had yet been found for most of them. The government of Israel would not allow them to return. Although hundreds of thousands of Palestinians had found work in other Arab countries, where many had married and settled, Jordan was the only Arab country which had granted them citizenship. Western nations had not accepted them in great numbers, either. Most of the refugees remained in the lands where they had first taken refuge, waiting for the day when they could return to Palestine. This idea was encouraged by other Arab countries, and by the PLO.

The two million Palestinian refugees registered with UN-RWA constitute about half the estimated number of Palestinians worldwide.* UNRWA provided them with basic education to the tenth grade level, primary health care and some vocational training. For the Palestinians still living in refugee camps—some out of economic necessity, some by choice—UNRWA also supplied municipal services, such as basic sanitation and garbage collection.

In October 1983 the few stores in Ein el-Hilweh sold only food and basic commodities. People who wanted to shop in downtown Sidon, about five minutes away by car, could get there by group taxi, Lebanon's chief form of public transportation. A boom in construction and commerce began in the camp in the spring of 1985, after the withdrawal of the Israelis from Sidon, when the PLO returned to Ein el-Hilweh. After a few months, most of the goods and services in Sidon were available in the camp, though on a smaller and simpler scale. There were clothing stores and furniture stores, pharmacies, auto repair shops, and coffee houses along the main streets. There was even a travel agency, no

*The Palestinians who remained in Israeli have been granted Israeli citizenship. They are known as "Israeli Arabs." Today they number about 600,000.

bigger than a one-car garage, where you could buy a plane ticket to Cyprus, Abu Dhabi or New York City.

Three large streets cut through the camp, and served as an informal address when one was giving directions. The Upper Street followed a north-south route close to the hills and ran in front of our hospital. Parallel to it was the Lower Street, which ran into a Lebanese neighborhood housing the local office of the National Guard. The Upper and Lower Streets were connected by the Vegetable Street, where most of the food stores and produce stands were located.

Our patients and staff often invited us to their homes in Ein el-Hilweh to have dinner with the family or to have coffee and sweets with a mother who had recently had a baby. The houses we visited were set back from the street down long narrow alleys. Some of them had enough space for a small garden or grape arbor. Most of the older women in the camp still baked the family's bread in outdoor charcoal ovens. The poorest families lived in damp, dimly-lit houses heated with charcoal stoves and furnished with aluminum lawn chairs and straw mats. Those with more to spend had velveteen sofabeds along the walls, separated by low formica tables and perhaps a video as well. It was the family luxury, and was covered with a lace doily when not in use. The families who could afford even better furniture, like carpets and overstuffed living room sets upholstered in brocade, could also have afforded to rent a flat in Sidon, but did not because somebody in the family preferred to stay in the familiar surroundings of the camp.

Most of the houses had three rooms. The front door opened onto a room for receiving guests, which was also used for eating and sleeping. The second room was another bedroom, and the third was an area for the kitchen and bathroom. Since the rooms were usually small, the chairs and couches were lined up against the four walls. On the walls were framed black and gold religious sayings in calligraphic script, or painted wooden plaques and ornaments made by the men in the family while they were in prison, or perhaps an old retouched photograph of the man of the house, which never really looked like him.

To an outsider, Ein el-Hilweh might look shabby and non-descript, and its residents often complained about the unpaved streets and the uncollected garbage. But it was a place where relationships between people were more important than appearances. Anyone who had ever lived in the camp felt that there was a place for him there, and people grew to know each other so well that even on the most crowded street, the face of an outsider was noticed immediately. In many ways the camp existed as a world apart, with its own cultural and political identity, a world many of its inhabitants never dreamed of leaving.

When you were in Ein el-Hilweh for any length of time, it was easy to forget about the world outside, but reminders of that world sometimes drifted in unexpectedly. One day, one of our employees brought in something that a friend of his had gotten in the mail, and asked me what it was. I laughed: it was a credit card from Filene's, the department store in Boston. There was no direct way to get mail delivered in Ein el-Hilweh; most letters to Palestinians in the camp were sent to them in care of some commercial address, or were delivered by friends coming home from overseas. I could not imagine how Filene's had located this customer halfway around the world. I explained that with this card one could buy anything he wanted, and not have to pay the bill for a month, but it only worked at a store called Filene's.

"You mean it can't be used in Lebanon?" he asked.

"No." I could see that he was disappointed.

UNRWA Clinic

I spent many mornings in the UNRWA clinics in Ein el-Hilweh and Sidon, and sat with different UNRWA doctors as they examined their patients. The doctors welcomed me, and sometimes asked my opinion about a patient we saw together. At times I would ask the doctors for a brief translation of what a patient had said, but I tried not to interrupt their work often, because they had a lot to do. An UNRWA doctor was expected to see at least 100 patients a day, but it was not uncommon to see more than 150. I was content to watch the doctors talk to their patients and to take notes about the incidence of some common symptoms and diseases.

The majority of the doctors and nurses working for UN-RWA were Palestinian, but a few were Lebanese. Most of those I met had gone to one of the Egyptian medical schools, which offered the best training that they had access to. (The American University of Beirut accepted Palestinian students, but the tuition was too high for most of their families.) Others had trained in government-run universities in Syria, Iraq, Pakistan or India. (The PLO arranged scholarships for nursing, medical and dental students in the USSR and eastern European countries, but most of the graduates of these programs worked with the Palestine Red Crescent Society, not UNRWA.) Doctors had to finish an internship before being allowed to return to Lebanon to work. UNRWA doctors were usually fluent in three languages: Arabic, English (all UNRWA communications were in English) and a language that they had learned in secondary school or medical school.

The rooms in the UNRWA clinic were sparsely furnished but spotlessly clean. The doctor worked at a desk in the middle of the room facing his patients, who sat on benches lined up against two of the walls; a third wall was reserved for an examining table with a screen in front of it. On his desk the doctor had a stethescope, a blood pressure cuff, an otoscopc (a light for examining the ear), a thermometer and some wooden tongue blades.

The doctors did not seem to mind examining their patients in front of the ten or twenty other patients waiting on the benches; the presence of an audience gave their work an extra dimension, a theatrical quality which could be used to their advantage. Everyone could hear what the doctor and patient were saying to each other. When the doctor teased his patient or made a joke, the other patients would laugh. At other times the doctor might get into an argument with a patient about something. The audience on the benches took an interest in these arguments; if they thought that the patient was being unreasonable, they would murmur among themselves and cluck with disapproval.

Some of the words used in these exchanges gave the doctor-patient relationship an added warmth and informality. Patients usually addressed doctors by their first names; I was known as Doctora Layla, for example. And doctors often used words like *habibi*, "darling," when they talked to their patients. *Habibi* is sung with a moan and a sigh in every love song on the radio, but a doctor uses it, or similar terms of endearment, to urge a dizzy old lady or a sullen young man to follow his advice this time and take his medicine as directed.

I spent my first morning in the UNRWA clinic with Dr. Rafik, a good-natured, energetic Palestinian doctor in his late thirties who had trained in Pakistan. We saw over 100 patients in the time I spent with him; I kept a record of the diagnoses he made. Each patient came in holding a clinic card which recorded the date, diagnosis and medication given during all previous visits to the clinic. Usually the patient stood in front of the doctor's desk as he described his complaint. Sometimes the doctor sat him down in a chair and examined him briefly or took him behind the screen for a minute, but he did not have time to examine all his patients. The benches along the walls quickly filled up, and once Dr. Rafik emerged from behind the screen to find that a crowd of patients had pushed their way in from the waiting room outside. He shouted, waved his arms and drove them back out of the room.

Since most of the men from Ein el-Hilweh were still in prison at that time, women made up the majority of our patients. The most common complaint among both men and women was abdominal pain; after that came joint pains. Dr. Rafik had had some surgical training, and he examined every patient who complained of abdominal pain. People wandered in from time to time to ask Dr. Rafik about something and then left again. A man with a pistol in his belt and a machine gun in his hand came in for a while. He greeted the doctor and then went over to the window and stood staring out at the camp for several minutes. Everyone knew him; he was a member of the National Guard.

He seemed to be looking for someone. After a while he turned and walked out without a word.

In midmorning a woman brought in little cups of strong Turkish coffee for us to drink. When I said "thank you" in Arabic, the patients smiled and nudged each other. Dr. Rafik did not take the time to drink his coffee, but as he worked he asked me if our hospital was still hiring doctors, and what salary we were paying. The UNRWA doctors knew all about the hospital. They had watched it go up for months, and some of them had filled out job applications before Kay and I arrived. In the weeks that followed we asked for their suggestions as we ordered medical supplies and planned the services we would offer. Their advice was always shrewd and practical.

Late in the morning a group of children stopped by on their way home from school and sat down together on one of the benches. They wore cotton coats of green, brown or blue over their clothes. Half of them came in because of an upper respiratory problem—tonsillitis or a cold. Most of the others had skin infections or healing wounds that the doctor had to check. Just before the clinic closed, the woman who had served us coffee came in with a pail of water and a brush. She flooded the floors and spread the water around with her brush until it dripped down the concrete steps outside to the ground floor.

Dr. Rafik went home for lunch and then went to his other job. Like many UNRWA doctors, he moonlighted at a large hospital in Sidon. Palestinian doctors would work in the emergency room or as the "house doctor," the doctor who took care of the private patients of other doctors on the hospital staff. It was hard work—the kind of work that is done by interns in the U.S.—and the salary was less than UNRWA paid—but it gave UNRWA doctors a chance to perform minor surgery, learn about new drugs and sometimes discuss complicated cases with specialists on the staff. At the UNRWA clinic, on the other hand, there was no time to do more than separate the obviously sick patients from the others, and refer all the sick ones to a hospital in Sidon for further care.

There was no system for screening patients who came to the UNRWA clinic; though UNRWA nurses could check blood pressure or change the dressing on a wound, every patient who wanted to see the doctor got to see him. The doctors spent a great deal of time seeing patients with psychosomatic complaints. They knew these patients well, and did not seem to mind their frequent visits. After listening sympathetically, they would offer some words of reassurance and dispense a placebo of some kind, like a vitamin injection.

As I was later to learn, a visit to the UNRWA clinic every week or two was a popular way to spend a couple of hours, especially among the older women in the camp. When one of them came to talk to the doctor, she would set down her bag (which already held up to a half-dozen different medicines) or jar (which contained some urine she wanted to have tested), and recite her ailments: palpitations, headache, sleeplessness, dizziness, constipation, backache, and so on. The doctor would listen patiently. Then, when it was his turn to speak, like a skeptical customer who had just listened to a sales pitch, he would make his counteroffer. During some of the discussions that ensued I could almost see the patient's ailments hovering in the air as the bargaining went back and forth. At last the patient, who was sure that her problems merited several blood tests and perhaps an X-ray, realized that she would have to content herself with a prescription for a couple of relatively harmless medicines available in the UNRWA pharmacy. Heaving a final, bittersweet sigh, she would pick up her clinic card and go her way.

Given what they had to work with, the UNRWA doctors performed very well, but Kay and I did not like some of the practices we saw; we did not want to give vitamin injections, for example. We also found that antibiotics were misused and overused. They were available over-the-counter, so many patients started treating themselves before they came to the doctor. Local pharmacists recommended various combinations of antibiotics or antibiotics mixed with vitamins. Pressured by their patients, and faced with periodic shortages of some UNRWA drugs, the UNRWA doctors often used antibiotics haphazardly. For example, patients with suspected strep throat, which was endemic among Palestinians in the camp, were rarely treated with an injection of benzetine penicillin, the drug of choice, for fear of a penicillin allergy. Instead, they were often given ampicillin (which was felt to be less likely to cause a penicillin allergy) or other antibiotics which were completely ineffective. As a result, some patients went on to develop rheumatic heart disease. Gastroenteritis (an upset stomach with vomiting or diarrhea) was treated with tetracycline, because some doctors thought it would prevent typhoid fever. Health conditions in the camp were so poor, they argued, that antibiotics were needed to bolster the patients' resistance to disease. In fact, patients with typhoid fever were detected from time to time (the diagnosis can be confirmed by a blood test), but they were isolated cases, and these cases would not have been prevented by a haphazard administration of antibiotics.

Still, the UNRWA doctors were a dedicated and hard working group. Though the health care offered by UNRWA was far from ideal, it was superior to what was available to the Lebanese poor. Many Lebanese children who grew up during the years of the civil war had never been immunized against tetanus or common childhood diseases like polio. The vaccines were available at some local clinics, such as those run by the Lebanese Red Cross, but it was difficult to immunize a population composed of so may displaced families. Sidon was well-supplied with clinics whose doctors (many of whom were displaced themselves) treated poor Lebanese (and Palestinian) patients for a nominal fee, but the hospital coverage provided for Lebanese patients by the Ministry of Health was often skimpy and inadequate.

Our hospital was called the Intermediate Health Care Unit. It had been designed to complement UNRWA's medical services, and since we were located close to Ein el-Hilweh, we expected to see mostly Palestinian patients, but the hospital was open to Lebanese as well. We would also see patients referred from other clinics who needed urgent medical treatment and/or brief hospitalization. Thus our unit was designed to fill a place halfway between a primary care clinic and a full-service hospital. We would have our own laboratory and pharmacy, and an inpatient floor with twenty beds. We could treat patients with emergency problems like asthma attacks, burns and minor trauma, and we could hospitalize others with certain infectious diseases or medical problems such as congestive heart failure and uncontrolled diabetes. Those who needed prolonged hospitalization or consultation by a specialist would be referred to one of the larger hospitals in Sidon.

As we learned about the medical services offered by UN-RWA and the Lebanese clinics, we thought that our hospital would be a useful addition to the services that already existed. But it could never have succeeded in its purpose without the support of the Lebanese and Palestinian doctors and health officials who helped us during our early months.

Driving to UNIFIL

Every two weeks a friend gave me a ride to Tyre, where there was a meeting of representatives from voluntary agencies sponsored by UNIFIL (the United National Interim Force in Lebanon), a 6000-member peacekeeping force composed of soldiers from ten countries. UNIFIL had been established after Israel invaded and briefly occupied southern Lebanon in 1978. It was given the mandate of "confirming the withdrawal of Israeli forces, restoring international peace and security, and assisting the government of Lebanon in ensuring the return of effective authority in the area." Between 1978 and 1982, UNIFIL had prevented the PLO from launching attacks on Israel from the territory under its control. But it had not been able to fulfill its mandate; Israel had never allowed UNIFIL troops to be deployed down to the Israeli border, preferring to keep its proxy militia, the South Lebanon Army, in that region instead. And since June 1982, the area under UNIFIL's control had become, as one soldier ruefully remarked, "a slice of meat in the Israeli sandwich"—a narrow sliver of land sur-rounded by Israeli-held territory.

UNIFIL tried to keep local militias from operating inside its territory, and its troops often interceded in confronta-tions between Israeli soldiers and local villagers. It also sponsored modest relief and reconstruction projects in nearby Lebanese villages, and operated a clinic and field hospital at its base in Nakoura, near Lebanon's border with Israel. UNIFIL's biweekly briefings gave us a chance to hear what other relief organizations were doing, and to talk about problems we had encountered.

The drive down to Tyre could be pleasant; much of the road lay along open stretches close to the sea, near culti-vated fields and banana plantations. But driving in Leba-non was always treacherous. The roads were narrow and covered with potholes so deep that some were marked with half-sunk automobile tires. Cars moved very fast; there were no traffic lights left in Lebanon, and no stop signs except at military checkpoints.

Some cars on the road were much fancier than typical American cars. I was once invited to take a spin in a shiny Mercedes with a bank of headlights in three colors, a syn-thetic-fur dashboard, and a horn that played seven tunes, including "*La Cucaracha*," "Never On Sunday," and "Happy Birthday To You." But more commonly, cars were quite run down. You might see one with no headlights or fenders or windshield, and it might be driven by a child sitting on his father's lap.

In one tourist guide written before the civil war, Lebanese driving was described as "a joke that has been carried a bit too far." I watched Lebanese drivers for months before I realized that when you were on the road, it was safest to drive the way they did. The rules were easy to grasp:

—The person driving the fastest has the right of way.
—If two cars are approaching each other at equal speed, the person who honks his horn first has the right of way.
—Yield to all cars with sirens.
—It is all right to use the sidewalk to pass another car.
—It is all right to pass in an intersection.

—It is all right to pass a car that is passing another car.

—It is all right to drive in either direction around a traffic circle, and to go either way along a one-way street. (As one Lebanese driver put it, "Why waste all that space?")

Using turn signals was regarded as a sign of ineptitude; instead drivers communicated their intentions with their headlights. If a driver was annoyed with the way you were driving, he would blink his lights at you to show that you had better get out of his way.

The idea behind Lebanese driving was always to drive as fast as possible, no matter how short the distance. However, most of the honking and blinking of lights and sudden swerves were just expressive gestures which did not allow drivers to go much faster anyway, since the roads were in such bad condition and the traffic was usually fairly heavy. In fact, the most outlandish driving occurred in heavy traffic, perhaps because it made people feel trapped and nervous. At first, I thought that a certain lunatic fringe was responsible for this kind of driving. But that was not the case at all; everyone drove the same way. One day soon after I came to Lebanon, I looked over at a driver who had just made a particularly bizarre and self-destructive move, and realized that he was the distinguished old gentleman I had met at a dinner party the night before.

Strangely enough, when drivers, finding themselves stuck in long lines behind military checkpoints, got out of their cars to wait, they were friendly and outgoing once again. If they were near the sea and it was a warm day, some might go down for a swim. Others would spread out blankets and begin a game of cards until they were summoned back to battle by the sound of engines starting in the line ahead.

Prisoner Exchange

On November 24, 1983 the BBC announced that a large-scale prisoner exchange was underway in Lebanon. In one day, more than four thousand Palestinian and Lebanese prisoners were released from Ansar, Israel's prison camp in South Lebanon, and one hundred Palestinians were released from prison in Israel—all in return for six Israeli soldiers who had been held by Fateh, the mainstream faction of the PLO. Over a thousand of the prisoners from Ansar chose to go to Algiers at the time of their release; the remainder were sent to Sidon and Tyre by bus.

In the days following Israel's invasion of South Lebanon in June 1982, all the men in Sidon between the ages of fifteen and sixty-five were ordered to gather along a road by the sea to have their identity cards checked. A similar process took place in all populated areas occupied by the Israeli army. The men were paraded one by one past a row of hooded informers, who were supposed to identify those who had worked with the PLO, but they implicated almost every man they saw.

The arrested men were first sent to a detention center in Sidon, and later were taken to Israel for interrogation. In July 1983 they were transported to Ansar, a prison camp built by the Israelis about a half hour's drive from Sidon.

In its 1984 annual report, Amnesty International estimated that some 12,000 men were taken to Ansar between July 1982 and November 1983 (about thirty women were held in a separate prison in the nearby town of Nabatieh). Only a small percentage had worked for any of the organizations operated by the PLO; PLO members who elected to leave Sidon to avoid arrest had had enough time to do so. The prisoners included men from every walk of life: Lebanese public officials, doctors, nurses, lawyers, office workers, blue collar workers, teachers and students. Men in their eighties and boys as young as twelve were taken to Ansar. The prisoners also included a number of the mentally and physically handicapped and men with chronic diseases. Some were released early, but, despite protests by the International Red Cross, many were not.

In the language of the Israeli military authorities, those arrested were not prisoners but "administrative detainees" who could be held indefinitely for unspecified "security reasons" according to emergency regulations adopted in

1945, when Palestine was still under British rule. Israel did allow the International Red Cross to visit inmates in Ansar and in the women's prison at Nabatieh, which meant that they could air grievances about their living conditions and receive mail (after it passed through Israeli censors). How-ever, Israel and the armed groups under its control also maintained a number of detention centers in South Leba-non to which the ICRC was denied access. (Lebanese mili-tias rarely allowed the ICRC to visit prisoners, either.)

Maintaining this huge prison population became an ad-ministrative headache for Israel, and conditions at Ansar brought Israel considerable adverse international publicity. Israeli soldiers wrote of being disgusted and demoralized by the squalor under which the prisoners were forced to live. An ongoing series of strikes and demonstrations organized by a PLO-run prisoners' committee brought concessions from the Israelis and kept prison guards on the defensive. Released inmates spoke proudly of the way prisoners of all ages and backgrounds had joined forces to demand better treatment; many looked back on their time at Ansar as an endurance contest, a war of wills which they had won.

A holiday atmosphere came over Ein el-Hilweh as news of the prisoners' release circulated through the camp. Al-though the prisoners had known for over a week that they would be released, their arrival came as a complete surprise to their families. Buses dropped the men off in the middle of town, and from there they shared taxis into the camp. The men wore green or blue running suits and carried bags made from towels or pieces of canvas tent. Women and children clustered around the prisoners who had returned or stood by the side of the road watching the approaching taxis. Those waiting along the Upper Street ran across the field dividing them from the Lower Street when they saw the taxis arriving. Children threw handfuls of rice and can-dies at the cars as they drove by with their horns honking. Women rushed to buy extra food for dinner, and the stores in the camp soon ran out of meat and sweets.

A week or so after the prisoner exchange, friends sug-gested that I volunteer to do screening examinations on some of the returning prisoners. It would be difficult for

UNRWA doctors in Sidon and Ein el-Hilweh to adjust to the sudden arrival of over a thousand men when their clinics already had to handle several hundred patients a day. Kay had volunteered to do physicals in local kindergartens, and since our own clinic was not yet open I had no medical responsibilities at the time. I thought that I could put together a good screening exam.

Everyone recognized that the matter of providing examinations for these men was politically charged. One UNRWA official pointed out that it would not be a good idea to screen all the released prisoners, even if that were possible, because several local militias wanted a list of the men who had been in Ansar and would try to steal any records that we kept. He suggested that I volunteer to examine returning prisoners who asked to be examined, along with UNRWA hardship cases—refugees who qualified for UNRWA food supplments because of a severe physical or mental disability. I submitted a written proposal incorporating his suggestions to the UNRWA office in Beirut. Within twenty-four hours, I learned, the matter had been discussed with UNRWA's legal counsel in Vienna; the answer that came back was "no." UNRWA did not want to compile any data on prisoners that might be summarized in a report because such a report would have "political significance," and it was not wise for UNRWA to get involved in such matters. Of course, one official informed me, anyone with a complaint was welcome to be examined, but the number of people coming in for assistance had been negligible.

However, one UNRWA doctor said that in the week after the prisoner exchange over 100 men from Ansar had been coming to the UNRWA clinic in Ein el-Hilweh every day. He had devised a screening exam of his own: whenever a newly-released prisoner checked in with the medical clerk, he was automatically sent to the lab for a CBC (complete blood count), urine analysis and stool exam. Most of the men were coming in with respiratory and gastrointestinal troubles, he said, although a fair number had complaints related to injuries sustained in prison. During a single morning in the UNRWA clinic I saw another doctor examine three men complaining of testicular pain after having been kicked in the groin by Israeli guards in Ansar. Two had no obvious injury on exam; the third had a hydrocele, a collection of fluid around the testicle. Conversations with other released prisoners revealed that testicular injuries were common; a midwife friend who worked in Ein el-Hilweh found that many women were afraid that their husbands who had been kicked in the groin in prison would be sterile.

When I told an UNRWA official in Sidon that I had seen prisoners in the UNRWA clinics with problems related to injuries received in prison, he became defensive. "Who said they were injured?" he said. "How can you prove it?" But, as we were to learn over the next few months, most prisoners did not bother to seek medical attention for injuries sustained in prison unless they were almost incapacitated by them. We did examine some newly-released prisoners who said they were beaten in detention, but most of the signs of injuries we found in our patients—teeth knocked out, scars from cuts and cigarette burns, healed rib fractures—turned up as we were examining them for other, unrelated complaints.

It soon became apparent that not all the prisoners from Ansar had come home in the prisoner exchange. Rima, the wife of one of the missing prisoners, worked as a cleaning lady in our house. Rima was an affectionate, impulsive woman in her early forties who watched over us like a housemother. She gave us cooking lessons, planted herbs in the garden, and, like mothers everywhere, took a great interest in the contents of our drawers and closets. As soon as she arrived in the morning Rima went into the kitchen to talk to whomever was there. After chattering about people she knew at the hospital and commenting about the condition of the food in the refrigerator, she put on her apron and her comfortable shoes and started washing the dishes. When everyone had left for work, she turned on the radio for company as she cleaned and did the laundry. She went outside to hang wash on the line, but she would not cross the street to empty the garbage; she preferred not to test the waters by venturing out in a Maronite neighborhood. When we came home for lunch, Rima took us from room to room to show us what she had done that day. Each week things looked a little different because she loved to rearrange the furniture and the kitchen utensils.

A couple of months after we met Rima we learned a little more about her husband. At the time of the exchange he had been separated from the other prisoners and sent to Israel along with over 100 other men. Rima could not understand what the Israelis wanted with him. He was just a dockworker, she said, a middle-aged man who was starting to lose his hearing. She did not mention that her husband was also an officer in the PFLP–GC (Popular Front for the Liberation of Palestine–General Command), the Libyan-backed branch of the PLO headed by Ahmad Jibril. In violation of their agreement with the International Red Cross and the PLO, Israel decided to keep Jibril's men, and a number of other men held on unspecified charges, to use in a second prisoner exchange, because Jibril was still holding two Israeli soldiers captured in 1982.

During the following year Rima had no contact with her husband. She asked the International Red Cross in Ein el-Hilweh what had happened to him and why they could not send him home. But the Red Cross had no information about the missing prisoners. For several months the government of Israel kept their whereabouts a secret. Then in July 1984 Amnesty International learned where the prisoners were being held and protested that their removal from Lebanon and their detention without charges in Israel was a violation of international law. Several months later the ICRC was at last allowed to visit them, and the prisoners were able to correspond with their families for the first time. When her husband's letters came, Rima's children read them aloud to her—she had never learned to read. Finally, in May 1985 the men who had been held back during the first prisoner exchange were released in exchange for the two Israeli prisoners, and Rima's husband came home again.

Dr. Jawad

One day not long after the prisoner exchange I took a gaunt and silent Palestinian doctor on a tour of the hospital. He had just been released from Ansar, and was dressed in a three-piece suit which was too big for him. I feared that he would be disappointed to see that the hospital was far from finished, even though we hoped to open in a month.

Dr. Jawad was in his early forties and had lived in Ein el-Hilweh for most of his life. He spoke with an exaggerated politeness which seemed old fashioned to me, and he appeared at first to be modest and unassuming. But he had a clear vision of what he wanted to accomplish as a doctor, and a practical sense of how it could be done. He thought our hospital would be a welcome addition to the camp, and he wanted to work in it.

I went to see Dr. Jawad from time to time at the Maroof Saad Clinic, where he worked in the mornings. The clinic, part of a local social welfare organization named after a former mayor of Sidon who was assassinated in 1976, was in Tamir, a Lebanese neighborhood on the northern edge of Ein el-Hilweh. After leaving Palestine in 1948 Dr. Jawad's father brought his family to join the refugees living in tents in Tamir. He had turned down an offer of Lebanese citizenship, because he expected that he would soon return home. Dr. Jawad's office at the Maroof Saad Clinic was only a short distance from the place where his family's tent used to be; he could almost see the spot from his office window.

Forty to fifty refugees lived in each tent. The tents were subdivided by blankets so that four or five families could live in each one. As the years went by, the residents made small improvements: they built embankments around the tents, and they dug ditches to prevent flooding in the rainy season. In 1952 UNRWA allowed refugees to put up shelters made from corrugated metal for the first time, but permanent structures were still forbidden. In 1956 Dr. Jawad's father decided to build a cement roof over the kitchen and bathroom. He worked on it at night, to avoid getting caught. But a soldier from the Lebanese Army heard him working as he walked past the house one night; he had to pay a heavy fine, but his new roof stayed up.

On slow afternoons when we were on duty together in the months after our hospital opened, Dr. Jawad told me more about himself. He had wanted to be a doctor, he said, ever since he was in secondary school, but no one who had grown up in Ein el-Hilweh had ever gone on to study medicine. It was expected that bright students would go on to work as UNRWA teachers after graduating from secondary school, but Dr. Jawad did not want to be a schoolteacher. After finishing school he worked as a teaching assistant at Sidon's Makassed College, and took some science courses there. However, his father became seriously ill, and the neighbors who came to visit voiced their disapproval of this was not working to support his family.

Without telling anyone, Dr. Jawad took a bus to the UN-RWA office in Beirut and asked about a job as a teacher. Within a few days he had gotten a position teaching elementary school in Nabatieh, about a half-hour's drive from Sidon. When his father heard that he had left his studies, he wept. Dr. Jawad resigned from Makassed College without admitting to his teachers that he was leaving because he needed money.

On his first day of teaching he wore his only suit, not knowing what he was expected to wear. He made his students work very hard. He finished the year's lesson plan halfway through the term, and then started on the next year's lessons. The superintendent, observing that his English was very good, asked him to teach chemistry, biology and physics in the secondary school in Ein el-Hilweh. The students had to work without textbooks. Dr. Jawad put some notes together and asked if they could be typed and distributed for use as a text, but the supervisor said no, there was no money for that. The students would have to make do with the notes they took in class.

Though his father recovered from his illness, Dr. Jawad continued teaching. After two years in UNRWA schools, he

went to Saudi Arabia to teach. A year later he married a
woman from Ein el-Hilweh and brought her to Saudi Arabia. But he had not given up the idea of studying medicine,
and when, in 1970, he heard of an opportunity to go to
medical school in Spain, his older brother, who worked as a
mechanic in Saudi Arabia, encouraged him and promised
to support him during his studies.

Dr. Jawad began as a freshman at the University of Sala-
manca in 1970, with about 200 students from Arab countries. He had had time to study Spanish for only three weeks
before classes began. At lectures, he copied all the diagrams
the teachers drew on the board but could not understand a
word they were saying. Every night he put his Spanish medical textbook beside a Spanish-English dictionary, and next
to that he placed an English-Arabic dictionary. He studied
up to 18 hours a day to learn Spanish and his medical
courses at the same time.

Dr. Jawad studied in Spain for eight years. Every summer
he travelled back to Lebanon by boat to visit his wife and
children. While he was in Spain, his family's house was
destroyed during an Israeli bombing raid carried out in
retaliation for an operation in Israel conducted by the Popular Front for the Liberation of Palestine, a radical PLO
faction. The PLO provided money to rebuild the houses,
and this time they were built with concrete, not corrugated
metal.

When Dr. Jawad returned to Lebanon in 1978 he went to
work as a medical officer in Bashar Hospital. It had acquired a reputation as the best hospital in Sidon, and was
rapidly growing. During those years he made enough
money to add a second floor to his family's house. Before
that he had been living with his parents, his wife and children, and his brother's family on a single floor.

After working at Bashar Hospital for three years, Dr. Jawad decided to open his own clinic on the first floor of his
house. He was proud to be the only Palestinian doctor with
a private clinic in Ein el-Hilweh. It was technically illegal for
a Palestinian doctor to open a private clinic (i.e., have a
private practice) in Lebanon. First he had to pass a special
examination, called a colloquium, and some Palestinian

doctors had managed to do this. But he would also have to pay a fee to the Syndicate, the Lebanese medical association; for foreign doctors this fee was about five times more than Lebanese doctors had to pay, and nobody could afford it. But at that time it did not really matter that his clinic was illegal. Several Palestinian doctors in Sidon had posted signs outside their apartments giving hours when they were available for consultation. They did not pose a serious threat to Lebanese doctors, most of whom had some specialist training, and, unlike Palestinians, also had admitting privileges at local hospitals.

During the Israeli invasion of June 1982, Ein el-Hilweh was shelled by land, sea and air for two weeks. Dr. Jawad's house was bombed and his new clinic destroyed. Refugees fled to villages in the hills above Sidon, or gathered by the sea. Dr. Jawad got separated from his family and went to Bashar Hospital to see if any of his relatives had been taken there.

The hospital had become a repository for the dead and wounded. Bodies were being dumped in front of the emergency room in plastic bags because nobody knew what to do with them. The rooms were filled with people "crying and burnt." Whole families were lying together on the floor, the less injured ones propped up against the walls. Dr. Bashar asked Dr. Jawad to stay at the hospital for the night to help care for the wounded, and Dr. Jawad agreed. He did not leave the hospital for the next twenty-seven days.

At first he had trouble getting used to the work. He would walk several times around the room full of wounded people before deciding how to begin. "We were not human beings at that time," he said. "Today if one patient dies in our hands, we feel terrible. But then we stepped over bodies, saying 'this one is dying, leave him,' 'that one is burnt too much.'" He remembered a patient brought in from the Government Hospital before it was shelled by the Israeli Army. The man, shot in the arm, had gotten a dressing at the hospital which still looked clean. Dr. Jawad had told the nurse to change his dressing last. When later she started to remove the bandage, a terrible smell filled the room; the arm under the dressing was black from gangrene. Dr. Jawad

sought out the orthopedist and said he would have to ampu-
tate the man's arm immediately. "I'm too tired," said the
orthopedist. "I can't do it now." But Dr. Jawad insisted.
Finally the orthopedist went to look at the man's arm. One
look was enough: he agreed to operate at once and ampu-
tated the arm just below the shoulder. After the surgery, they
found that the patient had a hematocrit of 8 (a normal
hematocrit is about 45); it took three days of transfusions
before they could raise the hematocrit to 12. Only when it
got to 14 was he finally able to raise his head from the
pillow.

Dr. Jawad lost track of the case after that, but when he
came back from Ansar, the man visited his house. He had
gotten a job as a guard at an UNRWA school. "I came to
thank you," he said. "If it weren't for you, I wouldn't be alive
today."

In the fall of 1982 Dr. Jawad was working at the Maroof
Saad Clinic six mornings a week. His house had been partly
rebuilt, and he was seeing patients at home. One night as he
was eating dinner with his family, two leaders of the National Guard in Ein el-Hilweh came to see him. He assumed
that they were patients, and asked his wife to make coffee
for them while he finished eating. "Can you come with us
for just a minute?" they said. "We want to ask you some
questions." He noticed that they were carrying pistols.

They drove him to the *saraya*, Sidon's former City Hall,
which the Israelis were using as an interrogation/detention
center, turned him over to the Israelis and left. The Israeli
soldiers asked him stupid questions, he said. "Do you have a
gun?" "Have you worked with any of the PLO factions?"
They never said what he was accused of, they never said
what they wanted. But Dr. Jawad was taken to Ansar, and
spent the next year there. Attempts by his friends to have
him released were of no avail. At first, Dr. Jawad refused to
work as a doctor in Ansar. Like others I met, he suspected
that he had been arrested *because* he was a doctor, to ease the
burden on Israeli doctors who were caring for the prisoners. He also thought that adequate medical care was a
mockery in Ansar. There were not enough drugs, and there
was no place he could examine patients. Some who should

have been hospitalized refused to go to Israel, he said, because they feared being bound and beaten on the way.

Finally doctors from the ICRC persuaded Dr. Jawad to see patients. He diagnosed the first case of appendicitis at Ansar, and the patient was airlifted out by helicopter. He also saw many cases of renal colic, which he attributed to an inadequate supply of drinking water. But toward the end of his time in Ansar, Dr. Jawad stopped seeing patients; he blamed the inadequate medical facilities, but it seems more likely that depression got the better of him. He was released during the prisoner exchange of November 1983. He left Ansar wearing the suit he had had on when he was arrested; he was the only prisoner not wearing the running suit provided by the ICRC.

The first time I visited Dr. Jawad's house in Ein el-Hilweh he took out an old brown envelope which held certificates and diplomas in English, Spanish and Arabic between yellowed newspaper clippings and pieces of tissue paper. His wife brought in the picture of his medical school graduating class, which had been blasted out of its frame during the invasion and was ripped in several places. The students were represented in oval portraits around the school seal. Dr. Jawad was the only Palestinian student from Lebanon in his class. I looked at his tiny portrait to see if his face was fuller then, but could barely make out more than his glasses and a bushy head of hair. "When I think back on it all," he said, "I'm surprised at what I did. I don't think I could do it again."

As our hospital grew over the following months, Dr. Jawad watched it with a careful eye, as if it were a plant growing under his care. He wanted us to have a good reputation in Ein el-Hilweh and among the Lebanese doctors in Sidon. He introduced us to other doctors, and suggested ways for the hospital to expand. He still saw patients at the Maroof Saad clinic in the mornings, but he spent most of his working hours with us. He had lost much of his enthusiasm about having his own clinic after it was bombed, and he transferred his energies to our hospital instead.

Isolation and Resistance

On a good day there was only a twenty or thirty minute wait at the checkpoint at the Awali river, where the coast road crossed the northern boundary of Israeli-occupied Lebanon. But in early November, ten days after the bombings at the American and French military headquarters in Beirut, another suicide bomber drove into the Israeli miliary barracks in Tyre, killing twenty-nine Israeli soldiers and thirty-two Lebanese and Palestinian prisoners. After that the coast road was closed at the Awali bridge for three days, because, as one Israeli soldier put it, there were too many terrorists out on the road. In the days that followed, it was closed more and more often. Some Israelis called for a permanent closing after the Tyre explosion, but more moderate leaders pointed out that such a move would be interpreted as a step toward partitioning Lebanon.

In mid-November Israel compromised by instituting a system of travel permits: any vehicle going to or from Beirut had to have a travel document issued by one of the Israeli "Civilian Assistance Centers" in South Lebanon, or by Israel's new liaison office in Dbayeh in East Beirut—not a convenient location for Moslem travellers. Pedestrians did not need permits, but on some days they were not allowed to cross either, and even when the crossing was open, it took a long time to get through.

The Lebanese accommodated themselves as best they could to all of this. Taxi drivers who used to take their passengers directly to Beirut would stand in Sidon's Nijmi Square shouting "Beirut! Beirut!" until their taxis filled up. Now they cried "Awali! Awali!" and drove their riders only as far as the Awali bridge. From there passengers had to pass through the Israeli checkpoints on foot and then get a taxi to Beirut from the other side.

On days when the bridge was closed to all traffic, some Lebanese swam across. Younger men swam holding older people by the shoulders, and it was said that swimming couriers carried magazines and newspapers on their backs to Sidon newsdealers. On November 6 a wedding was held for a man and a woman who lived on opposite sides of the Awali. To get to the church, the entire wedding party, consisting of the bride and groom and 250 guests, all dressed for the occasion, was ferried across the river on the backs of young men from the bride's village.

It was also possible to cross the river by crawling on all fours across a nearby railway bridge, or by wading across it at a more remote spot upstream. Israeli soldiers who noticed these plucky travellers chose to ignore them at first, or let them cross after firing warning shots over their heads.

It was not easy to deal with the Israelis in charge of traffic at the bridge. Soldiers sometimes got angry at motorists in line, tore up their permits and refused to let them pass. Drivers who parked their cars on the side of the road often returned to find their tires slashed, their windows broken, or the car gone—towed away and demolished, in case it had a bomb inside. When David commented about the Israelis' use of police dogs to control the crowd waiting for permits outside the so-called "Civilian Assistance Center" in Sidon, an Israeli officer chuckled. "Moslems hate dogs," he said. Even the Jerusalem *Post* complained, in an editorial on January 1, that "the [Israeli] army showed little sensitivity to the sensibilities of the local population," and referred to "harrowing indignities" that were alienating South Lebanon's civilian population.

Opposition to the Israeli occupation was not confined to resistance fighters. The friendly, attractive young bank officer who handled our account startled Sylvia one day by saying how happy she was that some Israeli soldiers had been killed in an ambush in Sidon the day before. Shiite leaders in South Lebanon called for "civil resistance" against the Israelis. At the end of December a general strike was held all over Lebanon to protest the Israeli occupation, and religious and civic leaders staged sit-ins at mosques in Sidon and Beirut. In response, Israeli military authorities closed the coast road for three days to "cool down the local populace," according to an article in the Washington *Post*.

As the road closed more often, South Lebanon became economically isolated from the rest of the country. Thousands of people who once commuted to Beirut every day had to move to their workplace or lose their jobs. Trucks carrying produce from the south sometimes had to wait for three or four days to cross at the Awali. The cost of transporting South Lebanon's citrus crop became so high that it no longer paid farmers to pick the fruit on their trees.

At the same time the south was gaining a new political identity. It was being called Israel's "North Bank," and many were convinced that Israel would never give it up. Israel had always coveted South Lebanon's abundant water supply, and it was known that some Israelis had called for the building of Jewish settlements in South Lebanon, which they considered part of Greater Israel. While Beirut was bogged down by squabbling and shelling between rival factions, the south gained prestige as the center of the Resistance, where Israel was the common enemy. The Resistance became the subject of poems and popular songs all over Lebanon. Exhibits of photographs and paintings about the occupied south were held in Beirut in the months that followed, and a movie called "The Revolted South" was a hit when it came out the next year.

In February 1984 heavy fighting engulfed Beirut and spread south to the hills of Iklim el-Kharrub, only a few miles north of Sidon. The fighting caused the coast road to shut down completely, and it did not reopen for a year. North-south traffic shifted to the circuitous road through the Shouf Mountains, where the Israelis imposed the same harsh security measures.

During the fall of 1983 I took a group taxi to Beirut every month or so. In those early days, the trip from Sidon took less than an hour. North of the Awali the road wound along a narrow strip of land that lay between barren rocky hills and the sea. Between the villages, vegetable gardens and banana plantations stood alongside abandoned beach clubs and bombed-out seaside villas. Close to Beirut the road became more desolate. Nothing was left of the Christian village of Damour but shells of deserted houses and hills of flattened rubble. The U.S. Marine base was situated across the road from an enormous dump south of the Beirut Airport, where decomposing garbage was packed twenty feet deep in places.

Traffic moved slowly through Beirut's southern suburbs, a poor and crowded part of town populated predominantly by Shiites. The streets were lined with small grocery stores and sweet shops, auto body shops and furniture stores with outdoor displays of living room sets upholstered in cheap brocade. Giant posters of Ayatollah Khomeini and Imam Musa Sadr looked down on passing cars, and the red, green and white logo of the Amal movement was painted on buildings.

Further inland, east of the Shiite suburbs, was the Burj el-Barajneh refugee camp, the largest Palestinian camp in Beirut. The Sabra and Shatila camps were north of Burj el-Barajneh, and blended in with the surrounding neighborhood. Together the three camps had a population of 50,000. They were guarded by the Italian contingent of the UN multinational Peacekeeping Force, which also operated a small field hospital for Lebanese and Palestinians in the area.

South of Beirut the coast road joined the Corniche, a walkway that followed the winding coastline and a popular place for a Sunday afternoon stroll with the family. On warm winter days fishermen stood on the rocks by the sea fishing with long poles, and men in bikinis lay sunbathing on the sand. Vendors stood along empty stretches of the road, selling feather dusters, cassette recorders, baby strollers and canaries.

Hamra, West Beirut's shopping district, was unaffected by the intermittent clashes between Moslem and Druze militias and the Lebanese army in late 1983, but the city's municipal services were barely limping along. The incessant honking of horns from passing cars and taxis mingled with the roar of portable generators that kept stores lit during power cuts. Sidewalks were blocked by parked cars, rubble, and mounds of uncollected garbage. Yet the window displays were as stylish and eye-catching as ever. Though their country was sliding into anarchy, the Lebanese on the streets of Hamra had not lost their taste for the finer things of life.

One had to admire the pluckiness they showed in adjusting to each new setback, but there was something unsettling about the way they had distanced themselves from the chaos around them, as if it were no concern of theirs. An advertisement for shatterproof glass in a Beirut newspaper illustrated this way of thinking. It showed a businessman cringing as his office window shattered into fragments. The caption read: AN EXPLOSION. DANGEROUS FLYING GLASS SPLINTERS. HORRIFYING CONSEQUENCES. *REGRETS.* The businessman's regrets stemmed from his shortsightedness at having failed to install 3M Safety Films in his office windows, for they were "the simplest, most economical way to prevent such disasters." The disaster, of course, was not the explosion, which might have killed a hundred people and flattened the office building on the next block, but those dangerous glass splinters that had invaded his office.

As the coast road closed more often, we made fewer trips to Beirut. When we showed up at the houses of friends in West Beirut, they looked at us as exotic specimens. Each thought that the other was living under more difficult conditions, and each was reluctant to travel out of town unless absolutely necessary. We sympathized with our Beirut friends who had to keep their bathtubs and buckets filled with water in order to wash and flush the toilet, and who got up at two a.m. to do the laundry, because that was the time they got their allotment of electricity. They in turn sympathized with us for having to live under military occupation.

When we arrived in Beirut in October, the newest posters in Hamra showed President Amin Gemayel appealing to his people as leader and peacemaker. Three months later they had been replaced by anti-Israeli posters, which cropped up even on the campus of the American University (AUB). One showed an Israeli soldier confronting a couple in front of their bombed-out house, while a giant hand which had broken off its chains was about to crush an Israeli tank. Another showed photographs of the disfigured corpses of men allegedly killed by the Israelis in South Lebanon. In early January there was a one-hour strike against the Israeli occupation of the south at AUB, even though the students had agreed at the beginning of the semester to refrain from political activity. Then on January 18 Malcolm Kerr, the President of AUB, was assassinated by unidentified gunmen inside the campus. His death was a sad reminder of the vulnerability of a university which had once been a haven of political tolerance.

First Christmas

Christmas came a week before we had planned to open our hospital, when we were all feeling tired and distracted. In Sidon, the Christmas spirit was muted; decorations went up late and haphazardly. The soldiers from Saad Haddad's South Lebanon Army put up a spindly Christmas tree at their checkpoint on the road below our house. The Phalangists in our neighborhood strung up the outline of a cedar tree, their military emblem, in green and silver tinsel overhead between the telephone poles. Next door the Maronite church played gravelly-sounding Christmas carols over and over at high volume. I found the strident sounds of "Jingle Bells" sung in Arabic especially hard to bear.

It was a sad time for the Christians. According to an assistant from the Mayor's office, some 10,000 of them, refugees from the four-month old Shouf war, were still living in schools and churches around Sidon. An estimated 20,000 were trapped in the mountains in the town of Deir el-Kamar, where they had taken refuge from the Druze. The Phalangists had put posters along our street showing a mother from Deir el-Kamar clutching her child to her breast with a grim, desperate look. Would they be rescued from their siege, the Christians wondered, or would they be massacred?

Then, ten days before Christmas, a truce was arranged, and the Christians in Deir el-Kamar were evacuated by the International Red Cross, with the assistance of the Israeli Army. The plan was to transport them to Sidon, and thence by sea to East Beirut.

The event was treated as a joyous occasion by the local Christian community, which looked upon the Christians of Deir el-Kamar as heroes. The Israeli Army ordered all stores to close in Sidon for the day. Dozens of Phalangist militiamen lined the road leading down from the mountains where the convoy would pass. They wore their military uniforms and carried automatic weapons with decals of Christ and the Virgin Mary on the rifle butts. Children held up Lebanese and Phalangist flags, and their parents crowded behind the soldiers, holding baskets of rice and Jordan almonds to throw at the buses when they passed.

After a long wait, the buses came, flying the Red Cross flag. Bystanders began to wave and cheer as the buses came into view, but then they caught sight of the grim, blank expressions of the people inside, and the cheering stopped. By the time the convoy had passed, faces in the crowd were stained with tears, and the women turned to go home, their baskets of rice still full.

Our Arabic teacher, Mme. Rocuse, invited us one day after class to see her Christmas tree. The fighting had prevented her family from going into the mountains to get a real tree as they had done in the past, so her husband, Emil, had bought an artificial one. "You should get a tree too," she said. When I replied that we did not have time to get ornaments together, she produced a big bag of cotton balls. "Pull these apart and put them on the tree," she said. "It will look just like snow."

We never got around to putting up a tree, but we did make several hundred Christmas cookies, and distributed them in decorated tins to our friends in town. The doctors and nurses in the UNRWA clinics got some, and so did our Christian neighbors, David's Beirut business contacts, the mayor of Sidon and the fortune teller.

The fortune teller lived in an apartment as large and grand as the mayor's, with high ceilings and expensive carpets and furniture. She was a middle-aged Palestinian woman from Tal Zaatar. She had large, kind brown eyes, and her face had a look of utter serenity which gave no hint of the sadness in her life. Both her young children had disappeared when Christian militias overran the Palestinian camp of Tal Zaatar in East Beirut in 1976. She still wore their portraits around her neck, and, although she had never heard news of them, she was convinced that they were still alive.

Like many Arab women, she could tell fortunes by examining the patterns of coffee grounds in cups emptied by her customers. But she preferred to get her inspiration from the patterns made by a film of oil on the surface of a cup of water. She would look into the cup, her eyes half-shut, moving her lips and counting something on her fingers, and then she was ready to speak.

The fortune teller was popular. Whenever we went to visit her, her reception room was crowded with sad old ladies. We found that early in the day her insights were uncanny, but by mid-afternoon she seemed depleted, and could offer only trite old standbys: the important letter which was coming soon, the one from far away who cares for you still. Just the same, we kept coming back. She was optimistic that our hospital would open on time.

The fortune teller spoke no English, and before we had always taken a lovestruck Arab friend who welcomed the chance to ask about the intentions of the new man in her life, an ICRC delegate. This time, Sylvia and I went alone with our cookie tin. We drank coffee with the fortune teller, but declined her offer of a new reading. For the first time, I noticed a large, striking tapestry hanging on the wall. I had never seen anything like it before. It showed a mother holding her infant in one arm and a rifle in the other, very much the way a saint would hold a cross. We finished our coffee. The fortune teller thanked us for her present, and we left.

David and Kay did not return from Beirut until Christmas Eve. They had spent nearly a week there, looking for drugs for our pharmacy. Some companies would not sell to us, because we were not a hospital by their definition; others said that drugs were out of stock "because of the situation." Even the biggest companies had little of what we were looking for. But David and Kay came back with most of the drugs and supplies we needed, and also brought our mail and a frozen American turkey, bought in a West Beirut supermarket. We unloaded the car, brought the gas heater into the kitchen and made eggnog. As we listened to Sylvia's tapes of Christmas carols, an attack against the Israelis erupted on the road just below our house. The first explosion almost blew in the windows, and it was followed by furious machine gun fire and flares shot into the night sky. You could usually guess by the pattern and timing of the firing who was attacking whom, whether it was a large or small ambush, and whether there were any casualties. This seemed like a medium-sized ambush. The firing stopped after a few minutes, and all was quiet until the Maronite hymns started up again over the church loudspeaker, just before the midnight service.

I had considered going to the Maronite service, but the atmosphere was not right. The crowd of armed Phalangists in front of the church seemed more suitable for a political rally than a religious service. Fearing car bombs, the Phalangists would not let even the neighbors park their cars on the street; Emil, the electrician who had installed the sound system in the church for the occasion, had to walk across the neighborhood to get to church.

On Christmas Day we stuffed and roasted our American turkey and took it across town to share with about twenty members of other voluntary organizations working in Lebanon. Most of them were British, Canadian, American, Swiss or Norwegian. Two years later only a handful of foreigners was still working in Sidon. The other workers were not replaced when their contracts expired, or were replaced by local Arab staff.

The Haddad soldiers did not take down the Christmas tree at their checkpoint for several months. It was still standing there the following summer, a firless skeleton. The Phalangists never bothered to dismantle their decorations either.

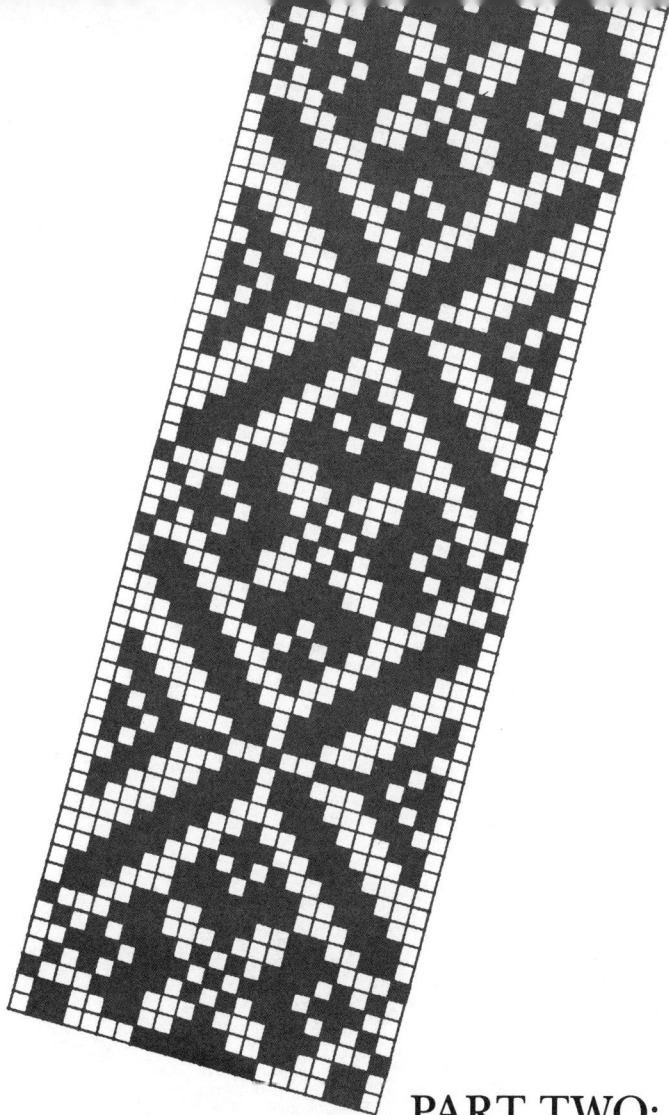

PART TWO:
JANUARY—MAY 1984

Briefing

Our hospital finally opened its doors in early January 1984 with a staff of about thirty. The administrator, two doctors, and three nurses were American. Most of the remaining staff was Palestinian. A Lebanese cardiologist later joined us as a part-time consultant. Our lower floor was a clinic with examination and treatment rooms, a pharmacy and a laboratory. Upstairs was a twenty-bed hospital ward, separated into men's and women's sections.

Leaders of Lebanon's political factions failed to concur on a program of government reforms during reconciliation talks held in Geneva in late 1983, and the country drifted toward a major military showdown. In February, fighting broke out when a coalition of Druze and Shiite Moslem militias battled the Lebanese Army for control of West Beirut. The Lebanese Army broke up along sectarian lines, and the cabinet resigned. Within weeks, all members of the four-nation peacekeeping force withdrew their troops from Beirut.

Thousands of Lebanese fled to Sidon from West Beirut, and the fighting extended to the hills north of Sidon. The coast road from Beirut to Sidon closed, and did not reopen for a year, leaving open only a circuitous road through the Shouf Mountains, its southern access controlled by the Israeli forces.

Transition

The hospital was not finished, and we were still short of some of the drugs and medical supplies we needed, but we decided to open our doors at the end of the first week in January. A few days before, we posted notices in the UN-RWA clinic describing the services the hospital would offer. We did not expect to have many patients in the beginning, but we wanted to use the first few days of operation to get to know the staff and to set up a routine.

A week before the hospital opened I held our first doctors' meeting. I expected five, but only two came to eat the quiche and salad I had made and to look over the handouts I had put together. Kay had gotten stuck in Beirut when the Israelis closed the road, and the two UNRWA doctors who had not yet made a commitment to work for us said at the last minute that they were too busy to come. That left only Dr. Mazen, Dr. Jawad and myself. Dr. Jawad used the occasion to deliver a few remarks about his medical philosophy of life, and gave several examples of how, through diligence and good luck, he had been able to bring back to life patients everyone else had given up on.

Dr. Mazen listened to us without a word, although at times I thought I could see a little smile at the corners of his mouth. He was a distinguished-looking man with greying hair. I did not know him very well. He had spent the last ten years working in Saudi Arabia, and had returned to Lebanon on June 3, 1982, for a short visit. His family held a welcome-home party for him, and then the Israeli invasion began. When he went to have his I.D. card stamped by the Israelis, a soldier asked him why he'd chosen to return to Lebanon at such a time. "My bad fortune," he answered.

At the meeting we talked about the kinds of diseases and medical problems that we would be able to treat, and we poked around the rooms to look over our medical equipment. The areas the doctors worked in consisted of a conference room, which functioned as a joint office for the doctors and nurses, an emergency room, a treatment room for suturing and dressings, and two small examining rooms. The pharmacy was in a large closet nearby, and the laboratory was near David's office. The inpatient beds were on another floor.

The doctors did not object to using an infectious disease protocol that I had made up: it was a table which recommended specific antibiotics for treating over a dozen common infectious diseases. But a second handout was less successful. To see what clinical skills we had as a group, I had prepared a checklist of medical procedures and asked each doctor to mark off the procedures he could perform and/or teach to others. The procedures ranged from simple ones like suturing and doing a spinal tap to technically complicated ones like doing a forceps delivery or repairing a damaged nerve. Later as I looked over the questionnaires, I realized that I had used the wrong approach, for each doctor had written that he could do all the procedures on the list. But when we started working together we soon had a good idea about our own skills and limitations. Sometimes we referred our patients to each other for consultation, but if a patient was unstable or difficult to manage, no doctor ever hesitated to have him transferred to a larger hospital in Sidon.

Since we were still short of doctors, I went to see Dr. Refki at the UNRWA clinic in Sidon to ask if he would work with us. Dr. Refki was a genial, heavy-set man in his early forties, but his curly brown hair and his round, smiling face made him look at least ten years younger. I had already spent a morning seeing patients with him in the UNRWA clinic. He had a special blend of qualities that one sees in the best UNRWA doctors: infinite patience, an air of quiet authority, and a hearty sense of humor. He did not mind working as a primary care doctor, but he had been trained as a surgeon, and he could not do even minor surgical procedures in the UNRWA clinic. He wanted to work in our hospital because it would give him the chance to perform outpatient surgery again.

Like Dr. Mazen, Dr. Refki had been trapped in Lebanon by the Israeli invasion. After finishing medical school and a year of internship in Damascus, he had gone abroad for further surgical training. First he worked as a medical officer in Uganda where, he said, "to be a doctor meant to be a surgeon." The medical work was relegated to a student. Dr. Refki started his training as the assistant of an Egyptian surgeon who was getting old and was happy to let a younger doctor take over most of the work. When the surgeon retired, Dr. Refki took over his practice. He was the only surgeon in the area and had cases in the operating room almost every day. He did many gynecological procedures, particularly Caesarean sections and laparotomies for ruptured ectopic pregnancies. But sometimes he was drawn into more complicated surgery. One day while operating on a patient with a large abdominal abcess he realized that he would have to remove one of the patient's kidneys. It was the most challenging case he had ever tackled, and he was relieved, and a little surprised, when the patient completely recovered.

After two years in Uganda Dr. Refki went to the Sudan to work with the Ministry of Health. The hospitals in Khartoum, the capital, were affiliated with British medical schools, and the time he spent in them could eventually lead to a FRCS, a British surgical degree, if he also spent a year working at a British teaching hospital. He had planned to continue his training in Dublin and was in Lebanon on a six-week vacation when the Israeli invasion began. Instead of returning to the Sudan, he took a job as an UNRWA doctor in Sidon where his wife, Dr. Majida, also worked.

Dr. Refki told me that he had known that he wanted to be a doctor from the time he was a child, when an UNRWA doctor had given him injections which healed a chronic abcess on his leg. He was encouraged in his ambitions by his older brother, and by his schoolteachers, who said that his handwriting was so illegible that he was sure to become a doctor someday.

Dr. Refki worked with us in the afternoons, after finishing at the UNRWA clinic. Once the other UNRWA doctors knew that Dr. Refki was working with us, they sent him most of their orthopedic cases, and his afternoons were busy.

We opened with a staff of about thirty—five doctors, twelve nurses, a pharmacist, a lab technician, and an assortment of medical clerks, translators, guards and drivers. After we started working together we learned the identity of a self-appointed scribe who had filled out job applications on behalf of many different people. As we looked over applications in the weeks before the hospital opened, we had often wondered who he was. He wrote in a graceful script, and at the bottom of each application always added a few humble words of his own. "Hoping to satisfy your kind requirement," he might conclude, or "I am very glad and happy if you select me to be at your esteemed center." His name was Abu Karim, and he later became senior medical clerk and major-domo at our esteemed center.

Abu Karim had worked as a senior medical clerk with UNRWA for over twenty years. He was a modest and polite man with that sunny serenity that one often finds among older religious Moslems. Because of his piety and his many years with UNRWA, the elders of his mosque had made him their treasurer. Most of his seven children were grown, and he was already a grandfather, though he was still in his forties. Abu Karim was an enterprising man; in addition to his UNRWA job he had a small office-machine shop on the Vegetable Street in Ein el-Hilweh for a time. His shop and his home were destroyed during the Israeli invasion and he was sent to Ansar. After his return, he started to save money again in order to rebuild his house and send his son to a university to study engineering. A university education was more important than money, he said, and no bomb could take it away.

Abu Karim worked for us in the afternoons after his duties were over at the UNRWA clinic. He prided himself on always knowing how to do things the correct way, and we all fell under his organizing influence. He made plastic name tags for us to wear with our names and titles spelled out in black stick-on letters. (The Americans wanted their names written in Arabic, and the Arab employees wanted to have their names in English.) After that we got ID cards with our pictures, and Abu Karim had them laminated. He set up a filing system for the patients' charts, and he organized the office supplies. He loved to make labels. The doctors who worked in the afternoon found that the charts of patients waiting to be seen came with little labels assigning each patient to one of Abu Karim's descriptive categories: "New Patient," "Follow-Up," "Old Patient" and a special category, "Old Patient—New Problem."

Abu Karim's sphere of influence encompassed all of the Ein el-Hilweh camp. He knew how to track down our most elusive patients, and he used his moral authority to compel them to come back for their follow-up appointments. To me he was the most settled and organized of men. But he could never forget that other people saw him differently. They had labeled him a refugee, and that is how he saw himself too. It was stigma he could neither accept nor overcome. One day he showed me the ID card that the government issued to Palestinians living in Lebanon. The word "refu-gee"—*laji* in Arabic—was written on it in four different places.

"In Lebanon," he said, "this word is an insult." That wasn't true in America, I said; most Americans had compassion for refugees. But in Abu Karim's mind this word called all of his accomplishments into question. "All my life I have been called *laji, laji,*" he said "and they will call me *laji* even when I am buried under the ground."

When the hospital finally opened, it was just barely pre-sentable. The elevator had not been installed, and the steps were rudimentary. Incoming patients picked their way around boards, cinder blocks and piles of linoleum tiles, and plumbers and electricians walked in and out of the rooms. Upstairs, rows of beds covered with patchwork quilts donated by the Mennonites stood waiting for our first pa-tients. When they came, some got nervous at the sight of so many attentive nurses and empty beds, and decided to go home after a few hours.

By the end of each day, everyone in our house was tired, defensive and noncommunicative. We all felt as if the opening of the hospital had put us in the spotlight with no lines to read. We got home after dark, ate a quick dinner standing up in the kitchen, and went straight to bed. After a week or so we were seeing ten or fifteen patients a day in the hospital—just enough to know what problems still had to be worked out, but not enough to know if the hospital would really catch on. Dr. Jawad was not worried about these growing pains. One day when he saw that I was troubled by an accumulation of minor problems, he said, "Take it easy. Surely we will meet with more than this."

The Staff and the Patients

I worked with Dr. Mazen and Dr. Jawad during the morning hours; Kay worked with Dr. Refki in the afternoons, and administered anesthesia for his patients with fractures and dislocations. As a group we ranged in age from our mid-thirties to our early forties. Despite differences in our personalities and backgrounds, we got along well with one another, and found that we all had roughly the same clinical skills.

Kay and I worked with translators. They usually were not needed by the other Americans on the staff, because except for the cleaning ladies and a few of the practical nurses, everyone who worked in the hospital could speak English. The translator had a demanding job; we depended on him not only for accurate medical information about our patients, but also for their good will. If the patients did not like the translator, they would not like us either. Though they never mentioned it directly, the translators had mastered English in the hope of studying overseas someday. Otherwise they had little in common.

Our first translator, Mansour, was a serious, quiet young man only twenty years old, but he looked much older. He had grown up in the Tal Zaatar camp, in a run-down industrial suburb of East Beirut inhabited largely by Palestinians and displaced Shiite Moslems. In 1976, when he was eleven years old, the camp was surrounded by a coalition of Maronite Christians and Syrian troops, and a long siege began. The Christians wanted to rid East Beirut of Moslems in general and Palestinians in particular, but the PLO, which directed the defense within the camp, was determined to hold out as long as possible.

Inside Tal Zaatar people soon ran out of food and medicines, and water was in short supply. The International Red Cross issued a public appeal on behalf of the wounded inside, estimated to number over a thousand, but attempts to evacuate them were called off when snipers fired at the Red Cross ambulances. Mansour's brother was shot in both arms by a sniper when he went out for water, but he held onto the buckets until he reached the house. When he put them down, the water was red with blood. Mansour remembered being sent out at night to look for water and stumbling over decomposing bodies that felt spongy underfoot. He drew a picture of them later for a woman from the International Red Cross who asked what he remembered about the siege.

After nearly two months the camp surrendered. Maronite soldiers rounded up the families left inside and took their money and jewelry. The women and children were separated from the men and put into trucks that would take them to other parts of Beirut. Some women saw their husbands and sons hacked to death with axes before the trucks and ambulances from the International Red Cross arrived. Most of the men were never seen again. Mansour lost an older brother, a brother-in-law and four cousins; his family still describes them as "missing." More than two thousand. men, women and children were dead or missing at the end of the siege. As the families were taken from the camp, said Mansour, everyone wept, even the ambulance drivers.

At the time of Israel's invasion of Lebanon Mansour had almost finished his junior year of high school. In the year and a half he spent in Ansar he worked on his English, using a Webster's dictionary and notebooks provided by the International Red Cross. When he was released from prison his brothers could no longer afford to send him to school.

There were thirteen people in his family, but he was the only one who had been able to find a job.

Bilal translated for Kay and me on evenings and weekends. He was a self-confident, easygoing man in his early thirties with a promising career. He had run a profitable contracting business in the Gulf for many years, and worked as an administrator with a local clinic after returning to Lebanon. His house in Ein el-Hilweh was destroyed by the first Israeli shell that struck the camp in June 1982—a shell, he reminded us, that was manufactured in the United States. A fake ID card which said that he was a Lebanese schoolteacher had saved him from being sent to prison. He had just bought himself a cowboy shirt and, certain that the Israelis would stay in Lebanon for only a few days and then quickly withdraw, he told his wife that he was going to keep it on until the Israelis left.

After a week his wife said, "Will you go and wash yourself somewhere? I can't stand the smell of you any longer." Bilal carried a pail up the hill to the outdoor pump that the neighbors shared and stood in line. When his turn came, he filled his bucket with water and poured it over his head—first one bucket and then another and another, as the people in line stared at him in astonishment. Then he went home and changed his clothes. He no longer thought that the Israelis would be leaving soon.

From the day our hospital opened Dr. Mazen and I worked together on the morning shift and consulted each other about difficult cases. Dr. Mazen was five months old when his family came to Lebanon in 1948. He grew up in the Rashidieh camp in Tyre. When his father left Palestine, he took the ownership papers for his land with him, to show the authorities when he returned. After studying medicine at Cairo University on an UNRWA scholarship, Dr. Mazen went directly to Saudi Arabia to work as a medical officer with the government. At first he worked in a clinic with a Pakastani doctor in a small town an hour's drive from the nearest hospital. Later he became director of a fifty bed hospital in a larger town in the central part of the country. His colleagues were doctors from other third-world countries—Egypt, Jordan, the Philippines, Pakistan. During his last year in Saudi Arabia Dr. Mazen's Lebanese wife came to live with him, and their son was born there. He had liked working in Saudi Arabia but found that the Saudis were not friendly. Even though he lived in the country for ten years, he never felt accepted there. They always made him feel like an outsider, he said, like someone whose stay in their country was only temporary.

Dr. Mazen obviously enjoyed taking care of patients, and he had a good rapport with them. He got particularly interested in managing our heart patients, and became adept at reading complicated EKG's. But he also liked matching wits with some of the tough and feisty older patients who needed to be persuaded that they were not as sick as they thought they were.

Our patients came from many different backgrounds. Some had lived abroad for many years, and others rarely left the camp. We treated a few affluent Palestinians who lived in apartments in Sidon, but most of our patients were poor Lebanese and Palestinians with homes within walking distance of the hospital. The poor patients wore rubber sandals even in the coldest weather, and their clothes were old and torn. Younger women with a little money to spend wore gold earrings and bracelets and Western-style outfits, highheeled shoes and stockings. The older people dressed in loose layers of homemade clothes. Old men and women usually had their heads covered, in accordance with Moslem custom, the men wearing a white knitted skullcap and the women a white scarf. Men dressed in trousers and jackets or *jallabiyyas*, long embroidered cotton or wool robes, and women wore long flowered print dresses over layers of petticoats. There were still some old Bedouins in the camp. The Bedouin women looked very striking; they had dark tatooed faces, and wore head scarves and long dresses in layers of black and paisley.

Most patients brought along another family member on their visits. Mothers came with their young children, husbands came with their wives, and older women usually brought their daughters. The accompanying family member always wanted to explain what was wrong with the patient. I never saw a patient object to hearing his mother or wife or brother go into a detailed recital of his symptoms: where the pain was, when it began, and what it felt like, how many times he had been to the bathroom, and so on. Once the door was closed on the spokesman, however, the patient did not mind describing the ailment himself.

Someone in the patient's family always brought along a plastic shopping bag with souvenirs of the present ailment or a previous one: pills the UNRWA doctor had prescribed (not labelled), slips from old laboratory tests, empty cardboard boxes that medicines had come in ("that one really helped"), old blue clinic cards from the American University Hospital in Beirut, and perhaps a prescription (illegible) from a private doctor who had once been consulted about the problem. After I had been at the hospital for several months, I made a poster on which I taped the twenty pills most commonly prescribed by local doctors, to facilitate identifying most of the pills lying loose in the bottom of the shopping bags we went through.

As the weeks went by, each of our doctors seemed to attract a certain type of patient which he felt technically or temperamentally suited to treat. To my lot fell the old ladies. Older patients were addressed respectfully as *haj* (male) or *hajji* (female). *Haj* means "pilgrim" in Arabic, and strictly refers to a Moslem who has made a pilgrimage to Mecca, but it was used as a respectful greeting to all older people. I got to know many of the older ladies quite well, and a composite *hajji* lingers in my mind.

A fifty to sixty-five year old woman, wearing a long floral print dress and a white head scarf would come to the clinic with a referral for chest pain. After a while I learned that she was probably at least ten years older than she claimed. She described the pain as a sticking left-sided and/or diffuse chest pain, worse when she was breathing, or when she was upset. She got short of breath easily. She had been taking medicines for diabetes and/or hypertension, but she had run out of them or forgotten to bring them. She also complained of weakness and/or palpitations, and abdominal pain which was not related to meals. She was at least ten kilograms overweight. When she saw me take out my stethoscope, she would bare a little space below her collarbone by pulling down on the collar of her dress. Her heart sounds were normal. Then I would say, *"nami, ya hajji,"* and she would lie down and pull up her dress. My young unmarried patients always looked out the window apprehensively to make sure that nobody was watching from the street below, but the older women did not worry about that. Under her homemade dark floral dress she wore a light floral print petticoat of cotton or flannel, and under that, homemade flannel bloomers tucked into her stockings.

She always had a little pain here and there in the abdomen, not related to any physical findings, and she usually insisted on holding my hand so that I would press the one special spot where the pain was. She did not see why I would be interested in examining anything else. As I was finishing, she would say that she also had low back pain and pain in her knees. On exam, these spots were always tender, and I could usually feel crepitations (crackling sensations) in her knee joints.

After I finished examining her, she said, *"yeeslamu,"* ("thank you"). She might have had eight or ten children, but this was probably the first time in her life that she had been fully examined by a doctor, and for most of the ladies, I learned, a real physical exam was just as satisfying as getting pills. But I would probably order an EKG also (which always showed non-specific ST-T wave changes), and antacids or an aspirin-like pain reliever, and tell her to lose weight. Of course she replied, as my American patients always did, "But I don't eat any sweets. I don't eat any fried food. Only fruits and vegetables and a little meat."

As she got up from the examining table, she insisted on folding up the sheet for the next patient, even though I told her that it was not necessary. I instructed her to come back in two weeks with her other medications, or return at any time if she had severe pain. She was always very good about keeping her appointments.

If one of our doctors told a patient that he should be hospitalized, the patient might go home to consult with his family, but usually he would go right upstairs and get into bed with his clothes on. Later his relatives would come to the hospital and bring him food—usually *laban* (yoghurt), fruit, juices, and simple cooked dishes. Occasionally one of the adults brought a radio, and some mothers would give their small children a piece of paper money to play with, but most patients were content to lie in bed talking to their families or each other. Mothers stayed with their younger children who were hospitalized, and an older child or female relative stayed with an older patient. We bought some books and simple games for the children to play with, because they never had toys of their own. Sometimes a family member brought in a doll for a sick child, but the mother and child always kept the doll in the plastic box it came in.

Our hospital was divided into a large female ward, where the younger children also stayed, and a smaller ward for men and older boys. There was an isolation room where we could put patients who were bizarre or distraught or possibly contagious. If it was empty, it was available for the doctor on night duty.

We hospitalized most of the children we saw with high fevers, to prevent their mothers from treating them with over-the-counter antibiotics. If our patients got worse at any time or did not improve under treatment after three days or so, we transferred them to a larger hospital in Sidon, though the doctors there usually had nothing to add to the treatment we had started.

Our doctors made rounds on the patients three times a day. The standard greeting to a patient, which I got to know by heart, was "May you be in good health. How are you feeling today? Better than yesterday, God willing." Or, if the patient was about to be discharged, "Thanks be to God for your recovery."

Local Hospitals

With the exception of Hariri Hospital, built by Rafik Hariri, Sidon's most successful businessman, to be an academic center, the hospitals in town were privately run by their owners, most of whom were surgeons and gynecologists.

They had built them after making a lot of money in a short time during the years before the Israeli invasion. In spite of differences in scale, these hospitals were alike in many ways. Most had gardens and fountains in front, and big lobbies with comfortable chairs and marble floors. Most also had steel cables and concrete blocks jutting from a corner of the building, a sign of the owner's dream of further expansion after the situation improved.

But the hospitals were really "part boutique and part butcher shop," as one Lebanese friend described them, and the plants in the lobby got better care than some of the patients in the back rooms. A colleague who tried to have a paraplegic Lebanese patient admitted to a large, well-equipped hospital to control her intractable pain was told that the hospital would accept her only if she supplied the pain medications herself. At another hospital, according to UNRWA doctors, the owner beat his Palestinian patients and gave them different food than he gave the Lebanese patients. Even at the best hospitals in Sidon, most doctors had stopped writing histories and physicals long ago, regarding that lowly work as the province of interns who were, "because of the situation," no longer available. There were still a few doctors who cared enough to keep good detailed records on their patients, but in most cases, aside from the nurses' notes, the only information on a patient's chart was the doctor's orders and the lab and X-ray results.

Most hospitals in Sidon were comparable to medium-sized American community hospitals in the services they offered: X-ray facilities, operating and delivery rooms, nurseries with incubators, a few beds with cardiac monitors. One hospital had a well-run dialysis unit which treated about sixty patients a week. But there were some serious deficiencies. For example, although dozens of surgeons practiced in South Lebanon, an area with a population of about 800,000, there was not a single pathology lab. Only one radiologist and one neurosurgeon served the area. Since hospitals did not have respirators for infants and children, babies born with respiratory distress usually did not live long. Patients who needed special tests and treatment unavailable in Sidon had always gone directly to

Beirut hospitals. The closing of the coast road a few months later proved serious for them.

Two of the largest hospitals in Sidon had contracts with UNRWA, and when a patient of ours became too sick for us to treat, or had to be seen by a specialist, we referred him to one of them. The directors of both hospitals had received some of their surgical training in the U.S., and we got to know them well. Every week I made rounds on our patients at one hospital, and Kay did rounds at the other. It was never easy to find out what was going on with these patients, because so little clinical information was on the chart (the parts used for billing, however, were filled out quite carefully). I was content to make contact with our patients during my rounds, and to see what clinical studies had been done. But occasionally I protested about the care a patient was getting. One night we drove a pregnant woman to the hospital with a suspected skull fracture. Later, I was surprised to find no mention on her chart that she had been in a coma for three days. We had her transferred to a hospital with a neurosurgeon on the staff.

Kay's rounds were made at Fuad Hospital. She also volunteered to work with the nurse anesthetist in the operating room there one morning a week, to keep up her anesthesia skills. She was usually on good terms with the director, Dr. Fuad, although she found that his feelings about the U.S. had soured since the Israeli invasion. Once she arrived for work to find Dr. Fuad tired and angry. He had been up all night operating on a child who had been shot by "your friends, the Israelis," but the child died. "I'm not going to discuss politics with you," Kay said. He never brought up the subject again.

After Kay had been working with Dr. Fuad for a few months, he revived weekly grand rounds at his hospital for a while, and served a big buffet lunch for all the doctors who came. He hoped that the doctors from our hospital and the UNRWA clinic would come too, he said. But most of the UNRWA doctors stayed away. They were dismayed by Dr. Fuad's enthusiasm for taking his patients to the operating room, and claimed that there was hardly a Palestinian in Sidon who still had his appendix after passing through Dr.

Fuad's hospital. They were not consoled by an obscure medical document unearthed by Dr. Fuad claiming that appendicitis could occur as an epidemic.

After I had been making weekly visits to Bashar Hospital
for a couple of months, I visited Dr. Bashar, the director, to
discuss the desirability of including at least some daily progress notes on the patients' charts. Dr. Bashar was an outgoing man, all smiles and energy. On his desk was a copy of
Dale Carnegie's, *How to Enjoy Your Work and Get the Most Out
of Your Job*, a book I didn't think he needed. He smiled and
breathed a contented sigh. He did enjoy his work, he said,
but he was too busy. He agreed that it was a shame there was
not more information on the patients' charts; he would ask
his doctors to fill out the discharge summaries, which were
usually left blank. (These are forms which outline the treatment the patient received during his hospitalization.) But
he could promise nothing, he said, with the situation the
way it was.

At the end of our meeting Dr. Bashar reached into his
desk and brought out a present for me: a 1984 pocket calendar from the Saudi Lebanese Bank. He had a drawer full of
them, I noticed; he probably gave one to everyone who
came into his office with a complaint. The next person
waiting to see Dr. Bashar was Abdallah Nassar, one of the
leaders of Sidon's National Guard. Like me, he was unhappy about something, but he was armed. I knew that his
talk with Dr. Bashar would be more fruitful than mine.

February Fighting

Lebanon was drifting toward war again at the end of 1983.
Druze and Moslem militias fought sporadic battles with the
Lebanese Army, violating a cease-fire that had been in effect
since September 26. Opposition leaders complained about
the lack of progress with government reforms in the months
that President Gemayel had been in office. In November
1983 President Gemayel held reconciliation talks in Geneva

with representatives from the country's political factions, but the talks ended inconclusively after a few days. A major point of disagreement was the so-called May 17 accord, which U. S. representatives had negotiated with Lebanese leaders in May 1983. The accord gave Israel security and trade concessions in return for withdrawal of its combat troops from Lebanon. It also made the withdrawal of Israeli troops contingent on the withdrawal of Syrian troops.* Syria's President Assad had not been consulted about the accord and refused to recognize it. Opposition leaders did not like it either, and it seemed as if, with Syria's help, they would eventually block its ratification. But the United States and Israel insisted that the accord was not to be tampered with.

The Geneva talks were adjourned to give President Gemayel a chance to go to Washington to discuss modification of the May 17 accord. On December 1 he met with President Reagan but, as expected, failed to get American support for any changes in the agreement, leaving him little room for negotiating with his opponents. Over the following weeks, as President Gemayel worked in vain on a security plan for the Beirut area, rival militias got ready to fight again.

On February 2, 1984, the battles began. The fighting, which engulfed Beirut and the surrounding mountains, was described as the most intense since the beginning of Lebanon's civil war. Militiamen from Amal fought the Lebanese Army for control of West Beirut, and Druze fighters moved down from the Shouf Mountains to the coastal highway. U.S. troops took part in the fighting. The Marines fired back when their base near the Beirut airport was shelled by Druze and Moslem militias, but the U.S. also took a partisan role by using the guns of the battleship *New Jersey* to attack positions that were shelling Christian East Beirut. The American embassy evacuated its nonessential staff, and

---

* Syrian troops had been in Lebanon since 1976, when Lebanese Christian leaders, with U.S. approval, asked Syria to intervene on behalf of the Maronite Christian forces. Since then the Lebanese government had never asked Syria to withdraw its troops, though it did not ask them to stay, either. For more detailed account of the circumstances surrounding the Syrian intervention, see the American Friends Service Committee report listed in the bibliography.

hundreds of foreign nationals were airlifted to Cyprus by helicopter. An estimated 15,000 people fled from Beirut to South Lebanon. Those who stayed behind were trapped for days without food, fuel or water, and fires burned out of control in several neighborhoods.

President Gemayel found himself without a government. His cabinet resigned, and his opponents called for his resignation. The Lebanese Army, which American military advisors were helping to train, broke up along political and religious lines; thousands of Druze and Moslem troops refused to take part in the fighting, or allied themselves with one of the militias.

The collapse of the cabinet, which had been in office since October 1982, and the breakup of the army brought a sudden change of fortune for Israel and the U.S. A network reporter from Israel referred to "concern and embarrassment" in Jerusalem over what was happening in Lebanon, "over the imminent and certain loss of any gain Israel claimed to have achieved from its invasion of Lebanon twenty months ago." President Reagan announced that the Marines, whose base was then surrounded by Moslem militiamen, would be pulled out of their positions around the Beirut airport and redeployed on Navy ships off the coast. Three weeks later, as the last Marines left, their positions were taken over by Amal militiamen and their allies from the Lebanese Army's sixth brigade. Britain, France and Italy, the other members of the Multinational Force, also withdrew their troops in the ensuing weeks.

It seemed that President Gemayel would have to turn to Syria for support if he wanted to remain in power. On February 29 he went to Damascus to meet with Syria's President Assad, and a few days later, to no one's surprise, the May 17 accord was abrogated. Israel was then left with no endpoint for withdrawing its troops. Prime Minister Shamir warned that Israel would have to maintain a military presence in Lebanon "for a long time to come."

In Sidon it was difficult to grasp what all this meant. The signs of nearby fighting were the same as those we had seen the previous fall. Schools in Sidon filled up once again with displaced Lebanese families. Cars loaded with clothes and furniture arrived in our neighborhood as Christian families came to stay with relatives. Once again Mayor Kallash rounded up representatives from all the foreign voluntary agencies in Sidon and asked them for emergency aid. Our organization contributed to a fund for blankets, mattresses and heating stoves.

During the day we could hear the sound of shelling from battles between the Christians and the Druze in the hills of Iklim el-Kharrub ten miles away; our Arabic teacher called it *"les booms booms."* At night we saw flares and rockets from our balcony. News came that the Druze and Shiite militias had joined forces at Damour and were moving south. It seemed that the fighting might extend down to Sidon. Our phone line went dead, and all roads to Beirut were closed, but our day-to-day routine continued uninterrupted. Everyone waited to see what would happen.

As usual, nothing definite happened. The fighting in Beirut tapered off but did not stop altogether. The roads stayed closed for several weeks. Our medicines started to run out, and there was no way of replacing them. Lebanese hospitals operated through times of crisis by maintaining large stockpiles of medical supplies, but we had started our operations with a modest inventory. We talked about going to Israel to buy medicines, but that was a potentially dangerous step. Some of our doctors would not use medicines that had been bought in Israel, and friends from other voluntary organizations warned us that if Palestinians in Ein el-Hilweh heard that we were using Israeli-made drugs, our hospital would be boycotted or bombed.

Fortunately some medical officers from UNIFIL came to our rescue. Members of international voluntary agencies in Lebanon went to meetings at UNIFIL's Tyre barracks twice a month to talk about their projects and to gather news from one another. When representatives from SWEDEMEDCOY, UNIFIL's Swedish medical team, heard that we were running out of intravenous fluids, analgesics and asthma medications, they let us take the medicines we needed from the pharmacy at their base in Nakoura as a "long term loan." I drove down to Nakoura with Sheila, a British nurse who administered a clinic for the Middle East Council of

Churches. When our drug-collecting spree was over, we had a trunkful of the supplies we needed—enough to last us for several weeks.

There were shortages of many basic drugs and medical supplies in Beirut for weeks after the February fighting. Luckily we arranged to buy most of our drugs and some of our supplies from UNRWA, which had a large warehouse in Beirut, and after the road opened up again in March, we never had any serious shortages.

The national reconciliation talks reconvened in Lausanne, Switzerland, in March, a few days after the May 17 accord was abrogated. Over 350 people had been killed and 600 wounded during the previous month's battles, and sporadic fighting continued in Beirut. One could get an idea of how the talks were going by looking at newspaper photographs of the leaders of the different factions. They showed men with stony gazes staring past each other, with only President Gemayel managing a wan smile now and then. They always sat far apart; if they got too close, I thought, they might start kicking each other.

Social Worker

Whenever the fighting in Beirut subsided, the road through the Shouf opened for a few days, and a small stream of traffic passed back and forth between Beirut and South Lebanon. Then a few taxi drivers would stand beside their cars in Sidon's Nijmi Square shouting "Beirut! Beirut!" as they had in the old days.

But the trip to Beirut was expensive. Hanan, a staff nurse at our hospital, had to pay more than 600 Lebanese pounds, the equivalent of a hundred dollars, to get to Beirut by taxi in mid-March. Perhaps the driver charged her more because she was Palestinian; Phalangists who operated flying checkpoints outside Sidon were not well disposed toward any driver carrying Palestinian passengers. Or perhaps the driver could see that Hanan was desperate. Her son was staying in Beirut with her husband Mousa, who had just come back to Lebanon, and Mousa had called to say that the boy was sick. I do not think the illness was serious, but Hanan went into a daze when she heard the news; their daughter had died a few weeks earlier after a long illness, and Hanan felt that she never should have let her son stay in Beirut. She was moody and preoccupied when she came to work at the hospital, but once she made up her mind to go to Beirut—a prospect that filled most people with dread—she was relaxed and self-assured once again.

"I am not afraid to face any checkpoints," she announced when I saw her off at the taxi stand. "I'm just a poor woman going to get my son." If the taxi driver had allowed it, Hanan would have driven them both to Beirut herself.

Hanan was petite, but not easily overlooked. She was a handsome woman with a magnificent head of auburn hair, and she dressed with a sense of style and drama, so that she seemed much taller than she was. She was bold, irreverent and always unpredictable. Beneath her good nature and her considerable charm she was a shrewd judge of character, but she acted entirely on her impulses, confident that things would go her way. When anyone started to sympathize over her problems, she would answer, almost automatically, "I can manage."

Hanan handled our difficult patients—the enraged, distraught, or despondent ones. When a patient started crying or shouting at one of the doctors in the examining room, Hanan would take the patient to a quiet place and talk to him in a calm, soothing voice until he got hold of himself again. Sometimes a doctor, puzzled or exasperated at the way a patient was acting, would ask for a consultation with Hanan. She gave herself over to her patients' problems, listened to their stories, visited them at home, and gave them what money she had when she thought it would help. Hanan's patients seemed to be lifted up and swept along by the force of her confidence and determination, and carried off to firmer ground, where they found that they too could manage.

I asked Hanan's help with some sad cases: a battered wife who cried and hid her face when anyone spoke to her, and a young widow with a houseful of children who said one day, when it was time to go home, that she could no longer walk. Hanan took her patients into a room that served as a nurse's lounge and closed the door behind her. When she emerged after an hour or two, she would shake her head and mutter that it was terrible what women had to put up with, but I knew that she would already have thought up her strategy. She had a long talk with the husband of the battered woman. She went to the store to buy new clothes for the widow and her many children. I don't know what else she did; I was afraid to ask. As soon as Hanan's patients started to improve they would come back to visit her at the hospital. When I saw them in the waiting room, they smiled at me shyly. It was the first time I had seen them smile at all.

But Hanan's crisis counseling was only a sideline, a skill she had learned during the civil war. What she liked best was caring for small children, for she had been trained as a pediatric nurse. She always wanted to be a nurse, though her parents did not think much of nursing as a career and could not afford to send her to nursing school. One day while she was still in her teens, Hanan had visited her niece, who was a patient at a children's hospital in East Beirut. While there she met Dr. Nabil, the director of the hospital. In a burst of enthusiasm she told him that she was a nurse, and he offered her a job. When she reported for duty she admitted that she was not really a nurse, but asked to work at the hospital anyway. Dr. Nabil made her a nurse's aide.

Two years later, Dr. Nabil called her into his office. "It's a pity to keep you working like this," he said. "If you studied nursing, I'd make you a supervisor in this hospital."

"I have no money," Hanan said.

"I'll help you," he said. "You won't pay anything."

Dr. Nabil sent Hanan to a nursing school in North Lebanon, and she returned three years later as a skilled pediatric nurse. She worked at Dr. Nabil's hospital in East Beirut in the morning, and at a children's hospital in West Beirut every afternoon. Then the civil war began, and one day a colleague of Dr. Nabil's visited her home to say that because she was Palestinian, it was no longer safe for her to work in East Beirut. He gave her money and wished her well.

Hanan and her husband Mousa moved to South Lebanon and settled in a Christian neighborhood outside Sidon. Hanan found a job as a staff nurse at a hospital in Sidon, and Mousa commuted to Beirut to work. When the Israelis invaded Lebanon in June 1982, Hanan and Mousa fled to Syria with their daughter Nida. Mousa refused to return to South Lebanon until the Israelis left, but after two months Hanan decided to come back with Nida, so that she would not lose her old job. She got home to find that their house and car had been taken by the Phalangists. For a time, she and her daughter stayed with friends and relatives. She bought a used car to drive to work and moved in with an older woman in Iklim el-Kharrub, north of Sidon, but then the Phalangists came there too. Hanan was pregnant, and Nida was chronically ill with kidney disease. Some Phalangist soldiers in the village helped Hanan get medicines, and let her pass through their checkpoints at night when she had to drive Nida to the hospital. But others were less friendly. One day Hanan heard that a Phalangist officer was planning to commandeer her car. She walked into his office and put the car keys on his desk.

"I don't want to bother you," she said. "Here are the keys to the car, and here are the papers. It would be a shame for you to drive my car without the papers."

"You are a strong woman," said the Phalangist. "We don't want you here. You'd better leave."

Hanan found a small apartment in the middle of the city and moved back to Sidon with Nida. A few months later her son Fadi was born. When I met Hanan late in 1983 Nida was ill again. Then Nida died unexpectedly, and a few days later, just as unexpectedly, Mousa returned to Lebanon. He wanted Hanan and Fadi to live with him in West Beirut, but Hanan was unhappy with the idea of moving and changing jobs again. For several months they lived apart. "I can manage myself," said Hanan. But Mousa had his way, and Hanan and Fadi moved to Beirut.

Some of Hanan's patients came to the hospital to see her before she left. The battered woman was relieved because her husband had mended his ways. She brought Hanan a present: a goldfish in a bowl. The young widow with the houseful of children came to visit. The local neurosurgeon had not known what was wrong with her, but when she came to see Hanan again, her gait was almost normal.

Conversations with Dr. Hassan

On my day off I sometimes stopped by the UNRWA clinic in Sidon after the morning rush of patients to say hello to the nurses and to talk for a few minutes to Dr. Hassan. Dr. Hassan was a brown-haired, brown-eyed Palestinian doctor in his mid-thirties, energetic and capable.

Dr. Hassan differed in two respects from the other UN-RWA doctors. First, he had not yet married. During the morning coffee break, he flirted with the nurses and told risqué jokes. But as soon as he sat down at his desk, he became engrossed in his work and took no interest in small talk. A less obvious difference—one I did not learn about for some time—was his religion. Dr. Hassan was a Shiite Moslem, which made him a member of a small minority within the Palestinian community. Most Shiite Palestinians came from villages very close to the Lebanese border and culturally had more in common with the Lebanese than did the Sunni Palestinians from Galilee. Some Shiite Palestinians had joined the Amal movement; a well-known Amal leader in Tyre was a Shiite Palestinian who had acquired Lebanese citizenship.

One day I asked Dr. Hassan what he thought about the Palestine Red Crescent Society. The PRCS was a PLO-sponsored medical organization with branches in several Arab countries. It had operated an extensive system of clinics, hospitals, and health-related programs in South Lebanon before the Israeli invasion. Dr. Hassan said that he had never worked with the Red Crescent, but he thought it functioned well. He didn't know what kind of work the Red Crescent did in other countries, and didn't seem interested. He said that he didn't want to get involved in politics.

"I don't want to fight anyone," he said. "I don't know how to use a gun. But I'm treated the same way that the PLO is treated."

Dr. Hassan had been trying for months to get a *document de voyage*, a special Lebanese passport issued to Palestinian refugees, that would enable him to go to Australia. UNRWA had arranged for him to study public health at a medical school in Australia, and the semester was about to begin. But the Australian government insisted that his Lebanese *document de voyage* be valid for the two years it would take to get his degree, and Lebanese travel documents issued to Palestinians were good for only one year, after which they had to be renewed at a Lebanese embassy or consulate outside Lebanon. Caught in this bureaucratic tangle, he had to stay in Lebanon.

One morning, hearing me ask about another doctor's whereabouts, he said to a nurse in Arabic, "She is wasting her time with him; he is already married. She should work with me." But when I sat down in his office he went back to examining patients, and hardly looked up for the next hour. At the end of the morning I managed to ask him about a reference he had once made to Shakespeare's *Merchant of Venice*. He was intrigued with the scene in the law court where Shylock insists on his pound of flesh, but realizes that he will not be allowed to take it if he sheds a drop of blood that he is not entitled to. He thought that the Israelis acted the same way—insisting on the justice of what they felt entitled to, regardless of the consequences for anyone else.

I asked if he had ever met any Jews. Two, he said. He met one in Sofia, Bulgaria, where he had gone on vacation a few years before; and they had become friends. The second was a member of Peace Now, an Israeli peace group which had visited the UNRWA clinic after the invasion in 1982. The Israeli was from the village next to his, and knew his father, who had been a prosperous landowner before 1948. Dr. Hassan asked the Israeli, "Do you think your country had the right to take my father's land?" The man answered, "No."

One day in March I found Dr. Hassan studying the newspapers that were piled all over his desk. He was reading two

or three Lebanese papers a day, and all the weekly magazines, to follow what was going on with the Lausanne talks,
where leaders from all the main factions were meeting to
discuss government reforms. One proposal under discussion was the granting of Lebanese citizenship to Palestinians whose families lived in certain villages close to the
southern border of Lebanon, an area whose boundaries had
been redrawn in the thirties. They were once Lebanese: why
not be Lebanese again?

"For me, it wouldn't change anything," he said. "I'd still
live in the same place, and have the same friends. But it
would be better—safer. What can I do now? I can't travel to
Beirut—because I am Palestinian. I can't open a private
clinic—because I am Palestinian. I can't get a visa to go to
Australia to study—because I am Palestinian."

He might never have succeeded in getting the passport he
needed if an enterprising ex-UNRWA official had not suggested another stratagem: applying for a diplomatic passport as a United Nations employee. This approach succeeded. At the end of the year Dr. Hassan was able to leave.
The ladies at the UNRWA clinic had to resign themselves to
losing Dr. Hassan to Australia and to matrimony. Before he
left, he finally married, and took his wife to Australia with
him.

A Woman's Places

After the hospital had been open for a few weeks, we were
busy enough to need another doctor to work in the afternoons, so we hired Dr. Refki's brother-in-law, Dr. Zuhdi. Dr.
Zuhdi was the youngest of our doctors, the only one who
had been born in Lebanon. He was a kind, gentle man with
a wry sense of humor.

He had grown up in the Rashidieh camp outside Tyre
and decided to study medicine because that was what his
sister Majida was doing. Majida always got the highest marks
in her class, and her father had encouraged her to become a

doctor. In 1965 she was accepted at Cairo University, the most respected medical school in Egypt. The neighbors were scandalized when they heard that Majida was leaving home to study in another country. But educational opportunities for women in Egypt had been opened up by President Nassar, and Egyptian universities had had sizeable female enrollments since the 1950s. Majida would be in a class where about fifty percent of the students were women—a much higher percentage than one would see in an American medical school even today. Majida's father took her to Cairo and helped her get settled into the women's dormitory at the university, and then he returned to Lebanon. When she came back to work for UNRWA after her graduation, she was the first woman doctor in the city of Tyre.

After that all three of Majida's younger brothers decided to go to medical school. The oldest studied in Spain, and settled there to work as a pediatrician. Dr. Zuhdi graduated from Ain Shams University in Cairo. Their youngest brother was still in medical school in Roumania.

One Sunday I drove to Tyre for lunch with Dr. Zuhdi and his family. His father was a gracious old gentleman with a rosy complexion and snow white hair. He reminded many people of a retired British colonial officer.

Having arranged for all six of his children to get a university education (his two younger daughters were studying at Lebanese universities), Dr. Zuhdi's father had another plan: he wanted to see his four children who are physicians and his son-in-law, Dr. Refki, united under the roof of a single hospital in Lebanon where each could practice his or her own specialty. Was such a thing possible? "He dreams beautiful dreams for us," said Dr. Zuhdi.

Kay and I had to adjust to some shifting standards in the way women were regarded in Lebanon. As in other Arab countries, a married man was informally addressed as "father of" his oldest son, and the birth of a daughter could still bring about an audible moan of disappointment in the delivery room. When Sylvia asked Dr. Jawad how many children he had, he told her, without thinking, the number of his sons. And yet some men, like Dr. Zuhdi's father, were encouraging their daughters to get a university education and a good job. Dr. Majida was one of a half-dozen women physicians our age practicing in Sidon. We dealt with women in top administrative positions at our bank, in the Mayor's office, and at some of Sidon's biggest hospitals.

But our doctors used more traditional values in assessing the female patients we saw. Dr. Zuhdi consulted with me one day about a thirty-one year-old woman with palpitations. He summarized the details in her history that he felt to be significant: she smoked a pack of cigarettes and drank ten cups of coffee a day, and was unmarried. "And in this country, Dr. Leila, believe me, that is a problem," he said. Dr. Refki asked a young woman he was examining, who complained of abdominal pain, "Are you unhappy? Are you in love?" When a woman came in with a problem that could be psychosomatic, like abdominal pain, he always noted on the chart whether she was married or not. The implication, of course, was that if she wasn't married, she was more likely to be a "hysterical case"; marriage solved these problems.

There was no doubt that a woman's marital status was an important determinant of her social standing and her psychological health. Marriage promised a woman a home of her own, financial security, prestige, and, of course, the happiness of having children. My female patients usually told me about their family situation in the course of describing their ailments: whether their husbands were alive or dead or in prison, whether their children lived in the camp or worked in the Gulf. In their minds, their health was directly related to their family's security. I always took a detailed social history for that reason. Still, I did not like to ask a woman outright if she were married, because I did not like the way the question showed my train of thought. There were ways to get the information less directly anyway, such as asking a woman whom she lived with at home.

"I'm *not* going to ask this woman if she's married," I said to our translator one day as we ushered a young woman into the examining room.

"She doesn't *look* married," he said, and asked her anyway. Of course, she was not.

I had to admit that most of the married women I saw with grown children did look different from the others, especially if they had a big family—and the more sons, the better. Mothers with four or five sons looked like queens, or like executives who knew that they had made sound investments. Some of them cracked jokes and teased the translators as they talked to us. As a group, the older married women seemed self-assured, good natured, and sometimes downright jolly. The young and old unmarried women, on the other hand, tended to be shy and a little anxious.

I often wondered how the Arab doctors on our staff felt about working with two unmarried female colleagues, but I knew I would never find out. They had had to live apart from their families for many years while they were studying and working in other countries. Most of them had married late, and their children were still young. Perhaps many years of student living (and coeducation) made them more comfortable working with female colleagues. Except for an occasional "toast" over pastries at the UNRWA clinic, when a nurse would say "May we all be together at your wedding," nobody alluded to the fact that I was unmarried. No one ever asked why I had studied medicine, or why I came to Lebanon. I am glad they did not, because I do not think I could have given them a good answer.

Heart Patients

When doctors at the UNRWA clinics heard that we could do electrocardiograms (EKG's), they started to send us cardiac patients for evaluation. Most were older people with chest pain that may or may not have been cardiac in origin—the kind of patient that internists and general practitioners commonly see in the U.S. But as the weeks went by we saw a number of patients with more complicated cardiac problems: children born with abnormal connections between cardiac vessels and chambers (a condition which our medical clerk termed "perforated heart"), and young adults with every conceivable manifestation of rheumatic heart disease, the result of a strep infection which can severely damage the heart valves. It was clear that many of these patients would need open heart surgery; in the meantime, they needed careful cardiac exams and detailed medical reports. Since the cardiologist at Bashar Hospital always seemed too busy to devote much time to them, we hired a cardiologist, Dr. Ibrahim, from a nearby hospital to help us manage these patients. He came one afternoon a week to hold a cardiology clinic for all our doctors.

Dr. Ibrahim was a young, academic Shiite Moslem who had studied in France. During our clinics he heard us present our patients' cases, then reviewed their EKG's and chest X-rays and examined them with us before giving his diagnosis and recommendations. His customary shyness departed when he got up to outline the pathophysiology of complicated cardiac lesions on the blackboard of our conference room. As he drew lists and diagrams on the board, his conversation would shift from English (which we all understood but he did not speak well), to French (which only one doctor understood), to Arabic (which the two American doctors did not understand). Finally, having made his point in two or three languages, he would sit down, covered with chalk dust, as one of the doctors wrote down his recommendations on the patient's chart.

Dr. Refki grumbled, as surgeons often do, about the medical problems of these heart patients. At the end of our first cardiology clinic, he seemed relieved to hear that three patients with fractures were waiting to see him. "I'd rather take care of ten fractures than one cardiac case," he said. In the emergency room, the patients were lying on stretchers waiting for him with their charts and X-rays. Nurses had plaster, cotton padding and a bucket of warm water ready for making the casts. "You can treat a fracture with a cast, and then it's finished," he continued, rolling up his sleeves and putting on his plastic apron. "But a cardiac case goes on and on, to this doctor and that one, to one procedure and then another, and it's never finished."

But in the following weeks a change came over Dr. Refki. One day he asked me to give him some EKG's to read. Kay had been coaching all the doctors on step-by-step interpretation of EKG's, but they had been reluctant to try any solo readings. The next day the EKG's I had given Dr. Refki were back in my box. As usual, his handwriting was almost illegible, but his interpretations were thorough, and absolutely correct. After that Dr. Refki must have started reviewing the cardiology chapters in his medical textbooks. He began to send us children with heart murmurs detected during routine exams in the UNRWA schools, and he was always ready to defend the diagnoses he made on his heart patients.

One day Dr. Ibrahim was examining a twelve-year old girl with a murmur that Dr. Refki had found. He listened around her heart carefully with his stethescope. Then he looked up and said, "There is no murmur." "Listen *here!*" said Dr. Refki, pointing to a spot immediately below her left collarbone. Dr. Ibrahim listened again, and then repeated his whole cardiac exam. When he looked up, his face was red. "She has a patent ductus," he said. (The ductus arteriosus is a vessel which connects the left pulmonary artery with the descending aorta during fetal life. It is supposed to close after birth; if it does not, it constitutes a significant handicap, and must be surgically corrected.) It was the only time I ever saw Dr. Ibrahim change his mind about a diagnosis.

Unfortunately, our cardiology clinic fell victim to "the situation" during the following weeks. Dr. Ibrahim moved to Beirut to be closer to his wife (a pharmacist who worked in Tripoli), and then could not commute to Sidon because the road was closed. Luckily for us the closing of the road had trapped a Beirut cardiologist in Sidon, and for several weeks he worked as Dr. Ibrahim's replacement. When he left, we suffered with a mediocre substitute who admitted that our patients were too complicated for him. Then Hariri Hospital, an excellent medical center outside Sidon, signed a contract with UNRWA, and we started sending our patients to the cardiologist there. However, the hospital was in Phalangist territory, where Palestinians ran the risk of being kidnapped or killed. For awhile one of our doctors went to meet with the cardiologist there every week, but after soldiers from the South Lebanon Army beat up some UNRWA patients at their checkpoint below the hospital, our trips had to stop.

When the Israelis withdrew from Sidon in February 1985, the road to Beirut opened again. I wrote Dr. Ibrahim to say that we had sent twenty-five patients to Beirut for cardiac catheterization over the summer and fall, and that the reports had confirmed his clinical diagnosis in every case. By that time eight of our pediatric and adult patients had undergone successful open- or closed-heart surgery, and others were scheduled to have surgery within weeks. The cost of the surgery had been paid for by international humanitarian organizations. Dr. Ibrahim came back to see us the very next day, and the following week our cardiology clinic resumed.

Of all the patients we saw, I think our doctors got most attached to the heart cases. We knew their symptoms and their medications; we hospitalized them when they had fevers, and we talked to their families over and over again. We answered their questions about surgery ("Is this a serious operation?") and got their papers in order for the military, medical and financial authorities. When they came back from Beirut after their surgery, relieved and happy, we congratulated each other. We felt that those hearts and valves were partly ours.

Night Duty

Once or twice a week each doctor took a turn at night duty in the hospital, which meant that he or she worked from 7:00 p.m. to 7:00 a.m., along with two or three nurses. We accepted outpatients twenty-four hours a day, but because of the presence of "armed elements" in the camp, few people came out after dark.

In the early evening, the night-duty doctor and one of the nurses made rounds on the inpatients upstairs. Afterwards the doctor and the nurses sat down to dinner. On warm evenings when there was no shooting they ate on the balcony overlooking the Upper Street. Usually everybody brought cooked food or fresh fruit from home and shared it with the others. Marwan, the night nurse, always cooked up a couple of hot dishes on the gas stove, or brought in some spinach pies and heated them up in the autoclave.

Sometimes over coffee Shafik, the staff nurse, and Marwan talked over their discouraging relationships with their Shiite girlfriends. The girls neither encouraged nor discouraged them, but it seemed that they would not be accepted by the girls' parents anyway. Shafik had suffered a serious setback on Valentine's Day. After Sylvia had explained the holiday to him, he told his *habibi* (sweetheart) that the day of love was at hand and it was time that she gave him a kiss; after all, they had been seeing each other for almost a year. "But she refused!" he said, still surprised at this rebuff. He sighed. "She is from the Shiia," he said sadly. "She has a difficult mind."

After dinner, the doctor might read a little and then look for a stretcher or a cot to sleep on; we had no on-call room. The nurses stayed up all night. Shafik checked the patients and their IV's, and the practical nurse on duty took vital signs and distributed the patients' medications. Downstairs Marwan wrapped and sterilized rubber gloves (because we re-used them) and gauze and surgical instruments. Every few hours the nurses made a pot of strong Turkish coffee or herb tea and shared it with members of patients' families who joined them to talk or listen to the news on Radio Monte Carlo. On some nights, especially during our early months, we saw no outpatients at all. We locked the iron gate downstairs when it got dark, and anyone who wanted to be seen after that had to ring a buzzer to summon the night nurse. By nine o'clock most of the dozen or so inpatients had eaten the dinners brought by their families and had gone to sleep.

Sylvia introduced the doctors and nurses to Monopoly when she was on night duty, and it caught on with the staff. We had a version of the game in Arabic, with a board that used well-known streets and utility companies in Beirut. The nurses who had been imprisoned in Ansar smiled wryly when they picked up the cards that said "Get Out of Jail Free." The doctors were aggressive players, and usually bought out the nurses in the end.

During night duty I studied Arabic or discussed "the situation" with my translator. One night I sat in the conference room with the nurses as we each worked on lists of new vocabulary words. I was slowly translating captions from a book of Arabic political cartoons. The nurses were looking up new medical terms or words they had picked up from being around Americans. Somewhere Shafik had heard the words "Easter" and "corset," and was looking for definitions in the Arabic dictionary. I started to explain Easter, but he interrupted. "I know about Easter," he said, "but when is Wester?" My translator, who took a political interest in events, wanted me to explain the difference between "subjugate" and "subdue." Dissatisfied with my answer, he looked up the words himself.

The conversation might turn to a subject often discussed at that time: the mistakes made by the PLO in Lebanon in the days before the Israeli invasion. There was general agreement about what those mistakes were. The PLO should not have tried to form their own government in Lebanon, as if it were their country; they should have worked with local Lebanese leftist groups. Instead they antagonized the Lebanese with their behavior. PLO leaders did not discipline their men who behaved badly. Some leaders even ran away during the invasion instead of staying to fight the Israelis. They would have to do better next time.

Sometimes as we worked we heard the sound of an explosion in town followed by a volley of machine-gun fire. That usually signified an ambush against an Israeli patrol. At the first sound of gunfire the bright-as-day beam of the Israelis' searchlight went on and swept across Sidon from their barracks on the hills of Mar Elias, like a giant eye opening and looking suspiciously from side to side. On quieter nights we watched from our window as Israeli soldiers drove into the camp to make arrests. Even if they were arresting only one or two people, they usually came in at least three jeeps, with enough soldiers to surround the house of each one who would be taken prisoner.

Attacks against members of the National Guard who lived in the camp were common at night. The houses of their leaders were surrounded by bodyguards, so any attack against them usually led to a prolonged gun battle. After watching and listening for a few minutes, my translator could guess which National Guard member was being attacked, how many were in the battle, and what kind of weapons they were using. As soon as fighting began inside the camp, members of the National Guard quickly gathered on the street below us to shoot at any cars trying to leave Ein el-Hilweh. At the sound of shooting or guns being loaded outside, our patients would wake up and run from their beds to the stairwell, tearing out their IV's in the process. Luckily no stray bullets found their way into the upstairs ward during the many gun battles fought around us that year.

The night-duty doctor got up at dawn to make rounds with Shafik again and write discharge orders on patients who were ready to go home. Kay and I liked to discharge our hospitalized patients as soon as we could, but the other doctors were more easygoing, and found little excuses for keeping their patients an extra day or so.

Dr. Jawad was always on call the night before me, so I saw many of his hospitalized patients. He was the butt of jokes because all the depressed, distraught and aggressive patients seemed to come in on his night. The nurses referred to this group as "mental cases." The big gun battles usually happened on Dr. Jawad's night, too. All this was hard on Dr. Jawad, who was a gentle man unnerved by violence of any kind. All he wanted was a chance to take care of ordinary patients in quiet surroundings, and to follow a predictable routine. In many ways he practiced medicine like an old country doctor. When his patients failed to improve on our medications, he supplemented the drugs with strange drops and tablets that I had never heard of. He tended to be more formal with his patients than most of the other doctors, and the language of his medical orders, like his spoken English, was quaint and distinctive. He seemed to regard the patient's ailment as a kind of unsightly beast to be tamed only within the four walls of the hospital. Regardless of the patient's admitting diagnosis, his first order was the same: "Admit for control."

After a day or two his patient might start getting better, but Dr. Jawad was not misled; the beast could still be danger-ous. While noting on the chart that the patient had im-proved, he would add: "Keep one more night to control the improvement."

A patient who was hospitalized for several days would be seen by all of the doctors in turn, and our different orders soon confused the nurses. When that happened, Marcia would ask us to clarify our orders. Dr. Jawad complied with this request by writing "Continue the above order as above" or "Continue the same order as above with respect to the other part of the order."

Dr. Jawad was very popular with his patients. Because of, or in spite of, those mysterious medicines he used, they all did well under his care. For a long time I thought that Dr. Jawad's style of speaking and writing came from his work as a schoolteacher, or was perhaps influenced by his many years in Spain. But those who knew him said he spoke Arabic and Spanish the same way—as if each sentence were an old-fashioned bouquet of carefully-chosen words.

When the morning doctor came in at 7:00 a.m., he sat down for coffee with the night-duty doctor. They discussed the situation for a few minutes, and then made rounds together before the night-duty doctor went home.

National Guard

Soon after the hospital opened, members of the Israeli-sponsored National Guard came to look it over. Knowing what we were doing and who was working with us was part of their job. They had an office a block away, and some of their leaders lived nearby, so we saw a lot of them in the next few months. We were in a volatile area, just outside the entrance to Ein el-Hilweh at the intersection of a road that led to the Lower Street and the National Guard office. As soon as any battle began in Ein el-Hilweh, the National Guard closed off all roads leading into the camp and established a checkpoint in front of our hospital. Anyone wounded inside the camp during a shootout had trouble getting out for medical treatment. In fact, most of the people we treated with gunshot wounds over the following months were our neighbors from the National Guard.

At first they were cooperative enough to check their weapons at the door, where we had posted a sign in Arabic which read "No Guns Allowed." When a National Guard leader came with a medical problem, the Palestinian doctors and nurses were reluctant to treat him, fearing that he would blame them if he was dissatisfied with his treatment; so, unless his complaint was minor, he was seen by an American doctor or nurse. There was a sudden silence whenever someone from the National Guard walked in. Their power and influence were unquestioned: they had sent most of the men on our staff to prison for a year or more, and they could have them arrested again at any time.

They came to ask us for favors, but they hung back a little at first, because we were Americans. They wanted to use our telephone to call the IDF. They wanted to "borrow" some medical supplies. Then they wanted to drive our ambulance into the camp. We compromised on the smaller matters, but stuck by our rules most of the time. We made sure that there was an American on duty in the hospital twenty-four hours a day to handle any ticklish problems.

A week after the hospital opened, we heard that a woman, said to be a spy, had been shot the night before by armed men inside Ein el-Hilweh. Because people in the camp had been warned, in leaflets stuck under their doors, to stay inside if they heard any shooting, she lay on the ground a long time before anyone came to help her.

After hearing this, I staged a mock emergency with the night staff, which consisted of two nurses, a translator and a guard. I thought that we would soon be seeing victims of these gun battles, and I wanted to make sure that we could work together efficiently in an emergency, even if we were surrounded by nervous and angry armed men. I went over some first aid measures and the ABC's of basic life support, and we looked at our emergency room equipment together. Then, to give everyone practice, I played an unconscious victim who had to be picked up at our front gate and rushed upstairs for treatment. This exercise had a calming effect on me at least. During the next year we all held up well in every kind of medical-military emergency.

In the beginning, members of the National Guard went about their business quietly; since most of their enemies were still in prison, there was rarely any need for a show of force. If a man from the National Guard saw a car that he liked, for example, he had no need to steal it; he merely went to the owner, as he did to a relative of one of our doctors, and asked for the keys. National Guard members took a special interest in any meeting within the camp because meetings were considered political events until proven otherwise. But they did not have to hang around outside looking nosy. To find out why a meeting was being held, they had only to wait for it to be over and then arrest one of the participants. Translators were often arrested after meetings held by representatives of Western relief agencies, and their employers would then have to intervene to get them released.

So confident were the men in the National Guard of their power that if they wanted to interrogate someone, they did not always arrest him—they could simply tell him to appear for questioning, knowing that it was impossible for him not to come. This tactic was used on the brother of one of our translators. His family then had several days to consider how best to deal with the problem; for example, whether to offer money to the National Guard, or to ask a more mellow member from their midst to intervene on the man's behalf to make sure that he would be released after the questioning.

Serious opposition to the National Guard began only when more than a thousand men returned to Ein el-Hilweh from Ansar in November 1983. Ambushes and attacks against them became commonplace in the months that followed, and sometimes led to long shootouts inside the camp. The gun battles that erupted outside our hospital window were like scenes from a gangster movie. National Guardsmen knelt in the road and fired into the camp as cars raced up behind them and more armed men got out and joined in the shooting or rounded up everyone in sight. A nurse on his way to our hospital for a job interview was arrested outside the front gate during one shootout. On another occasion a pediatric patient of mine was beaten with a rifle butt at the National Guard checkpoint in front of the hospital. Dr. Refki's parked car was sprayed with machine gun fire three times in a month during battles in the camp.

Those who were caught up in the violence felt trapped and desperate. A woman who had been wounded in her house in an assassination attempt came to see us after being discharged from another hospital, and begged to be allowed to stay at our hospital instead of going back home. A Palestinian who worked for UNRWA was brought to the hospital after collapsing at work. His friends said that he was being pressured by men from the National Guard demanding jobs and favors, and by their victims, who came to him to protest the threats and beatings they had gotten. A high-strung young woman associated with the National Guard often came to our hospital to see the doctors. She cut her wrists one day in a suicide attempt, and was still so distraught after her wounds were sutured that she tried to tear out the stitches with her teeth.

When a campaign of arrests and rearrests failed to stop the attacks against them, beleaguered National Guard members responded by punishing the entire camp and threatening worse reprisals. After one of their members was killed inside Ein el-Hilweh, they used bulldozers to erect earthen barricades across every road leading into the camp, and prevented anyone from going in or out even on foot. The schools and the UNRWA clinic closed, and life in the camp came to a standstill until the National Guard consented to open the roads again. After a shooting incident in early March, a member of the National Guard named Abu Ali Fakhouri gave a well-remembered speech with a bullhorn in front of our hospital. He warned the people of Ein el-Hilweh that if armed elements in the camp continued to threaten them, National Guard members would come into the camp "with our Phalangist brothers," and there would be a massacre like that of Sabra and Shatila.

The Israelis had a curious attitude toward their unsavory allies. Although members of the National Guard made no secret of their dependence on the IDF, and could be seen in the company of Israeli soldiers whenever any large-scale arrests were made in the camp, Israeli military representatives maintained to reporters and to Western relief workers that what the National Guard did was no responsibility of theirs. In an interview with a reporter from the Washington *Post* in May 1984, Colonel Sami, the Israeli officer in charge of military affairs in South Lebanon, even denied that there was an Israeli-backed militia in the camp at all.

But in the spring of 1984 a chain of events in Ein el-Hilweh brought Israel unwelcome international publicity, and finally caused the IDF to draw in the reins of the National Guard. The trouble began when the IDF went into Ein el-Hilweh on the night of May 16 to make arrests. According to Western news reports, the soldiers arrested about thirty people and also dynamited houses in the camp where, they said, "large caches of arms" had been found. The Israelis did not add that the explosions went off while people were still inside, though they obviously knew, because an Israeli medic treated some of the casualties. Sylvia and Dr. Jawad treated four patients that night who had been injured in the explosions. Twenty people were injured in all, according to UN sources.

The following day the residents of Ein el-Hilweh held a demonstration against the IDF. A leading National Guard member named Ibrahim Ristom fired at the crowd of demonstrators, killing a woman. Although the cause of the demonstration was well-known and the identity of the attacker was confirmed by eyewitness accounts, Israeli military spokesmen dismissed the incident as an "internal dispute" that had occurred, they said, during a demonstration over economic conditions in the camp, a matter which was not their concern. But reporters from Beirut got a very different version of events from camp residents, and the funeral of the slain woman became the occasion for an even bigger demonstration against the Israelis and the National Guard.

The Commissioner General of UNRWA, Olaf Rydbeck, expressed alarm at what was happening in Ein el-Hilweh and asked the Israeli army to investigate. The U.S. State Department deplored the events, and Arab states called on the UN Security Council to hold a discussion about the situation in the camp. Finally representatives from the IDF agreed to talk with UNRWA. Colonel Sami summoned local UNRWA officials to an evening meeting at IDF headquarters to discuss the security situation in the camp. According to an UNRWA representative who was present at the meeting, Colonel Sami was told that the violence in Ein el-Hilweh would continue as long as the National Guard was allowed to operate inside the camp. Evidently he agreed, because shortly afterwards all men from the National Guard moved outside the perimeter of the camp, and resigned themselves to carrying on their activities in Ein el-Hilweh by remote control.

David and Captain Albert

One day about this same time, David went up to the headquarters of the IDF in Kfar Falous with a list of our Palestinian patients who needed permission to go to Beirut or Israel for medical treatment. Some had already had surgery in Israel and were supposed to return for follow-up and additional surgical procedures. (In the aftermath of the Israeli invasion, when medical services in South Lebanon were disrupted, many Palestinian and Lebanese patients were treated by Israeli doctors, and some patients who needed special surgery were sent to Israeli hospitals, where they were treated at no cost.) Others were newly-diagnosed cardiac patients whom we wanted to send to Beirut for cardiac catheterization.

David had broken his wrist during a football game a few days earlier, but thought he would have no trouble driving with his arm in a cast, so he went alone. He was standing outside the IDF headquarters with a group of Lebanese who were also waiting for permits when he spotted Captain Albert, the Israeli officer in charge of civilian affairs in South

Lebanon. He had met the Captain before, and had chatted with him a few times, and so he called out to him. Captain Albert responded by walking up to David and, without a word, punching him in the face. He then summoned a group of soldiers from the South Lebanon Army to hold David down as the beating continued. They took David inside a building, where he was beaten again and kept under guard. Soldiers from the South Lebanon Army had him strip, and put a metal rod down his cast, apparently to make sure that he was not concealing anything.

A couple of hours later, David was taken to see Colonel Sami, the officer in charge of Israeli military forces in South Lebanon, and another man dressed in civilian clothes. The Colonel professed shock at what had happened, and promised that the matter would be handled in "Israeli military fashion." But, he said, Captain Albert was sure that David had authored an article in an Amal newspaper about the Israeli liaison office in Dbayeh, East Beirut; was the office an embassy or an intelligence center? the article asked.

"I'm not excusing what the Captain did," said the Colonel, "but you had no right to write an article like that. You shouldn't claim to be one thing when you're another. It's all right to be a journalist if you say you are a journalist—we don't keep them out—it's your being here under false pretenses that we don't like."

The mixture of arrogance and paranoia in these officers was so shocking that it was hard to tell if they believed what they were saying. Did Captain Albert really think that David wrote an article in the Amal newspaper, when David could not read or write Arabic? Or did the Captain just dislike David? There were a lot of people that Captain Albert did not like. Perhaps he had heard that David was playing on a local Lebanese football team, and considered this goodwill demonstration a dangerous development. Perhaps he was sending a message to Washington that the Americans who had been sent over in a program funded by the State Department were getting in his way.

It takes a lot of nerve to hit a man in front of twenty witnesses, especially when the man has a cast on his arm, and then say you did not do it. But that is exactly what happened. Evidently the Captain was confident that he could get away with it, and he was right. The Israeli officials contacted about David's beating promised that the Captain would be court-martialled if the story were true. Then, during the course of their official investigation, the Israelis changed their minds about what David had been up to. In searching his belongings, they said, they had found "coded information" linking David with an extremist Shiite militia. David was a spy, they concluded, and the whole incident was David's own fault. They actually insisted that David had hit the Captain first. The State Department was said to have been "very sympathetic" about David's predicament, but claimed that there was nothing to be done about it.

In the interest of being thorough, the Israelis also visited local Shiite leaders and warned them that David was a CIA agent. Our Shiite friends who told us this story thought it very funny that the Israelis would go to such lengths to discredit David, but it was an ominous move. Though our friends disregarded what the IDF said, it would not have been hard for the Israelis to exploit anti-American feelings by spreading rumors like these among armed Shiites, if they wanted to do so. It was clear that David would have to leave the country for his own safety, but that would not be easy either, for the IDF had taken his passport.

Within hours the story of David's beating had spread around Sidon and up to Beirut, related by some of the Lebanese who had seen it, and David was asked to tell Beirut-based journalists what had happened. But we all agreed that it would not be wise for us to publicize the incident. Any publicity could have led to reprisals against our hospital or its staff—reprisals that could endanger us all and force the hospital to close.

The Beirut airport was not open, so David had to leave Lebanon some other way. Nobody thought it wise for him to go through Israel. He obtained another passport from the U.S. Embassy in Beirut, and finally left via Damascus in a U.N. convoy. His encounter with Captain Albert was mentioned briefly in some American and European newspapers over the summer, long after he had left. Even a reporter who wrote about the incident at length after checking the facts with the American Embassy could not explain why it had happened.

PART THREE:
JUNE 1984—February 1985

Briefing

South Lebanon remained cut off from the rest of the country as it began its third summer of Israeli military occupation. Christians travelling between Beirut and South Lebanon could travel by boat, but everyone else had to use the long road through the Shouf Mountains.

Attacks against Israeli troops increased, and lists were circulated of those accused of collaborating with Israel. Lebanese leaders appealed to the United States to compel Israel to lift the harsh conditions of its occupation. A United Nations Security Council vote calling on Israel to ease its restrictions was supported by all members except the United States. The American veto generated considerable anger in Lebanon. Two weeks later, the United States Embassy in East Beirut was attacked by a suicide car bomb that killed twenty-three, including two Americans.

Late in September Israel announced that it was willing to withdraw its troops from Lebanon without a simultaneous withdrawal of Syrian troops, a condition it had insisted on before.

After Israel's announcement, political and religious leaders in Sidon began to hold meetings to try to forestall confrontations that might occur after the Israeli withdrawal. Apprehension increased over the possibility of an outbreak of fighting and our thoughts turned to the role our hospital might play in responding to a nearby disaster.

The days before the Israelis' final withdrawal were marked by bomb scares and scattered exchanges of gunfire around the city. Major roads were closed off. A growing paralysis came over the city amid rumors that the withdrawal was imminent. The Israelis finally left Sidon on February 16, as people sang and danced in the streets and mosques broadcast prayers of thanksgiving.

Voyage Home and Back

A few days after David's beating I went back to America briefly because of a death in the family. I left Sidon with a half-dozen other passengers on a cargo boat returning empty to Cyprus, and took a plane to New York from there.

Lawyer friends in New York seemed quite hard-boiled in their response to my description of David's encounter with Captain Albert. "It's a dirty business," said one, who then tried to persuade me to find a job elsewhere. Another doubted that any government official who would take an interest in David's beating, except, perhaps, a congressman from his home state.

The Barnard Alumnae magazine had asked me to write an account of my experiences in Lebanon for their summer issue, and while I was in New York I dropped it off at the alumnae office. I thought my account was restrained, considering what we had been through, but evidently the editor felt it was potentially controversial. I had already given her some photographs to use, but later, when we spoke on the phone, she suggested that I also send a picture of myself. It could run with the article, she said, "so people can see that you're not . . . weird."

When I left New York, the Beirut airport was still closed, so I returned to Lebanon by the same long route Kay and I had used the first time we came: first a flight to Athens, then a flight to Cyprus, and then on to Beirut by boat. With the layovers at each stop, the trip took three days.

I bought a ticket in Cyprus for the night boat to Beirut. At the port I realized that there were two groups of people waiting for different boats: Moslems going to West Beirut, and Christians going to the port of Jounieh in East Beirut. I was going on the boat from West Beirut, because it was easier for me to get to South Lebanon from there. The

Christian group was well-heeled; one woman was even wearing a fur coat on that warm May evening. The Moslem group was more informal. The women looked like my Palestinian patients; they wore floral print dresses and covered their heads with scarves. One man carried what has become for me the symbol of the Lebanese displaced by the war—a canary in a cage. Both Moslems and Christians wore signs of their religious affiliation in gold around their necks.

The two boats were leaving at the same time. Lines of Christian and Moslem passengers moved through the customs house together on opposite sides of the counter. They looked at each other without a word. Then a customs agent behind the counter shouted "Indians!" and out of nowhere about a hundred dark-skinned men and women emerged. They were "guest workers" recruited from Sri Lanka on their way to East Beirut, where they would do domestic work and menial jobs. The clerk did not try to pronounce their names as they passed. He just held up every passport in turn with the photograph showing, and each person who passed would nod to say, "Yes, that's me."

On the boat the passengers made themselves at home; many of them evidently made this trip quite often. Within minutes four men had unrolled a straw mat on the deck and were playing cards, while another group of men started to sing sentimental songs. Also within minutes I was accosted by three men, each of whom made me a different offer. The first volunteered to drive me to Sidon the following day; the second, a member of the crew, offered to let me sleep in his cabin. The third was an older man who said that he would like to spend an evening with me in quiet conversation. Wounded by my lack of interest, he protested, "You must differentiate! I am a gentleman!" I was the only American on the boat and almost the only woman travelling alone. I had expected this kind of reception, but I was travelling with three dusty duffel bags and a back pack, and was trying to show that I could manage by myself as the bags kept rolling off my luggage trailer. Also I was wearing blue jeans, and I started to feel that an unescorted woman on a Moslem boat should at least have worn a dress, duffel bags or no duffel bags.

Later I gathered my bags around me and went to sleep on a wooden bench. Blankets and foam mattresses were provided for everyone who wanted them. The next morning the boat landed at the *Bains Militaires*, a military sporting club which had a pleasant little swimming cove. A small crowd of Lebanese was waiting on shore to take the boat back to Cyprus. These boats left Cyprus for Lebanon every night, and plans were underway to add faster hydrofoils during the day as well. Most of the traffic was going back to Beirut at the time, I was told; about two hundred Lebanese were returning home on these boats every day. Why? I wondered. What signs were there that things were getting better?

A few customs officials stood around the port, but nobody asked to see my bags, or even inquired what was in them. One of the officials, a middle-aged man who worked for Amal, gave me a ride to the UNRWA office, where I could arrange to get the next car going to Sidon. It was the first time I had been in West Beirut in five months. At first it was hard to say how the city looked different. Hollyhocks were blooming by the roadside among the garbage. Vendors at the big intersections along the coast road were still selling feather dusters, baby strollers, luggage and cartons of cigarettes. There seemed to be more soldiers on the street, and new checkpoints, and more Amal posters on the walls. During our brief drive through West Beirut we passed an Amal headquarters, a PSP (Progressive Socialist Party, the Druze militia) checkpoint, and an area manned by the Sixth Brigade of the Lebanese Army.

The Moslem month of Ramadan had started, so most of the bars were closed. Uncle Sam's, a bar and restaurant across the street from the American University, was boarded up, and the sidewalk cafés along Hamra Street were almost empty.

I paid a visit to my friends Dorothea and Peter, who lived on the AUB campus. It was getting dark when I left their house after dinner. I had not meant to stay out so late and was not sure if it was safe to be out at that hour. Everyone had a different opinion. "It's safe in the daytime," one person said. "It's always safe for women," said another. "It's OK to be out in the evening, as long as you don't stay out too late," said a third. I walked back to the hotel looking straight ahead, striding briskly.

I went to bed around midnight, but I cound not sleep because of the unfamiliar night noises: a distant boom, a nearby volley of shots. The pattern was different from what I was used to in Sidon, and also more menacing, since I was sleeping near a large plate-glass window.

The next day I went to one of the two exhibits on South Lebanon which had opened in West Beirut. The one I saw had been organized by Amal and was held in the Ministry of Tourism Building, which was being used as a barracks for Amal soldiers. The photographs and paintings in the show were close to the tents the soldiers slept in. It was a pro-Resistance anti-Israeli propaganda show. Most of the photographs were of dead bodies and bombed-out buildings. There were photos of beaten bodies photographed in color, with every bruise and welt showing, bodies of people who had been shot in the back, photos of bodies lying in the dirt with clods of earth over their faces, and bodies on stretchers, with yellow intestines showing through holes in their clothes. I looked at each picture medically, as I had looked at newspaper photographs of the bodies of women and children killed by Christian and Moslem militiamen in Beirut that winter. I hoped that everyone in the pictures had died instantly, before the photographers arrived.

Later I met an American woman who had worked at AUB for many years, and asked her about the situation in Beirut.

"Things have gotten much better," she said.

"In what way?"

"Well, the electricity is on more now." She could not think of anything else, so she changed her answer a little and said, "It's better now, but anything could happen."

I drove back to Sidon in a U.N. car. We took the coast road as far as the village of Damour, and then started the long detour through the Shouf Mountains. As we wound higher into the mountains, the car radio played "Breaking Up Is Hard to Do." Bassam, our driver, was friendly and confident. He said "Good Morning!" in English to the soldiers at every checkpoint, and "Thank you to you!" as we drove on again. The whole trip from Beirut to Sidon took just under three hours.

In Sidon I went straight to our house, and talked to Kay for a while. Then I went to the hospital to say hello. I kissed everyone on the staff, except for the very religious men and the shy ones. The Arabic greeting to a returning traveller is the same as the one given to a patient who has recovered from an illness. I was very happy to be back.

Ramadan

In 1984, the Moslem month of Ramadan began in the middle of May. It is the ninth month of the Moslem year, the month when the Koran was revealed to the prophet Mohammed. Since the Moslems use a lunar calendar of 354 days, it falls several days earlier each year. During Ramadan, most Moselms fast during the day, but break their fast after sundown. Besides abstaining from food during the day, fasting means that you cannot have anything to drink, even water, and cannot smoke or take medicine. If you are sick enough to require medications, you are not supposed to be fasting.

There is no equivalent to Ramadan in the Christian calendar. The injuction to fast suggests that it is a time for physical and moral purification, and it is; but it is celebrated with a spirit of happiness and goodwill that reminded me of the Christmas season. It is supposed to be a time for charity and forgiveness, when old quarrels are forgotten. In the evening men went to the mosques to pray and listen to the reading of the Koran. Women prepared elaborate meals for their friends and neighbors, and families stayed up until after midnight sitting together under their grape arbors where the night air was cool. (Most people ate one meal at sunset and a second meal before going to sleep.) The stores and restaurants stayed open late. Parents walked through the streets of their neighborhoods with their children or took them to the Corniche, the boulevard that ran along the sea.

Children set off firecrackers (described as "happy noises") and got to stay up late and eat special Ramadan sweets. Colored streamers were strung between houses and street lights, and the mosques were decorated with strings of lights that stayed lit all night. Ramadan ended with a three-day feast called the *Eid al Fitr*, when people visited family graves, paid visits to all their neighbors, exchanged gifts, and had a special feast of roasted goat.

During Ramadan little children stopped me outside the hospital to ask "*saymi?*" ("Are you fasting?") Our clinic was quiet during the day. Most patients stayed home and rested while the sun was hot. Some came in complaining of dizziness and lightheadedness, but they were usually older people with chronic diseases who should not have been fasting.

We saw some patients late in the day, but just before nightfall the hospital and the streets emptied as everybody got ready to eat their evening meal. Then the night duty doctor and nurses sat down to eat the food they had brought in. Even the most hastily-assembled Ramadan dinner at the hospital was a banquet. A typical meal included the following:

hummus, mtabbel (dips made with chickpeas and eggplant, respectively, eaten with fresh Arab bread)

kubbe (ground lamb mixed with spices), raw (considered a delicacy) and cooked

fatouche (a special green salad eaten during Ramadan)

foul (fava beans with garlic, olive oil and lemon juice)

laban(fresh yoghurt)

kafta (ground meat grilled on skewers)

kousa (baby squashes stuffed with rice and ground meat)

grilled fish

stuffed grape leaves

fresh vegetables: tomatoes, cucumbers, peppers, scallions, romaine lettuce and *farfarhini* (a green resembling watercress)

deviled eggs, potato salad (my contribution, and not popular)

rice

french fries

olives and pickles

fresh fruit
coffee and soft drinks

For the remainder of the evening we were inundated with patients. Some with trivial complaints had come because they just happened to be passing by with friends; others complained of abdominal pain which usually came from trying to wolf down too much food and liquid.

Ramadan was celebrated with extra happiness that year, because it began just as the Israelis had agreed that members of the National Guard would no longer be allowed into the camp. For the first time the people of Ein el-Hilweh were not afraid to go out after dark, and they walked back and forth along the streets until after midnight. Mingling with the crowds on the first night of Ramadan, it was rumored, were Israeli intelligence agents disguised as ice cream sellers. But if they were there, nobody seemed to mind.

The Masked Men

In June 1984, soon after the IDF agreed to keep the members of the National Guard out of Ein el-Hilweh, the masked men began to appear. As the summer went on, their numbers grew, and you could see them inside the camp every night. By the wintertime, in the weeks before the Israeli withdrawal, there were masked men all over town, in every neighborhood, on the roofs and in the alleyways of the Old City and at flying checkpoints on the roads.

Who were these masked men? Nobody could say. One of our medical clerks, more outspoken than the rest, was standing outside his house one evening when a masked man asked him for a cup of coffee. "First take off your mask and show me who you are," he said. "Then I'll decide whether I'll make you coffee or not." In the camp, they came out on the streets after dark, moving singly or in groups. Some were commandos looking for spies or training for later operations. Some were probably the spies the others were looking for. Others were kids who liked the excitement and the chance to go out with a gun for the first time. Thieves used the same disguise. In town masked men broke into houses and looted them on occasion. You never knew how you stood with the masked men. One night a group of them cheered our ambulance as it passed in the camp, but soon afterwards a masked man pulled a gun on one of our doctors who was driving out of the camp at night.

Most people wanted to stay out of their way. The hours of the day shift were arranged so that our hospital staff could get home before dark. In the daytime little boys with their faces covered with scarves carried sticks and patrolled outside our hospital, imitating the masked men. But when a group of masked men came out in the camp during the day, it usually meant they were after someone, and everyone started running for cover. Sometimes they could be seen quietly following behind an Israeli patrol, carrying machine guns and hand grenades, testing and pushing the Israelis, but not firing a shot. At other times they went after collaborators who had disregarded the understanding that they were to stay out of the camp.

One day the masked men surrounded a woman who was known to be a spy as she was about to get into a taxi on the Upper Street of Ein el-Hilweh. She was carrying her grandchild in her arms, and it was said that the masked men told her three times to give up the baby, but she refused, so she and the baby were both cut down in a volley of machine gun fire. The baby was brought to our hospital with four bullet wounds, gurgling and cyanotic, and died as soon as our ambulance delivered him to a hospital in town. Later the same day a man was shot to death by some masked men while he was playing cards in a coffee shop on the Lower Street. His body lay in the road for over an hour before anyone dared to come out and get it.

Operations carried out by the masked men started unpredictably and provoked a quick and nervous reaction from members of the National Guard. Late in the summer, shortly after his wife had a baby, Yasser, a driver and guard from the hospital, invited me and some friends to his house in Ein el-Hilweh for dinner. We drove to his house in the hospital car while it was still light outside. Yasser and his wife had spread a plastic cloth over a long table in the grape arbor in front of their house. We sat down under a bower of vines and flowers and ate a big dinner with many dishes: fresh and grilled *kubbe* (ground lamb), broiled chicken with *tumm* (garlic mayonnaise), *shish tawook* (marinated grilled chicken), and grilled fish.

While we were eating a neighbor stopped by to say that the masked men were out again. Then, just as Yasser's wife was serving coffee, we heard the crack of gunfire, like the start of a sudden summer thunderstorm. Yasser smiled and said, "*Ahlan wa sahlan,*" which means "welcome," but in this case meant "I'm glad you could come anyway," and we laughed nervously.

You could usually tell from the ferocity and duration of the first round of shooting in the camp how intense the National Guard's response would be. If they expected a prolonged battle, they would send their men out to all the roads in Sidon that went near Ein el-Hilweh. This time the gunfire seemed heavier to me than usual. Yasser decided that we should leave early, but I think it would have been better had we waited.

We walked out to the street and saw no other cars on the road. Neighbors stood outside their houses, watching us with some interest, as if we were climbing into a rocket ship. A few blocks further on the streets were completely dark and deserted. Our translator Mansour saw masked men half-hidden in the side streets, but I was driving and kept my gaze fixed directly ahead, trying to maintain a certain speed, not suspiciously slow or suspiciously fast.

After passing the open stretch between the camp and the hospital, we drove by a militiaman from the National Guard standing beside the road. His profile and machine gun were outlined by a streetlight. I could see another National Guard checkpoint a few hundred yards down the yard, where one gunman was standing on the left side of the road; another suddenly leaped across the road in the beam of the headlights. I thought, "Look at him run! He must be after somebody!" A moment later I realized that it was us he was after; he was running to take aim at us from behind a dirt hill across the street. We heard the sounds of guns being cocked and shouting voices. Mansour said, "Keep going!" I tried to continue at my unobtrusive speed, turning on the light inside the car with my free hand so that the men could see who we were. We just missed getting the car shot at from all sides. ("They'd only shoot the car," someone said later. "They wouldn't shoot you.")

We found a dozen more gunmen from the National Guard standing outside the hospital. Mansour stayed in the car, knowing he would be taken away for interrogation if he got out, so I dropped him off further down the road. Luckily there was no more shooting that night.

The masked men sometimes patrolled the area around our hospital, but they went inside the building only once, a few weeks before the Israelis left town, on a winter evening. They ordered the night staff to stay upstairs, and broke into the kindergarten on the floor below us. They made themselves coffee, dug up something that had been buried in the kitchen (guns, most likely), replaced the lock on the door and left again. In the weeks after the Israeli withdrawal, masked men came out at dusk, to dig up buried weapons in the fields around town.

The masked men did not disappear entirely after the Israelis withdrew, but their numbers decreased. They still came out from time to time on special missions—avenging vigilantes and their cautious imitators, all mixed in together.

Abu Sultan

One night Abu Sultan came to visit the hospital with some of his men. Abu Sultan, a Palestinian from the West Bank, had come to Lebanon in 1970, after the PLO was driven out of Jordan, and had worked for the PLO until advent of the Israelis in June 1982. Since then he had been one of the leaders of the National Guard in Ein el-Hilweh. He had

been wounded in an attempt on his life in early May, and
was erroneously reported as dead.

Abu Sultan was drunk that night, and his men were heavily armed. Finding the front gate of the hospital locked, he
shouted, "What is this, a prison? Open the gate!" He announced that a friend of his had been admitted to a local
hospital, and he wanted me to sign an UNRWA hospital
referral form so that his friend would be treated at no cost.
Members of the National Guard often came to local clinics
and hospitals trying to force doctors to give them money or
drugs, or to get free medical care for their friends or families. If an UNRWA doctor refused, the National Guardsmen
threatened to send him to Ansar. I had sat through many
such scenes at the UNRWA clinics.

I told Abu Sultan that I could not sign a referral form
without examining the patient; if he wanted me to see the
patient, he would have to bring him to me, because I could
not leave the hospital. In response, Abu Sultan pointed his
gun at me and threatened to shoot everyone in the hospital.
Our translator and the night nurse did their best to appease
him, but he blamed them for his failure to get the referral;
he was sure they had not translated his message correctly.
The Lebanese pharmacist in our building was watching us
nervously. He came over and said, "Give the man what he
wants."

Irrelevant thoughts drifted through my mind. I wondered
what my parents would say if they could see me in a scrub
suit and white medical coat trying to reason with this armed
drunk. I remembered one of the bracing Christian hymns I
had learned at Miss Porter's School:

Awake my soul, stretch every nerve,
And press with vigor on.
A heavenly race demand thy zeal,
And an immortal crown,
And an immortal crown.

I did not believe Abu Sultan would really shoot us, but on
the other hand I did not think we would have been his first
victims, either. We tried to speak to him quietly. Finally, we
agreed that our ambulance would fetch Abu Sultan's friend
so that I could examine him. A half hour later the ambu-

lance returned without the patient. Abu Sultan had lost interest in the idea for the time being. He returned the next day, though, with the same demand, and got the same answer. One of his more mild-mannered colleagues saw me in town the following day and jumped out of his car to apologize for the incident.

But a few nights later, another incident occurred; after Kay told the brother of the National Guard leader, Hussein Akr, that all he needed for his sore throat was aspirin, he went home and returned to the hospital with a car full of armed men. Never has a sore throat been so militantly defended. They shouted for the night nurse to come down, but everyone stayed upstairs until the men left.

The next day, I drove up to the IDF headquarters at Kfar Falous to talk to Col. Sami about our problems with the National Guard. A well-known Phalangist had been assassinated in Sidon that morning as he was driving through town with his family. His baby was brought to our hospital with minor head wounds, and I dropped him off at Bashar Hospital on my way to the IDF headquarters.

At Kfar Falous I heard that Col. Sami was in Sidon investigating the shooting incident. The other officers were having lunch and did not want to be disturbed. I waited for an hour outside the gate, swatting flies with a Hebrew newspaper, and then tried again. I explained what had happened to a junior Israeli officer who spoke good English.

"Can't you take care of this problem yourself?" he said. "I don't see that it's any of our business."

I explained that we had these troubles before, and the Colonel had said to let him know if the National Guard harrassed us again. I had tried to call him a dozen times that week, I said, and had been turned away the week before when I came up hoping to find him.

"O.K., just a minute," he said. He made a phone call, and then sat down on the bench with me to wait for an answer.

"You know," he said, "we are trying our best to get things working here, but there just aren't enough of us for the job, and so we have to depend on these Lebanese soldiers," looking with a sigh at a soldier from the South Lebanon Army who was standing nearby half asleep.

Hearing this remark, the Lebanese soldier awoke. "Lebanese soldiers? What are you saying about Lebanese soldiers?" he asked.

"Just be quiet and go over there and sit down," said the Israeli.

A few minutes later I was summoned into a prefabricated building nearby. Inside, a man with short greying hair and blue eyes, wearing a *yarmulke*, sat at a desk talking to three other soldiers. I was directed to a seat next to his desk, and somebody brought me a 7-Up. After a minute, he looked up at me and said in French, "Yes, what is it?"

"Who are you?" I asked.

"Captain Albert."

"Oh," I said, with an audible sigh of disappointment.

The Captain professed to know nothing about our hospital, and asked its name and where it was located. I explained the week's events to him, saying that we wanted to be able to contact the IDF immediately if we were threatened again. We had been told by the Israeli consulate in New York that Israel was ready to guarantee our protection in South Lebanon, I added, pleased that my French was holding up so well.

"I assure you," he said, "there won't be any further problems."

I showed him reports from hospitals in Israel where Palestinian children had been taken for special surgery during the past few years. The hospitals had written the children's families saying that they should return for followup, but the IDF had refused to give them permits to travel to Israel. "Forget about it," he said. Palestinians from Lebanon were no longer allowed to go to Israel, even for medical reasons.

In general the captain was polite and efficient, but distant, which was just fine with me. He took notes and translated our conversation into Hebrew for the others from time to time.

Later in the summer I heard that Abu Sultan had spent a month in prison in Israel because of the incident at our hospital. But if this was true, it may have been because the Israeli consulate in New York had also heard the story. I saw Abu Sultan months later when he came to visit one of our patients. He surrendered his gun at the door without a word of protest. I never saw Captain Albert again. Bruce, our new administrator, had to see him on business sometime later. "You know, the whole conversation was in English," he said. "He speaks English perfectly well."

Moving in Circles: The Summer of '84

Some of the expatriates who worked in Sidon during the summer of 1984 had copies of a *New Yorker* cartoon which showed two goldfish swimming together in a very small bowl. One fish was saying to the other: "Let's go around one more time and then call it a day."

We all felt trapped in bowls, or cages, of different sizes. The closing of the coast road to Beirut made it extremely difficult to get in and out of South Lebanon. The Beirut airport was closed from February to July, so incoming mail arrived by boat via Cyprus, and outgoing mail had to be hand-carried out of the country. Public telephone and telex lines worked only intermittently. The radio was our only regular source of news. As I rode back and forth between the house and the hospital every day, it seemed to me that the world was flat after all, and that its limits were Beirut and Israel, the mountains and the sea.

None of the employees at the hospital thought of taking vacation days, except for one or two who wanted to fix up their homes in Ein el-Hilweh. There was nothing to do but work, and work helped keep your mind off the situation. The younger men on the staff often stopped by the hospital to have coffee on their days off. When I asked a young unmarried staff nurse why he was not out on the town one Sunday, he said, "no safety place to go." In the old days, he could have gone for a drive to the mountains with friends, or spent the afternoon at the Rest House, a seaside garden and restaurant near the Crusader's Castle. He might have taken a boat out to a small rocky island in the harbor, or gone to the Awali River for a picnic or a swim. None of that was possible any more. The Castle and the island and the Awali were off-limits, and the Rest House had been shut down. Of course, he could still go to a movie in Sidon, or stop at a sidewalk café for a cup of coffee or an ice cream. There was nothing illegal about that, but it was not altogether safe. If a bomb went off, he might find himself arrested by the IDF or the National Guard. And then there was the South Lebanon Army to contend with. Young Palestinian men could be arrested, singly or in groups, from flying checkpoints by soldiers from the South Lebanon Army and held for several days until their families paid a ransom to Phalangist "intermediaries." We had treated some of these men for beatings they had received while in the custody of the SLA.

The foreigners who worked in Sidon liked to go on short outings on weekends, and some of us took along members of our Palestinian staff. Early in the summer Mark started taking a carful of our unmarried male employees on Sunday drives to Tyre or Nakoura, two coastal towns south of Sidon. Tyre, a port city twenty-five miles south of Sidon, was known for its Roman ruins, its beaches and its seaside fish restaurants. Nakoura, a few miles drive further south, was the headquarters for UNIFIL. It was a good place for a picnic or a swim. The Palestinians on our staff were eager to go on these outings. They felt safe in the car with an American. And so, by popular demand, the Sunday drives continued on into the fall.

One Sunday I drove down to Tyre with our translator Mansour. He had lived in Lebanon all his life, but had been to Tyre only once before that summer. I mentioned my surprise that we did not have to show ID cards at any checkpoints that day. Mansour asked about ID cards in the U.S. He could not believe that Americans were not required to carry identification papers. "But what if there were an emergency and they had to establish checkpoints on the road?" he asked. He had never seen a road without checkpoints. It was wise to travel with a credit card in the United States, I said, but that was not the same thing as ID.

Early in the summer our neighbor Nadim left to look for work overseas. The Lebanese government was requiring its employees to take their vacations days, and he decided to use the opportunity to see about emigrating. So far, it seemed as if Spain and Sweden were the two countries most likely to accept him. But he was already in his late thirties, and none of the three languages he spoke would help him in either country. Nadim was gone for about four months. The only venture that looked promising, he said, was opening a small restaurant in Spain, but he would probably have a tough time making a go of it.

Ironically, Nadim had trouble getting back into South Lebanon. The Phalangist selling tickets for the boat from East Beirut looked at his ID card with suspicion. "Nadim? That's not a Christian name," he said. "How can you prove you're a Christian?"

But the group that had the most trouble getting around that summer was certainly the Israelis. Wherever they went they were shot at, and they risked being attacked if they stood still too long. They drove their military vehicles through populated areas as fast as they could, and in unpopulated areas, like roadside checkpoints, they rarely ventured out of their guardhouses. The faces of the soldiers who passed our hospital were tense and angry.

By midsummer there were two or three ambushes a day against Israeli patrols in South Lebanon. Nobody except Yasser Arafat claimed that the resistance to Israeli occupation was being led by the Palestinians. A coalition which called itself the Lebanese National Resistance Front published statistics every month about the number of attacks it claimed to have launched against the Israelis and their allied militias. And Moselm fundamentalist groups also conducted their own operations against the Israelis. Most of the attacks were being led by Shiite Moslems from the villages of South Lebanon.

The bodies of Lebanese or Palestinian men killed by the Israelis in and around Sidon were usually brought to the Government Hospital until they were identified and taken away by their families. Anyone could come and see them in the morgue, and when word got out that there were bodies at the Government Hospital, even children would stop by to look at them.

The details surrounding the deaths of these men were always controversial, but did not vary much from one incident to the next. The Israelis always claimed they had been shot while trying to plant a roadside bomb, while the families of the victims claimed that they had been killed as they were walking through an orchard on their way to or from work. It was true that resistance fighters often hid behind the stone walls of orange groves waiting to ambush Israeli patrols (in retaliation, the Israelis had razed many an orange grove on the road to Tyre), but it was also true that people used the paths through the orchards as a shortcut between paved roads.

One evening in late July, a crowd gathered around our ambulance as it was going through the camp. Someone asked the nurses to help find out what had happened to a boy named Mohammed Ali Mabrouki who had been missing all day. He had been taken by the Israelis, they said. Mark drove to the morgue at the Government Hospital, but there was no body. Then he went to the headquarters of the Lebanese Police at the *saraya* to ask if they had news of the boy. The police said no, and Mark was turning to go when the IDF pulled up and dropped off a body on a stretcher. He was told to wait a minute. It was the Mabrouki boy. His body was riddled with bullets, his head had been run over.

Dozens of people came to see his body at the morgue. After the funeral service, a long and angry procession followed his coffin along the Upper Street of Ein el-Hilweh to the cemetery, and a protest strike was held in the camp that day.

Major General Lahad's South Lebanon Army was being groomed to play a larger military role by the IDF: they were to operate on their own after the Israeli withdrawal. But aside from making arrests occasionally, they had not been asked to do much in Sidon. Usually they sat in bunkers beside the big intersections at the edge of town. Now and then they looked inside the trunks of cars, but most of the time they were forgotten. When they drove through town, nobody paid much attention to them. The sight of an SLA tank rattling along the street was not one to inspire feelings of fear and awe when one noticed that the soldier sitting on top of it was eating a banana.

But early in the summer Lahad's soldiers were seen around town more; they were being sent out on walking patrols. Although they wore the same olive-colored uniforms as the soldiers of the IDF, you could tell from a block away that they were not Israelis. They were clumsy and erratic, and had trouble concentrating on their military duties. One day I watched an SLA soldier who had broken away from a foot patrol. He was running down the street, shouting and pointing his gun at what turned out to be a little dog who was barking at him from a distance and finally had the good sense to run away. Another soldier, part of a patrol that had halted in front of a filling station, got interested in a radio on a nearby chair, and walked off to have a look at it.

During the summer Western journalists were invited to interview Major General Lahad and his "new" South Lebanon Army. Lahad had taken command of the army after the death of its founder, Major Saad Haddad, several months earlier, and had increased its ranks to 2000 men. Lahad boasted that his mostly-Christian militia would soon have a sizeable number of Moslem recruits, and that he would eventually have a force large enough to patrol all of South Lebanon. But on September 21, after seven SLA soldiers opened fire on a group of unarmed civilians in the village of Sohmor, killing thirteen and wounding twenty-two, the IDF decided that enough had been written about the SLA; a group of Western journalists was escorted out of South Lebanon the same day, and Beirut-based reporters were forbidden to return without special permits issued by the IDF.

A few days earlier, on September 16, the Palestinians in Ein el-Hilweh commemorated the anniversary of the Sabra and Shatila massacres by holding a political rally and raising Palestinian flags along the Upper and Lower Streets. This did not, of course, go unnoticed by the Israelis. About two weeks later a heavily armed Israeli patrol came into the camp one night accompanied by a military helicopter with a searchlight beam, and, as residents watched from their windows, an Israeli soldier climbed a flagpole on the Upper Street and removed the flag.

There were other Palestinian flags just down the street, but there were not confiscated. They were made of modelling clay by kindergarten students in the camp. The flags were on display in an art show, which also featured drawings of what the children remembered from the Israeli invasion: planes dropping bombs, tanks and gunboats shelling houses, fighters and dead bodies. A new generation was making its revolutionary debut.

Getting Through Bater

Nobody went to Beirut that summer unless it was absolutely necessary. It was hard to cross Israeli lines to leave South Lebanon, but it was even more difficult to get back again. Lebanese Christians were allowed to travel to Beirut by boat without Israeli permits. But Moslems had to get a permit from the IDF to make the trip on the long winding road through the Shouf Mountains. Even after getting permits, people spent hours waiting beside the road at Bater, a few miles east of Sidon, to be searched and questioned at the IDF checkpoints. There were three checkpoints along a short stretch of road, each with its own procedures. Trucks bringing commercial goods from Beirut or produce out of the south often had to wait for several days at Bater before being allowed to cross.

Late in August 1984 the Israelis adopted an even harsher system: those travelling to and from South Lebanon had to cross the IDF checkpoint on foot, and all trucks had to unload their cargo, transport it by wheelbarrow across a 100-yard stretch of road, and load it onto a second truck waiting on the other side. Even patients in ambulances had to walk or be taken by wheelchair across the checkpoint to board another ambulance. Israeli military authorities said that these new measures were undertaken for "security" reasons. But that did not explain why U.N. trucks carrying

medical supplies were turned away; why Palestinian patients need an IDF permit to travel to Beirut *and* IDF permission to use the ambulance of the Lebanese Red Cross; or
why even infants needed IDF military clearance. Rather, the
measures seemed an attempt on the part of Israel to show
who was boss in South Lebanon. No doubt it offered tired
and angry Israeli soldiers a chance to ventilate some of their
frustration, but the Lebanese and Palenstinians who had to
submit to these ever-changing military regulations were just
as tired and angry. Not surprisingly, the new regulations had
no effect on the number of guerilla attacks on Israeli soldiers in South Lebanon.

I travelled to Beirut once in August before the new Israeli
regulations went into effect. I needed a relay of four different taxis to make the trip. Including a half-hour wait at
Bater, it took about four hours. I considered myself lucky.
When I went to Beirut several weeks later, I knew I would
have a hard time, but I had to go, since our first open-heart
case was scheduled for surgery in Beirut the following day. I
left Sidon in a taxi at 7:30 in the morning. The taxi took me
as far as the town of Jezzine; there, everyone wanting to go
to Beirut had to await a bus for the ten-minute ride to the
Israeli checkpoint at Bater. There were already hundreds of
people milling around in the town square of Jezzine; many
of them, I learned, had spent the night there waiting for the
bus.

Nobody knew when a bus would come, though, or even
how one could buy a ticket for it. I asked a soldier from the
Lebanese Army for his advice, and he introduced me to a
Lebanese man who was trying to get back to the American
Embassy in Beirut where he worked as a bodyguard. The
soldier assumed that the two of us would have a better
chance of getting to Beirut than the rest of the crowd. The
bodyguard was a big, broad-shouldered, friendly man who
had come down to South Lebanon to visit his family. He was
holding a small box of fresh figs. ("*Ma fi teen fi Beirut,*" he
said; "there aren't any figs in Beirut.") He spent the next
hour going into different offices with our passports and ID
cards while I stood outside, holding his overnight bag and
the box of figs. First he found a taxi driver who took us to

the Israeli-run "Civilian Assistance Center." The officer in charge there sent us to talk to his colleagues in the South Lebanon Army. The South Lebanon Army, of course, told us to go back to the IDF. The officer back at the Civilian Assistance Center finally told us he could do nothing to help us get to Bater.

By 8:30 that morning, we heard, all the tickets for the bus had been sold. I saw one bus pull up, and a crown rushed to it, but it was already full. A soldier from the South Lebanon Army fired his machine gun in the air to scatter the crowd so that the bus could drive off. The bodyguard and I gave up and returned to Sidon. When we parted, he said he would never make the trip again.

I finally got to Beirut only because I managed to wangle space in an UNRWA car, which was allowed to make the trip because it had a diplomatic license plate. In Beirut, I learned that our patient's surgery had been cancelled; the ambulance failed to get her to the hospital in time for her scheduled admission. She would have to wait two more months for the next opening.

I stocked up on newspapers and magazines at the hospital's newsstand. Whenever I went to Beirut I bought every copy of the *International Herald Tribune* that I could get my hands on and also the latest copy of Beirut's weekly English-language news magazine, *Monday Morning*. I had gotten into the habit of reading *Monday Morning* because it gave a day-by-day summary of the past week's events in Lebanon. It offered one way of following what was going on in the country, and what the official story was of a battle or an "operation" that one had heard only rumors about the week before. But recently *Monday Morning* had changed its format. The daily summary of the past week's events was abolished in favor of more general news articles. The magazine still emphasized its political coverage, though. Each week it printed interviews, as it always had, with two or three different religious or political leaders on the subject of where the country was headed. The black and white photographs which accompanied the interviews showed beautiful young female reporters dressed in designer clothes sitting across from their subjects while tiny little tape recorders transcribed their conversation. In an apparent attempt to in-crease readership and attract new advertisers, the magazine had also begun running long articles about fashion, beauty, and social events of note around Beirut—dentists' gradua-tions, bridge tournaments, and unusual social gatherings, such as a contest for "the most beautiful child in the world," which was handily won by a girl with the same family name as one of the nation's leaders.

The last issue of *Monday Morning* I had seen carried an article about the battles being fought in the northern Leba-nese city of Tripoli. I could still remember a picture that went with it; it showed a pile of rubble with an arm sticking out. The caption read simply, "Death." But then, by turning a few pages, you could enter into a world where everything was waiting to be made beautiful. In the latest issue of *Monday Morning*, for example, there was an article about aerobics, which asked the question, "What is the attitude of the average Lebanese woman toward aerobic dancing?" This was followed by an article on how to have fantastic feet, wherein I learned how to put on toenail polish: "Make your first stroke straight up the middle of the nail. . . ."

These articles made good escape reading, but it seemed that the people who read them had nothing to escape from except boredom. They had managed to arrange their lives so that the war was just an inconvenience, something that complicated their daily routine in a thousand tiresome ways, but which could be avoided most of the time with proper planning. But I liked to think that these beauty tips might one day be put to better use. If, for example, a *Monday Morning* reader ever found herself trapped in line at Bater, she could get into a conversation with an average Lebanese woman about aerobic dancing, and then, for want of any-thing better to do, the ladies might all put down their bun-dles and jump around together for a while. Perhaps the Israelis would interpret this as a form of political protest, and the Lebanese resistance would take off in a new direc-tion.

Crossing the Green Line
with Hanan

While I was in Beirut I met with AUH surgeons and pediatricians to discuss some of our patients, and then I visited
the UNRWA office, where I saw Hanan again. After working
with us as a staff nurse for several months, Hanan had
moved from Sidon to Beirut to be with her husband, Mousa,
whose work was based there. When Hanan heard that I
wanted to go to the office of the *Sureté* on the Green Line
between East and West Beirut, she offered to drive me.

I had promised one of our Palestinian employees that I
would check on his passport; it had been held up for several
months at the *Sureté*, the Lebanese police headquarters, because it had been improperly processed in Sidon. There was
no way to discover the fate of the passport unless one went
to the office in person, and since he could not get to Beirut,
I offered to go instead. I had never been to the *Sureté* and
was not sure how to get there; Hanan was the first person to
offer to drive me there, but she did not know where it was,
either. Her husband lent us his car. He would not have
dared to cross into East Beirut himself, but he was not
worried about Hanan. She could disguise her identity by
imitating different accents—Christian, Druze, Syrian—and
had no trouble passing as a Christian.

Hanan had driven between East and West Beirut many
times during the early days of the civil war. Her family and
Mousa's family both lived in the Tal Zaatar camp in East
Beirut, and they often went there to visit. Hanan was six
months pregnant with their first child when she and Mousa
visited Tal Zaatar in the summer of 1976, just after the
Phalangists had surrounded it. Though they were able to
enter the camp and see their parents, they were stopped at a
Phalalgist checkpoint when they tried to leave by a different

road. Hanan was driving. "Don't say anything," she told her husband. "Let me manage."

"_Bonsoir, chéri_," she said to the soldier at the checkpoint. "_Comment ça va?_" They were coming from Dikwani, a nearby Christian village, she said, and were on their way to the hospital because she was ready to deliver.

The soldier, to listen to her accent, tried to draw her out in conversation. "What do you want, a boy or a girl?" he asked.

"May God save you, as He saved the Christians before!" said Hanan. "Whatever the Lord God wills."

The soldier walked over the passenger side and looked at Mousa. "And how about you?" he said, "Do you want a boy or a girl?"

Mousa had no opinion. He just shrugged his shoulders.

"Ay! Ay! The pains are back!" Hanan cried. "Where is the hospital?" The soldier let them pass.

The next morning Mousa was still in a daze. He kept saying, "Am I still here? Am I really alive?" He had been sure they would both be killed.

The rest of Hanan's family was not so lucky. When the siege of Tal Zaatar was over and the survivors were taken to West Beirut by the International Red Cross, Hanan searched for her family among them. "They're coming, they're coming," the others said. But after all the survivors had been brought out, most of her family was still missing.

Hanan's mentor at the children's hospital in East Beirut, Dr. Nabil, was a close friend of the Gemayel family. Through him she arranged a meeting with Bashir Gemayel, the Phalangist leader, to ask about her missing relatives: her father, who was 110 years old, her three brothers, their wives and children, and her cousins—seventeen family members. But the meeting was not helpful. Bashir was annoyed when he heard why she had come. He said he knew nothing about her family, and was not interested in getting involved in such matters. She never learned anything more about them. All of the men in her family were killed at Tal Zaatar.

I held onto my seat with both hands as Hanan sped toward the Green Line. She always had a friendly word for the soldiers at the checkpoints. She felt sorry for them all, but she did not like any of the militias. As we drove away from an Amal checkpoint, she said, "You know this group, Amal? Fighting for God, fighting for God always, as if God is waiting for someone to fight for Him." We crossed into East Beirut. Hanan said, "Now we are not in a Moslem area, but I am not afraid, because I didn't do anything bad."

In fact, Hanan had once saved the life of a Phalangist soldier. Early in their marriage, she and Mousa lived in Iklim el-Kharrub, in the hills north of Sidon. She was asked to work part-time in a small PLO-run clinic there. She protested that she was a pediatric nurse, but was told that that didn't matter; she would serve as a "consultant."

One day the PLO soldiers brought in a blindfolded prisoner. His lower lip was lacerated from a beating, and the soldiers wanted Hanan to suture it so that they could continue interrogating him. Hanan looked at the prisoner. He was frightened and pale. Though the cut on his lip was quite large, it was not bleeding. "I can't work in front of you," she said to the other soldiers. After they left her alone with the prisoner, she took off his blindfold. Though he was dressed in a Phalangist uniform and had been captured with an M16 rifle, he protested that he was not a Phalangist, and begged her to help him. "I felt pity for him," she recalled. "My oldest brother was a fighter, and I thought perhaps he had been captured in this way." She said to the Phalangist, "Maybe you were the one who killed my family in Tal Zaatar, but if you should be punished, let God decide." She looked outside the door and saw nobody. She untied his hands and said, "*Yella!* (Go!) If someone asks how you escaped, don't mention my name." The soldier ran from the room, leaving his rifle behind. Hanan left by another door, jumped in her car and drove away.

At home, Hanan's sister asked why she looked so pale. When Hanan explained, she said, "You did a great thing. Why are you afraid?" But Hanan and Mousa thought it best to leave town quickly. They drove to a village closer to Sidon.

Two weeks later a man who worked with the PLO came to their new address. He was related to her by marriage, and they had always been on good terms. She knew why he had come. "Before you ask me, I'll tell you," she said. "I let him go."

"Hanan, do you realize that that man killed thirty-three people?" he said.

"Who says so?" Hanan replied. "Did you see him your-self?"

"Never mind," he said. "But don't tell anyone what you have done."

"I still remember the soldier's name," Hanan said. "If I am ever taken by the Phalangists, I will ask for him."

At last Hanan and I found the building we were looking for. As we walked past the guards, she whispered, "Here I am not speaking Palestinian." When we asked how to find the Palestinian Passports Division, people became distinctly unfriendly. "Why are you bothering with Palestinians?" one official asked Hanan. The people we spoke with were friendlier to her than to me. Hanan said the Christians were angry at the American government for pulling the Marines out of Lebanon.

The official who supposedly knew how our employee could get his passport back listened to my story without much interest, and then advised me to put my inquiry about the passport in writing. I knew what that meant. Over a year later, with the help of a Swiss friend of his, the employee finally got his passport.

"What can we do?" said Hanan. "We did our best."

Nakoura Talks

I returned to Sidon in an UNRWA car with two Palestinian UNRWA employees and a child who had just been dis-charged from the hospital. The soldiers at the first two Israeli checkpoints said at first that we would not be allowed to pass, citing regulations that should not have applied to us. At each checkpoint I got out, introduced myself, and explained that UN cars were supposed to be allowed to pass. After a lot of equivocation and delay, we managed to get through.

The Palestinians were impressed by these simple exchanges. "You talked to them! That was very good!" said the UNRWA teacher in the back seat when I returned to the car. If it weren't for the presence of a foreigner in the car, they would have resigned themselves to turning back, knowing that no military regulations, no understanding between UNRWA and the IDF would guarantee their passage on any particular day; ultimately everything rested on the whim of the Israeli soldiers at the checkpoints, who could always invoke "new regulations" which they were not required to explain.

In mid-August, shortly after the Israelis posted their "no vehicle" rules at Bater, Lebanese Prime Minister Rashid Karami and Amal leader Nabih Berri appealed to the Reagan Administration to pressure Israel to ease its policy on the people of occupied South Lebanon, but U.S. officials refused to intervene in the matter, saying that the Lebanese would have to work out their own settlement with Israel. The Lebanese government then took its grievances to the United Nations. A Security Council resolution was drafted calling on Israel to lift its restrictions on the movement of people and goods in and out of South Lebanon, and insisting that Israel comply with the Geneva Conventions governing the treatment of civilians in wartime. All fourteen Security Council members supported the resolution, with the exception of the United States. On August twenty-ninth the U.S. vetoed the resolution, declaring that it should also condemn Syria as a foreign force in Lebanon.

The veto generated a great deal of anger among the Lebanese; it seemed that the United States, while professing to be neutral, would always back Israel's policies in Lebanon, no matter how much hardship they caused. When he heard of the veto, Prime Minister Karami told the U.S. to "go to the devil." A man claiming to speak for the Islamic Jihad telephoned foreign news agencies to warn of an impending attack in retaliation for the veto. On September twentieth, the U.S. Embassy in East Beirut was hit by a suicide car bomb; twenty-three people were killed, including two Americans. The Islamic Jihad claimed responsibility for the blast.

The IDF did not change its regulations at Bater during the remaining months of the occupation, but diplomatic efforts were begun at least; two days after the Embassy blast, Israel announced that it was willing to withdraw its troops from Lebanon without a simultaneous Syrian troop withdrawal. For the first time, it seemed that the Israelis really might leave South Lebanon.

After flying to Beirut to assess the damage at the American Embassy, U.S. envoy Richard Murphy made an unexpected visit to Damascus and then went on to meet with Israeli leaders in an apparent attempt to set the stage for negotiations between Israel and Lebanon about an Israeli troop withdrawal. In October the Lebanese and Israelis agreed to hold talks under the auspices of UNIFIL to discuss security arrangements in South Lebanon after an Israeli pullback. The talks began in early November at the UNIFIL base in Nakoura, close to the Israeli border, and continued for the next two months. The two sides never came close to agreeing about any security arrangements. The Israelis wanted an expanded UNIFIL force to police the areas vacated by their army, and they wanted their South Lebanon Army to patrol an area close to the Israeli border. But the Lebanese government wanted South Lebanon to be patrolled by its own army, and wanted to assign UNIFIL only a limited role, such as guarding the Palestinian camps. The Lebanese government regarded the South Lebanon Army as a group of Israeli-backed mercenaries who had no legitimate security role in South Lebanon. Lebanon's terms suited the leader who did not have to bother to send representatives to the talks—President Assad of Syria.

As the troop withdrawal talks got underway, the main topic of conversation everywhere was what might happen when the Israelis pulled out of Sidon. An UNRWA official was seen leading a UNIFIL delegation on a tour of Ein el-Hilweh, and we assumed that UNIFIL troops would be sent to Sidon when the Israelis left. Everyone I talked to had read or heard that the UNIFIL troops would enter Sidon, and knew where they would stay. But the Palestinians on our staff wondered how quickly they could get there, and whether the Israelis would let them come before they pulled out; a massacre could happen in the first few hours.

There were many different theories about who the avengers would be, and who the victims, in battles that might erupt after an Israeli withdrawal. While there was general agreement that any remaining members of the National Guard would be killed, no one could say for sure what might happen after that. The Lebanese Forces might start firing on Ein el-Hilweh and Mieh Mieh from Christian villages in the surrounding hills. The Druze might come down from the mountains to drive out the Christians in Iklim el-Kharrub, north of Sidon. The PLO factions might start shooting at each other in the camps. The Shiites might go after almost anyone, but most likely it would be the Christians and the departing Israelis. Unfortunately, all of these things were to happen in the months that followed, but not in ways that anyone could have predicted.

Ambulance Cases

During the summer of 1984, we started to see a new kind of patient in the hospital. The medical clerks called them "ambulance cases." They were patients with chronic, debilitating diseases that could not be managed in Sidon. To get the proper treatment, they had to go to larger and better-equipped hospitals in Beirut, such as the American University Hospital. Since the closing of the coast road in February, it had been impossible for most of them to travel, but in June 1984, the Lebanese Red Cross started to take these patients to Beirut by ambulance with the help of the International Red Cross, which secured the necessary permission each week from the Israeli military authorities.

The ambulances of the Lebanese Red Cross had only the simplest medical equipment, and the ride to Beirut through the hills was long and uncomfortable, but it was the safest, most reliable way for these patients to make the trip. Going by ambulance meant that they would not be harrassed by local militias on the way, or forced to pay bribes to soldiers at the checkpoints. The patients who used the Lebanese Red Cross ambulance usually were not critically ill (they were in no danger of dying within hours or days), but they had serious illnesses requiring the care of specialists available only in Beirut: for example, patients with cancer who needed chemotherapy or radiation therapy, young patients awaiting open heart surgery, and children with complicated cases of thalassemia, a type of congenital anemia. The Lebanese Red Cross transported both Palestinian and Lebanese patients, but only the Palestinians needed permission from the IDF to travel by ambulance.

The procedure for getting ambulance cases to Beirut was quite complicated. The patient needed a medical referral form from an UNRWA doctor, a medical report from one of our doctors (both in English), and a photocopy of his or her Lebanese government ID card. Permission from the IDF usually took a week or two to obtain, but sometimes over a month. If a patient was approved, he then got a permit from the IDF in Hebrew and a letter from the ICRC in French. Then we waited another week or two for a space on the Lebanese Red Cross ambulance.

Once the patient got to Beirut, he needed still another permit from UNRWA to be admitted to the hospital. If the hospital was full (which was often the case if there had been heavy fighting that week), the admitting office might refuse to accept any patients, but we had no way of knowing that in advance. We could not make appointments for our patients, since the telephone and telex lines were not working most of the time, and we could not be sure when the patients would arrive in Beirut. So when they finally left in the ambulance, they knew neither when they would be seen by a doctor nor when they would come home again. Some got lost in the hospital and returned without having seen a doctor, and a few decided to stay in Beirut once they got there. But most of them came back. Every time I went to Beirut I took along the medical reports and X-rays of patients I was trying to send, in the hope that doctors would agree to see them soon after they arrived. Most doctors I talked to were sympathetic and helped us get patients into the hospital with a minimum of paperwork.

I wrote medical reports for about seventy-five ambulance cases. Talking with them and tracking down their medical reports from other doctors took up most of my working hours that summer. The difficulties we encountered were emotionally draining for the patients and for us. Many patients making the trip faced separation from their families for the first time. They felt vulnerable and lost. The ones who had to go were afraid of leaving, and the ones who were not allowed to go felt that we thought they were not really sick. So many patients started to cry during the course of our conversations that I always sat them down next to a box of Kleenex before we got started.

The ambulance cases and their families came to the hospital at all hours to see Kay and me. They followed me down the street and cornered me in the UNRWA clinics to say why they had to go to Beirut or to ask how their case was going. One day a man I had never seen stopped me on the street to show me a chest X-ray he was carrying and then started to take off his shirt so that I could see the scars from his old shrapnel wounds. They were causing him constant pain, he said. To escape from these patients I would say "Come to the hospital tomorrow morning at eight."

And they came. We saw babies with cleft palates, crippled children waiting for orthopedic surgery, patients with uncontrollable seizures, patients with untreated tumors, a half-dozen children and adults who were waiting to get artificial eyes. I suspected that these patients would be turned down by the IDF as being "not urgent," and most of them were. But the patients believed that we could pull strings for them, because we were Americans. "You could help us if you wanted to!" they said. One old woman arranged a fainting spell when I told her that she probably would not be allowed to travel to Beirut. She managed to clear a little space in the crowd around her and then sighed and eased herself onto the floor of our waiting room.

We never refused to see an ambulance case referred by another doctor, but I wrote medical reports only for the patients I thought needed prompt medical attention. The others would have to wait for several weeks at least, and I put their names down on a waiting list. I concentrated on patients with treatable diseases: for example, children with congenital heart disease, patients with chronic infections resistant to the antibiotics that were available locally, and patients with neurological disorders who needed CT scans. But many others came to us with incurable diseases that had been treated in Beirut in the past. Most of them were children brought by their parents: children with retinitis pigmentosa, a degenerative disease of the retina that eventually causes blindness; a child with severe brain damage from general anesthesia; two children with SSPE (subacute sclerosing panencephalitis), a rare neurological complication of measles. There was no treatment available that would improve the outcome for these patients, but I could not explain that to their parents, who felt that they and I were neglecting their children unless they could be sent to a hospital in Beirut where they would be treated by special doctors with special medicines. Their names went on the list, too.

After months of negotiations, the IDF finally agreed later that summer to let two busloads of patients travel to Beirut every week on UNRWA buses. (Considering that there were about 90,000 Palestinians living in South Lebanon, the number of patients allowed to make the trip was still quite small.) Young men were not supposed to use the bus, however, and UNRWA had to promise to search the patients for weapons before the bus left. The introduction of the UNRWA bus meant that some of the "non-urgent" patients finally had a chance to see specialists.

In December 1984, UNRWA signed a contract with Hariri Hospital, a modern, well-equipped medical center outside Sidon. Because the hospital was in Christian territory, Moslem patients were not eager to use it at first, but Maj. Gen. Lahad, commander of the South Lebanon Army, assured UNRWA officials that his men, who operated the checkpoints in the area, would not disturb any patients enroute to the hospital. However, the UNRWA bus had been in operation only a few weeks when Lahad soldiers stopped it one day and beat up some of the patients it carried. All further trips to Hariri were stopped.

After the Israelis withdrew from Sidon in February 1985, the coast road to Beirut opened up again. Our patients could get to Beirut easily on their own. Our doctors and patients congratulated each other for their perseverance, and I put my box of Kleenex away.

Hospital Programs

By mid-summer our hospital had evolved from an urgent-care center for local UNRWA clinics to a small community hospital with in- and outpatient services, a visiting nurse service and teaching programs for patients and staff. Our programs supplemented already existing medical services, or provided them at lower cost. We hoped that they would be continued by any agency that succeeded us, but if they were not, we had at least not created a demand for services that could not be found elsewhere.

The medical complaints we treated most often were asthma, gastroenteritis and tonsillitis, and the most common surgical problems were minor burns and injuries. Most of those were directly or indirectly related to living conditions in the camp. Many of our patients—both Lebanese and Palestinian—lived crowded together in damp, poorly-ventilated houses heated in the winter by charcoal stoves or kerosene heaters. Children played among the rubble of bombed-out buildings and waded in mudholes around construction sites. Garbage accumulated on street corners faster than UNRWA could pick it up. Our doctors were afraid that waterborne diseases like typhoid and dysentery could spread at any time through the open sewers that still existed in parts of the camp.

Public health conditions were a complex and very political issue. The land in the camp was leased from Lebanese citizens through the Lebanese government, and UNRWA lacked the funds or the authority to undertake large-scale improvements on its own. Displaced Lebanese families who lived in shanties nearby were suffering from the same problems. A number of international voluntary organizations were working on projects with UNRWA and the Lebanese government to make what improvements they could.

By midsummer, we had treated over 300 cases of tonsillitis, and the patients we saw represented only a small fraction of the total. They were not mild cases; most had high fevers and swollen tonsils coated with pus. We treated all of these patients with an injection of a long-acting penicillin, on the assumption that many or most of them had a strep infection that could result in damaged heart valves or kidney disease. We also saw a large number of young women with goiters (thyroid enlargement) or thyroid nodules. In the opinion of Dr. Fadi, a local endocrinologist who held a teaching clinic at our hospital, the high incidence of goiters was probably diet-related; most of the salt sold in Lebanon was not iodized, and although you could buy fresh fish during much of the year, it was too expensive for most people to eat often. During 1984 we had about twenty patient visits for thyroid-related problems. The following year, when word got out that there was a thyroid specialist at the hospital, we had twenty patient visits a month.

Soon after the hospital opened we started working on a patient education program. Most of our patients were cooperative about taking their medicines, but they usually did not know what they were for. Many of them still relied on home remedies—putting toothpaste on burns, for example—or went to traditional Arab healers in the camp. Our staff put together a teaching program that used posters, brochures, and talks with in- and outpatients. For example, asthmatics were taught the most effective way to breathe during an asthma attack, when to take asthma medications and what side effects they might have. Patients with ulcers learned to avoid cigarettes, coffee and aspirin, and heard about the benefits of antacids and the warning signs of internal bleeding.

We also started a home visits program. Doctors and nurses visited patients who could not leave their beds. A sixty-one year-old man, for example, was still convalescing from ten bullet wounds received when an Israeli patrol opened fire on a crowded street in Sidon after an ambush. His family asked us to see him at home because he had made no improvement since his discharge from the hospital. We found that he had developed a serious infection from his orthopedic injuries. It was clear that he would have to be readmitted to the hospital, and we helped his family arrange for his transfer. Later the patient's son stopped by the hospital to express his gratitude. "So kind of you," he said. "Bundle of thanks."

We made home visits to patients who came to the hospital too often, such as some of our asthmatics, and others who did not come often enough, like infants with what pediatricians call "failure to thrive." We visited patients who had serious family and psychiatric problems: battered women, psychotic patients, patients who had attempted suicide. We tried to establish a rapport with the family, and to find the solution to a particular problem that would improve the patient's living situation. The nurses worked in pairs, one Palestinian and one American. Their efforts were limited to working with possible sources of support in the family and the community, and, occasionally, from other voluntary agencies. But there were limits to what the nurses could do. Psychiatric problems were particularly difficult to deal with; there were no outpatient psychiatric facilities for children or adults in South Lebanon, and the single hospital for inpatients, in Nabatieh, treated only men.

Women in the camp often took their troubles to Dr. Majida at UNRWA's Ein el-Hilweh clinic. Dr. Majida was the only female physician employed by UNRWA in South Lebanon and the medical director of the Ein el-Hilweh clinic. She was good-natured and always overworked. At the end of the morning when she had seen all her medical patients and the rest of the UNRWA staff got ready to leave, Dr. Majida stayed behind in the examining room to listen to women who came to tell her their troubles and have a good cry. They might get a sedative or a tranquilizer to tide them over a crisis, but longterm use of such medications was rare; we never saw it in our patients. Our doctors felt that conditions of stress were chronic and were felt to some degree by everyone, and so patients would just have to learn how to cope with it.

One day Marcia and another nurse paid a visit to Mrs. Shehadi, a mother of five who worked as a cleaner to support herself and her children. Mrs. Shehadi's husband had left her long ago to marry another woman. She was subject to anxiety attacks which had been treated by various doctors with various medications in the past. She came to our hospital one night while I was on duty. She burst out crying as soon as I walked into the room and said that she just could not cope any more. I gave her a tranquilizer and put her to bed in the women's ward, but she still had trouble sleeping. When Marcia paid a home visit a few days later, Mrs. Shehadi's neighbors said that she was doing a little better—as well as could be expected for a woman in her position. Mrs. Shehadi talked to the nurses for a while, and then said, "So there's nothing you can do to help me?" Marcia was caught off guard by the abruptness of the question. The answer was yes and no, but, alas, mainly no.

In the fall we held a course in basic life support for our hospital staff, which then numbered about forty. An instructor from the Lebanese Red Cross came to the hospital with a mannequin called a "resusci-Annie" to teach the course, which was conducted in Arabic and English. The argument could be made that any victim one might find lying on the ground was more likely to be suffering from bullet injuries than a cardiopulmonary problem, but we saw a sizeable number of cardiac patients, and had had a half dozen "codes" in the hospital already.

Everyone was enthusiastic about the course, but some were surprised to learn that our four cleaning women were also going to take it. The cleaners had the lowliest job in the hospital and did not socialize much with the others. They spent most of their time silently scrubbing the floors and making coffee for the staff. People assumed that they would not be interested in the course, but the cleaners all said that they wanted to come. They went to their assigned classes, though they were too shy to practice on the resusci-Annie in front of everyone else. "Never mind," said Dr. Refki, "This will be a good beginning for them."

Other projects of ours did not turn out as we would have liked. A second-hand X-ray machine promised to us by an American company arrived with some parts missing and with no instructions. The engineers who came to look at it said it would not work in Lebanon, anyway, so it was eventually used as a lunch counter. We had hoped to build a small obstetrical unit for normal deliveries; the unit would serve as a source of extra training for traditional midwives in the camp and allow deliveries to take place with some medical backup. That idea fell victim to budget cuts and the worsening security situation.

As the year came to an end, we were not even sure that the hospital would be funded for another year. One day, after we had discussed our uncertain future at a doctors' meeting, Dr. Jawad took me aside and asked how many of our patients would be getting open-heart surgery. About ten, I said. Our first pediatric case, a teenage boy with an atrial septal defect and pulmonic stenosis, had had a successful repair that very week. Dr. Jawad was always conscious of how our work was being judged by the community. He said, "We must try to do ten operations, so that if we close, we will have accomplished this at least." It seemed to me that we had much more to our credit than the heart surgery cases. But the projects I cared most about were ones that we had just set up, and they certainly would be of no benefit if the hospital closed. Perhaps the heart surgery that we arranged would be our most tangible accomplishment, but it was too early to tell.

Fatmeh Yusuf

One summer day I finally accepted an invitation for lunch at the home of Fatmeh Yusuf, my pious, loving but chronically ailing sixty-two year-old diabetic patient with back pain, neck pain, abdominal pain, typical and atypical chest pain, constipation and headaches. Afterwards I could no longer get exasperated at her, because I knew all about her five children, her forty-two grandchildren, and her three trips to Mecca. I still did not understand why she felt it necessary to come to our hospital so often, but I learned to accept her.

Fatmeh had the longest chart of any patient in the clinic; it grew by two pages a month, until by mid-summer it was more than ten pages long. I decided to accept her invitation because I thought that if I visited her at home she would stop coming to the clinic so often. There was rarely anything demonstrably wrong with her; her examination and lab tests were usually "within normal limits." Maybe she felt sick so often because she worried about her family; it was so big that somebody in it was always running into problems. Earlier that summer, one of her sons was awakened from sleep by the Israelis and sent away to Ansar. Her forty-third grandchild was a "blue baby;" one of her daughters brought him to us a few hours after he was born, and we got him to the local hospital, at least; I did the C.P.R. (cardiopulmonary resuscitation) while Dr. Mazen drove us there in his car (our ambulance having somehow disappeared). The baby had pinked up with my positive pressure breathing, but the local hospital had no respirators for babies, and he died in a few hours. A few months later, three of Fatmeh Yusuf's older grandchildren were killed when the camp was shelled by the Lebanese Forces.

Whenever Fatmeh Yusuf was admitted to our hospital, she felt right at home. Usually one of the other patients was a neighbor or a distant relative, so she had someone to talk to. When I came to see her on my rounds, she always smiled and kissed me on both cheeks and said that my medicines had not helped, and she did not feel any better. She brought a prayer rug with her and knelt on her bed five times a day to pray. During visiting hours her children, all middle-aged, would come to see her. Her sons would kiss her hand, an old-fashioned greeting of respect.

After Fatmeh Yusuf had been in the hospital for a few days, I noticed that each of our doctors, intimidated by her smiling rebuke, would order a new lab test or a new medication on their rounds. On the fourth or fifth day, when I found that she had been put on milk of magnesia, multivitamins, tylenol, antacid tablets and warm compresses in addition to her insulin and cardiac medications, I would congratulate her on her recovery and tell her that she was ready to go home that very day, and she would accept, neither happy nor unhappy.

She was a tall woman for a Palestinian, almost six feet tall, with a straight back and broad shoulders. She usually dressed all in white, and that made her look even more majestic. She was popular with her children and grandchildren. Though she had her own house, she took turns living with her children in theirs. Her deep-set eyes and a certain facial expression reminded me of my mother. She was also about the same age as my mother, but there the resemblance ends.

One of our doctors told a story about a misadventure that had befallen Fatmeh Yusef in 1948, when the Palestinians were living in Ein el-Hilweh in tents. One night she went outside to pee and returned to bed only to find herself lying next to a man with a beard. She thought, "My husband doesn't have a beard!" She had gone to the wrong tent.

Before we left after lunch, I took some pictures of her, one of her daughters, her brother, and the available grandchildren. Her daughter said, "We used to have a lot of pictures, but they were all destroyed during the invasion." A sad blank look came into their faces, and my translator said, "Say something." So I changed the subject.

The pictures I took came out pretty well, and I gave some copies to Fatmeh Yusuf the next time I saw her. I do not know why, but my home visit had its intended effect. After our lunch that day, she stopped coming to the clinic so much. I did not see her any more often than most of my other patients.

First Year's End

Sidon seemed to grow more hot and humid in September, as if some kind of pressure had to build up before the autumn rains could begin. Outside my bedroom window the leaves of the oleander bushes drooped and panted in the small breeze that stirred them. At night there was a thick, almost sticky dew on the chairs outside on the porch, and the lights of Sidon twinkled in a haze. Mosquitoes were in season. I lit a mosquito coil before going to sleep, but if it burned out in the middle of the night, I woke up to the whine of mosquitoes around my ear, and then would I stay awake listening to the other night sounds: the clatter of tanks and armored personnel carriers going up and down the hills, the barking of dogs, the call to prayer of the *imam* at the mosque and the first song of the birds. The children went back to school. Our pediatric patients came to the hospital dressed in their school uniforms carrying bookbags, and we had to remember to schedule their medical appointments after school hours.

In early October our neighbors harvested the dates and olives. A caretaker climbed the date trees around our house and put nets around the clusters of dates before they ripened. Then he came back to cut down the clusters with a machete. Some people liked eating the dates just after they were picked; they had thick orange or yellow skins. Only the inside pulp was edible, and it had a slightly acid aftertaste. It was only after the dates had been stored for a few weeks that they darkened and turned sweet. The olives were really knocked down, not picked; people spread plastic tarps on the ground and then struck the branches of the trees with sticks until the olives fell. It was important to pick the olives before the first rains came, for then their color changed from green to black.

The Christian store owner down the street used to hire Palestinian women to pick his olive trees, but he was told by "the authorities" (presumably the Phalangists) in the Christian neighborhood of Abra that that would not be allowed this year. Palestinian women were paid thirty-five Lebanese pounds (about six dollars) a day to pick the olives. The old man finally hired Lebanese men to do the harvesting but had to pay them seventy-five pounds a day for the same yield.

As our first year in Lebanon came to an end, the original group was breaking up. David and Mark had left in the early part of the summer. Sylvia worked as our nursing supervisor and administrator all summer, and left in September. She planned to visit her family in Egypt and the Sudan for a few weeks and then return to the States. Sylvia had been our hospital's guiding spirit. Though she had to contend with constant shortages of supplies and the frequent military clashes that engulfed us, she always stayed calm and unruffled. The rest of us went about our work with a serenity borne of the conviction that Sylvia would be able to solve any problem that came up. Nobody seemed to notice how tired she had become from all her work, and how the atmosphere of violence had worn her down.

We had a going-away party for her at the hospital just before she left. A representative of the staff presented her with a bouquet of long-stemmed roses. When she got up to say a few words of farewell, some of the nurses started to cry. But others could not grasp that she was leaving the hospital for good. As she was going out the door, holding her roses in one arm, the nursing supervisor rushed in, calling, "Miss Sylvia! Wait!" and handed her the day's list of medical supplies to pick up.

A few weeks after Sylvia left, it was Kay's turn to go. She was as dedicated to the hospital as she had ever been, but she felt that a year of work without a break was enough. She was going to work in the States for a while, but hoped to return to Lebanon after a year or so. She planned to travel to Syria, Jordan, Israel, the West Bank and Gaza, and get back to Colorado just in time for Christmas.

Kay spent her last few days taking photographs and driving around Sidon and Ein el-Helweh to say her goodbyes. One day she was taking a picture of the Maronite church in our neighborhood when a young man in a car pulled up. He was not in uniform, but he had a revolver on his lap, and he wanted her film. She refused to give it to him. "I live here," she said; "I've lived here a long time." She was frightened and angry that a man she had never seen before should try to prevent her from taking pictures of a neighborhood where she had always felt at home. The man finally drove off without the film. Kay walked over to an old woman sitting on the front porch next door to our house and said to her in Arabic, "I don't understand Lebanon."

An UNRWA bus was supposed to take Kay to Beirut. We exchanged addresses and had a tearful farewell on the morning of her departure. But, as is so often the case in Lebanon, the bus did not leave after all. Kay came back home and spent a quiet day in her room, and the next day, just as quietly, she left.

By October 1984 Marcia and I were the only remaining members of the original American team. Sylvia was replaced by Bruce and Ellen, a couple who had just earned M.P.H.'s at Harvard. They had arrived a few weeks before Sylvia left so that they could learn her routine.

One afternoon I came home from the hospital feeling tired and discouraged. As I headed upstairs to my room I noticed that Bruce and Ellen were moving into the downstairs bedroom. They had put on a tape of baroque music, and I began to feel that a civilizing influence had come into the house. I noticed later that they had rearranged their furniture and brought in some big potted plants from the porch. Their room was starting to look almost elegant. I went back upstairs and looked at my room. I tried to see how I could make it look more civilized and elegant, and less like a room in a one hundred year-old dorm. I swept the dust and the the squashed grasshoppers out from the corners Rima had swept them into, and I hung a couple of Matisse prints from the curtain rods. I felt a little better after that.

Soon after arriving, Bruce started to get things fixed in the hospital. In the months since it was built it had aged prematurely. Our lazy, inept and tightfisted landlord had left his mark everywhere: windows leaked, doorknobs fell off, and paint rubbed off the walls as if it were nothing more than concentrated chalk. The elevator broke every few weeks, and the pipes leaked into the fusebox, shutting off our regular and emergency power supply. With Bruce's encouragement, the men on the staff with mechanical skills did our emergency repairs and undertook some small construction jobs in the hospital.

We almost succeeded in getting a telephone line. One of our biggest problems was the lack of a telephone connection between our house and the hospital. The hospital phone had been out of order for most of the year, and we could not persuade the phone company to repair it, so one day two young and agile men on our staff decided to fix it themselves. They got a roll of cable and attached it to the telephone line outside, and we had a dial tone again. Unfortunately, we had tapped into the telephone line of the clinic next door, so we had to disconnect it. Finally Bruce decided to forget about a telephone and buy a two-way radio that would link the hospital with our house in Bramieh. The hospital was in such a volatile area that it was important for us to know whenever a problem came up that might threaten the patients or staff. Bruce and Ellen brought a radio back from Beirut. We used it to check with the hospital staff at night, and to coordinate the delivery of medical supplies from our house to the hospital every day.

We waited a month for the arrival of Kay's replacement, a French pediatrician who had gotten an M.P.H. from Harvard with Bruce and Ellen. The doctors were taking turns working seven days a week to make up Kay's hours. On some days I got so tired that I had to sit down while talking to patients. The knowledge that a new doctor was coming made it easier to put up with the long hours, the constant political tensions, and our uncertainty about the hospital's future.

Then, in early November, our new doctor called from Paris to say that he could not come. He had been trying for almost a month to get a visa, but the Lebanese Embassy would not give him one, and finally, when his money ran out, he had accepted another job. It was a terrible blow. I had hoped to take a few days off when he came. The Palestinian doctors on the staff did not complain about working the extra hours, but the lack of a new doctor reminded them of how isolated we were and what little control we had over our fate. We did not mind working hard, but we never knew what we were working for.

Meetings with the Phalangists

One night in mid-October there was a shootout in Wastani, a Moslem neighborhood near the highway that ran below our house, and we learned the next day that a man had been killed. We heard the gunfire and saw tracers go right over our roof. Some of the shooting seemed to be coming from an area very close to us.

A couple of days later two cars and a jeep pulled into our driveway, and a half-dozen armed Phalangists began poking around outside the house. One of them said he had found some fresh bullets, and asked if we were Christian, why we had come and what we were doing in Lebanon. Most of them left a few minutes later, but two teenagers armed with automatic rifles stayed behind and sat on our porch for the rest of the day, scanning the hills below.

We had no idea how long this would go on, so I asked our neighbor, Nadim, if we could talk to a local Phalangist representative to see what they had in mind. He recommended talking to members of both the military and political branches of the Phalange party. The two had distanced themselves from each other, he said, and were not interacting very much at that time. Another Christian neighbor promised to send the local Phalangist military leader to meet us. The military delegation drove up a couple of days later while I was alone in the house. They were four young guys, not in uniform, not visibly armed. I recognized only one of them, a neighbor of ours named Pierre, who spoke English. I made tea, and we sat down in the living room in a circle. Their leader, Nicola, spoke neither English nor French, so Pierre acted as translator.

I told them that I was worried about having armed militiamen on our porch, and about the safety of our Palestinian staff when they came to our house. (Members of the staff came by ambulance almost every day to pick up medicines and hospital supplies.) Regarding the militiamen, Nicola

said that our house was in a strategic military position between the Christian neighborhoods behind us and the Moslems below us. In fact, he said, if a battle were to erupt in
the valley below, we might be asked to leave the house for a
while. Of course, he added, the medicines and medical supplies stored in the house would not be disturbed.

"Four of our men have been killed," he said. "We have to
defend ourselves."

Regarding the Palestinians, he did not like the idea of
their coming to the house—not because they were Palestinians, but because they were Moslems. At first he wanted a
list of their names, but I resisted, saying that many had been
in prison already, and I did not know what might be done
with such a list.

"Never mind," Nicola said, "if you trust them, then we
trust them. But don't forget—you are a Christian." As I
looked at their tense, grim faces, I realized for the first time
what a burden one's Christianity can be.

"But Christians should have kindness and charity for everyone," I replied lamely. Apparently my remark was irrelevant to the problem at hand—Pierre did not bother to
translate it.

Voicing the concern of some of our Christian neighbors, I
then asked, "Do you trust all of your soldiers? Can you keep
them disciplined?" Nicola seemed offended.

"Yes, of course," he said.

We agreed to meet again if there were problems on either
side. As he left, Nicola noticed the medallion of the
Jumblatt's Progressive Socialist Party on the wall. It was
hanging over the washing machine in the pantry when we
moved into the house. I had hung it in its present location a
long time ago and forgot it was there.

"What's that?" he asked, obviously annoyed. "I don't like
that."

"This is a Druze house," I said. "It belongs to the
Jumblatts, not to me."

I never saw Nicola and his friends again. They were the
first group that expressed a military interest in our house,
but not the last.

A few days later Nadim took me to have coffee with a representative of the political branch of the Phalangists, a school teacher named Hashim who lived nearby. We spent an hour or so with him and his family. He was a homely, middle-aged man, soft-spoken and attentive, ready to minimize any difficulties.

Hashim wanted to know which Phalangists had come to see us and what they had said. "Were they well-behaved?" he asked. He assured us, as Nicola had, that the armed patrols outside our house had nothing to do with us. "If they're bothering you, just let us know. You can always go out and talk to them. They won't hurt you."

We talked about the upcoming American elections, the declining Lebanese pound (then over nine to the dollar), the influence of the Jewish population in the world outside Israel, and their favorite TV program (a British comedy series called "Mind Your Language"). When the subject turned to local politics, we heard a different refrain from that of the military branch, a whine in a higher register.

"All of the foreign organizations are helping the Palestinians," he said. "No one is helping the poor Christians. So your organization gave a bulldozer and backhoe to help rebuild Damour—so what? There isn't a single Christian in Damour now. You should offer your services to the people in this neighborhood. Just an hour or two a week. Only if you *want* to, of course. It would be good for you to get to know the neighbors. We know where there's a garage you can use. When can you start?"

In the year we had spent in Sidon, Kay and I had already made house calls to most of our Christian neighbors. The story was always the same—they had been to one or two doctors already, and they had five bottles of medicine that the doctor(s) had prescribed, but they wanted to have *our* opinion. They did not want to hear that the five medicines were unnecessary; they wanted us to say that we knew of five different, newer medicines that were better. They did not want to hear that our hospital was open to everyone at no charge, and that Palestinians from neighborhoods further away then theirs had come to be treated there. They would not go to a hospital in a Palestinian camp. I knew that if I examined a Palestinian child and told his mother, "Don't worry, he's not sick," she would usually accept my opinion. But if I were to say the same thing to a Christian mother in my neighborhood, she would think, "These doctors don't care about our children; all they care about are those Moslem refugees."

I explained to Hashim that one of our doctors had left and I had no free hours just then, but the neighbors knew, I added, that they could come to our house at any time with their medical problems, and we would do our best to help. As I left his house with Nadim, I thought I would rather deal with the military Phalangists than the political ones. They were more forthright.

When I told Dr. Mazen about these conversations, he said, "Any Moslem would tell you to move out of there."

Preparing for a Small Disaster

The knowledge that the Israelis might withdraw in a few weeks' time heightened local animosities between Christian and Moslem militias, and between resistance fighters and those who had collaborated with Israel. The Phalangists had used the Israeli invasion to establish themselves as a military presence in Sidon, and they had made a lot of enemies among the Moslem population. Now they were on the defensive.

In late October, two Moslems and three Christians were kidnapped in Sidon within a few days of each other. The Phalangist guards who had been recalled from our house as a result of our protests ("if they're bothering you, we'll put them somewhere else") returned and sat by the pine trees outside our living room, holding guns and notebooks. Soon after they returned, Samir, the brother of Ghazi, a Shiite nurse on our staff, was kidnapped. He disappeared while jogging along the street at the foot of the hill below our house—the same street that the soldiers under the trees were watching.

Ghazi's family made the rounds of all of the military groups to look for Samir. The Israelis said they knew nothing; the Lebanese Army and the ICRC could not help. Finally, after political pressure was put on them, the Phalangists admitted that they had kidnapped him and taken him to East Beirut by boat. Ghazi's father left for Beirut. Samir's wife was expecting a baby any day.

When you drove through Sidon, you could sense the danger in every neighborhood. Each side was girding itself for battle, in case it was attacked when the Israelis withdrew. On our street in Bramieh, Pierre, our preppy Phalangist neighbor, who used to spend his afternoons riding around on his ten-speed bike, now patrolled our street like a sentry, watching the neighbors and making notes in a little book. Our neighbor Nadim came over to say that Israeli intelligence agents had been poking around the neighborhood, engaging people in conversation and listening for their accents. In the Shiite neighborhood of Harat Saida, Moslems were planning a revenge kidnapping if Ghazi's brother was not released. In Tamir, the neighborhood around our hospital, members of the National Guard were feeling the heat from the masked men, who were getting bolder and more numerous every week. In late September, the Lebanese National Resistance Movement published the names of about forty people it accused of collaborating with Israel, according to an article in the *Daily Star*. Almost every week someone took a shot at Hussein Akr, leader of the National Guard in Ein el-Hilweh, as he drove around Sidon to collect from local storekeepers. His name was on the list.

Faced with increasing tensions in town, people withdrew to the relative safety of their own neighborhoods, and looked at outsiders with suspicion. One day when I was driving home from the hospital I found the main road home was blocked, so I tried a smaller street that I had never been on before. One of our Palestinian employees was in the car with me. The street got so narrow that we could barely pass, and as we slowed down I noticed clusters of men staring at us. We got stuck behind another car and had to stop. My companion said, "This street is too narrow, and too Christian." I backed out and returned to the main road.

On some nights I stayed awake listening to the sound of shelling in Iklim el-Kharrub, only a few miles away in the hills north of Sidon, where the Druze were battling the Phalangists. The shelling was a reminder that a battle might soon begin in Sidon, and I wondered how we should tailor our medical efforts to take that possibility into account. We had spent most of the summer arranging for the treatment of our sickest patients. Now those efforts, still far from finished, seemed less important. If there were any major fighting in Beirut or Sidon, those patients would not be going anywhere, and we would have to forget about scheduling diagnostic procedures and surgery and start working on disaster relief.

But which disaster would we be relieving? I could think of several different scenarios we should be ready to handle. Perhaps we would be trapped at home for several days with our Christian neighbors during a battle in Sidon. Many of them were chronically ill; I wondered which emergency medications we should keep in stock for them at home. Our ambulance was used for the routine transport of patients and medical supplies, but we should equip it with some emergency medical equipment too. Lastly, I thought about what we should have in the hospital if the camp were surrounded and sealed off by "armed elements," as it had been several times already, and I wondered what would happen if our hospital were hit.

We had already had an unpleasant warning that the hospital might become a target. One evening in November a green Mercedes drove up to the hospital and a hand grenade was thrown out which exploded in front of the gate. There was some shrapnel damage outside the building, but nobody was injured. The grenade was of Israeli manufacture. Bruce copied the Hebrew letters and the serial number from the cap of the grenade and included them in a letter he wrote to the IDF to report the incident. We did not expect a reply, and we never got one. Was the grenade directed at the hospital, or at one of the other tenants in the building? If it was aimed at us (we were the only ones in the building at the time), what were we being warned about? We would never know.

As plans were announced for troop withdrawal talks in Nakoura, we started talking about disaster planning at our doctors' meetings. I wanted us to decide how our medical staff could respond to a nearby emergency: not a catastrophic event, like prolonged heavy shelling, in which it might not be possible to go outside at all, but an accident limited in time and space, like a large explosion nearby or a round of fighting that might affect only one area of town. I called this possible scenario a small disaster, and I thought we could do something to help in such an event.

Our doctors were enthusiastic about the idea. We decided to meet with the two or three clinics closest to our hospital to see how we could pool our resources. I made up a flyer with a questionnaire asking each clinic what services it could offer to respond to a small disaster: how many doctors, nurses, and other staff were on call? What kind of vehicles did they have? Did they have telephones and radios? What emergency medical supplies did they have on hand at all times?

Representatives from some of the politically active clinics in Sidon heard about the meeting and said that they would like to attend. They advised us to make sure that each religious group was represented, so we finally decided to invite all of the clinics in Sidon, numbering about twenty. I went to most of the clinics myself to deliver the questionnaires and explain the purpose of the meeting.

But when matters reached this stage, most of our Palestinian doctors backed out, saying that the original purpose of the meeting had changed, and that they did not feel comfortable going to a meeting with a lot of Lebanese doctors they did not know. I did not know most of them either, and I felt uncomfortable about not speaking Arabic. I asked the Lebanese administrator of *Secours Populaire*, a politically active Lebanese clinic, to chair the meeting, since he was fluent in French, Arabic and English, but he declined. It seemed presumptuous for an outsider who had been in Lebanon for only a year to chair such a meeting, and I wondered if someone was trying to teach me a lesson. I thought that at least I could collate the answers to the questionnaires, distribute them to the different clinics, and then sit back and see what happened.

The first meeting was packed. Representatives came from all the Lebanese groups we had contacted, and from some groups we had forgotten to invite, like the local Civil Defense unit and the Moslem Scouts (the Moslem equivalent of the Boy Scouts). The meeting was conducted, unfortunately, in three languages. Self-appointed translators summarized the important speeches for the others, and their summaries interrupted other speeches in turn. There was goodwill on all sides, though, and more meetings were scheduled. The administrator of one of the Moslem clinics, who was young and enthusiastic, took over the task of organizing future meetings, and subcommittees were appointed to deal with specific medical and administrative matters. I got my questionnaires back, and used them to make a table of emergency resources in the Sidon area, so we were all happy.

During the weeks that followed we sent a representative to subsequent meetings of the Sidon clinics, but our staff concentrated on planning for the Ein el-Hilweh area. We stocked the hospital with canned food and extra medical supplies, and packed boxes of emergency supplies for the smaller clinics in the camp. A committee consisting of a Palestinian doctor, a nurse, and representatives from Ein el-Hilweh planned first aid stations for the camp, and assigned doctors and nurses to them who lived nearby. In our doctors' meetings we talked about emergency communications and triaging (separating urgent from routine medical problems), fuel and water supplies, and the possibility of expanding the clinics into nearby mosques if necessary.

Local representatives from the ICRC stood on the sidelines for a while, not sure of what to do. At first they insisted that they had to save their store of medicines "for an emergency." But one day an ICRC nurse got into a conversation with Dr. Jawad, who said, "My clinic in Ein el-Hilweh is very small. I don't have many medicines, and I have no instruments. If there is an emergency in the camp, I can't offer anything much—my stethescope and nothing more." A few days later, the ICRC sent a big box of supplies for Dr. Jawad and the smaller clinics. Of course, we were all still limited in what we could do—we were concentrating mostly on first aid—but the feeling that we could help during an emergency gave everyone's morale a boost.

Open Hearts

At the end of November I went to Beirut once again because Sonia, our first adult open heart patient, was scheduled to have surgery at last. We had paid for it in advance, but representatives from the hospital administrator's office came to Sonia's room several times before her operation asking to see the receipt that proved her bill had been paid. Then we learned at almost the last minute that Sonia's family had to provide the blood needed for the surgery—at least four units of packed cells, preferably from freshly-donated blood—or the operation would be canceled. The do-it-yourself approach which the war was forcing on the Lebanese had taken hold even at the hospital's blood bank. Sonia had an uncommon blood type (A negative), but thanks to the Lebanese Red Cross, a broadcast appeal on the Sunni Moslem radio station, and donors from Sonia's family, we got the blood together, and the operation went ahead as scheduled.

After Sonia's surgery I talked to her cardiac surgeon about scheduling our next two adult open heart patients. I walked out through the hospital lobby to the snapping sounds of guns being reloaded by departing visitors. Visiting militiamen checked their weapons at the information desk before going upstairs, and got them back on their way out.

When I walked through the streets of Hamra I felt more self-conscious than I had during earlier trips to Beirut. I spoke French in the stores, and when shopkeepers asked if I was American, I usually said no. One of them asked how long I had been in Lebanon, and when I answered, "For over a year," he said, "Then why aren't you speaking Arabic?" Some patients at the hospital were starting to ask the same question; it always made me feel tired and defensive. Shopkeepers would probably not have asked such a question ten years ago. But why not? Wouldn't a foreigner in the U. S. be questioned about his or her English the same way?

I went into Antoine's, a bookstore that stocked thousands of titles in English, looking for a book about the United States to give as a present to a Palestinian friend. The travel section of the bookstore had books about Western Europe, Canada, Africa, and the Arab Gulf. There was even a Serbo-Croatian dictionary on the shelves. But I could not find a single book about the United States in Antoine's or any other bookstore in Hamra—no picture books, travel books, or maps.

It was a relief to go off with Hanan and Mousa at the end of the day. Every evening they picked me up at the May-flower Hotel and took me out for dinner. As first I objected, knowing that they both went to work early in the morning, and that these evenings were hard on their two-year-old son, who usually came along. But they insisted, so I gladly spent all my free time with them.

On my first evening we had dinner at an empty restaurant by the sea in Khaldeh, a Druze-held area south of the city, and I had my first real conversation with Mousa. Hanan had often spoken about her husband during the months they were separated. He was her best friend, the man who was understanding and supportive of her even when he was far away. At the hospital their unusual relationship was something of a legend, but also a source of jokes. I had no idea what he would be like.

Mousa was a trim man with greying hair and steely blue-grey eyes. He had the walk and the wary gaze of a beast of prey. He was very quiet at first, and I thought that he did not speak much English. But he was just listening to me. I talked about friends we had in common and about our problems taking care of patients over the summer. It was not until I made a comment about the PLO that he started to speak. He seemed to be still living in his mind in the time before the Israeli invasion, when he had a responsible position with the PLO. Before the civil war he had studied political science at a university in Beirut. He would have liked to be a lawyer in Palestine. His clerical job in a Beirut hospital left him bored and restless, and he got into arguments with people at work. It was his nature to push things and people, to make difficulties, to see if others would yield, and not to care, it seemed, about the consequences. He wanted to leave, but where could he go? "This is not our time," he said. "This is not our time."

Hanan and Mousa disliked living in Beirut. Housing was scarce and expensive, the supply of water and electricity was erratic, and the schools closed whenever fighting broke out. Hanan had gotten accustomed to coming and going as she pleased during the months they lived apart, and she felt too confined in their small apartment. Hanan and Mousa seemed neither happy nor unhappy together. They had known each other so long that they had learned to accept each other's failings, but that did not mean that they were necessarily going to be quiet about them. My presence was useful; when I was with them, their grudges turned into teasing remarks that each made to me for the other's benefit. I got used to it all after a while.

Hanan and Mousa had had a long and difficult courtship, but they both remembered it fondly. She met him when she was still a teenager and he a schoolteacher. She wanted to learn English, and he agreed to give her lessons. At first, they did not think much of one another. He considered her vain and self-absorbed, and she found him cold and critical. But in time their feelings changed. One day he slipped a love poem into her book. She was surprised to find it, and pretended to be indignant. But he followed her around and wrote her poems and long letters, and threatened to kill anyone else who was interested in her. There were many spats and stormy scenes before she was won over. But Hanan's parents did not think Mousa was the right man for her, and withheld their consent to the marriage.

In time, Mousa married another woman but was unhappy. Hanan's family tried to interest her in other men. Her older brother brought home a friend, a wealthy man from Tripoli who had taken an interest in Hanan after seeing her picture. But Hanan would have no one but Mousa. When she was called in to meet her would-be suitor, she entered the room with a lurch, talked with a lisp, and laughed in an unbecoming fashion. Her brother's friend fled before he had finished his coffee.

After a few years Mousa divorced his wife, and Hanan's family agreed to let them marry. Hanan showed me her wedding pictures one day. She wore a long white veil and a dress with a very short hemline. She was 27. On official papers, she has her husband's name, but still uses her maiden name at work. "Why not?" she says. "It's a nice name."

One night they took me to a wedding reception. The groom was a friend of Mousa's, but Hanan did not know any of the guests, most of whom were middle-class Palestinian families with young children. The reception was held in an apartment over an Amal party headquarters in West Beirut, and a young man from the Amal office downstairs came too, with a pistol tucked into his blue jeans.

This was the second marriage for the groom, a balding, middle-aged man who had recently returned to Lebanon after working in Europe for many years. When we arrived the reception had been going on for a couple of hours. Long tables in the center of the room were still piled with plates of *tabbouleh, hummus,* salad, kebabs, olives, stuffed grape leaves, fruit and Pepsi. The guests sat on either side of the tables, and the bride and groom were seated together at one end watching the events. Following the Arab custom, guests stood up spontaneously to chant praises to the bride's beauty or wishes that the couple have many children. After each guest finished, the others signalled their agreement by ululating—making a sound with their tongues like an Indian war whoop. Hanan joined in by whistling through her teeth, but she thought that some of the guests were getting carried away in their praises of the new bride—a woman who was, after all, as ugly as a horse.

Mousa moved around the room talking to his friends, and Hanan got acquainted with the women sitting near us. From time to time men and women did solo dances to taped Arab music. Hanan danced for a while with a jug of water balanced on her head, as women sometimes did on occasions like these, but the demonstration seemed to bore her—she made faces as she danced and clowned around a bit before sitting down again. Hanan and Mousa were the only people who danced together. He sat beside her for a while, and I saw them holding hands for a moment. But then she complained that he was drinking too much whiskey, and he said that she was not drinking enough, and the moment was gone.

The horse-faced bride did not dance at her wedding, but when someone put on a tape of Western music the groom got up and did a disco dance with me. The Amal militiaman sat near the door and socialized. Once he took out his pistol and waved it in the air as a mock threat, but most of the time his presence went unnoticed.

Hanan drove us home. It was late and there were few cars on the road. Hanan swerved from one side of the road to the other at top speed like a stunt driver. Mousa was dozing off. He was accustomed to his wife's driving, but I was not. I did not know how I was going to last through the week.

One night Hanan and Mousa brought me back to their apartment for dinner. They lived in a small, dark ground floor flat in Beirut's southern suburbs. Most of their neighbors were religious Shiites; Mousa called them "the old-fashioned people." Their living room was sparsely furnished: a few aluminum patio chairs, some formica side tables and a small black and white TV set. When we sat down to eat, Mousa had to bring in an extra table from the kitchen. Hanan made a delicious meal: the main dish was *kebabs* cooked on a small grill which they brought into the room. After dinner she heated a pot of Turkish coffee on the embers. It took a long time to boil, but tasted so good that it was worth waiting for.

Mousa complained that Hanan was rushing around too much; he would have liked her to stop working and stay at home. But, he added ruefully, "Hanan is not a good home lady." There were days when she did not feel like cooking dinner. Sometimes she came home from work and slept all afternoon, or went out to visit someone, and would pick up cooked food from a store in the neighborhood for dinner.

Occasionally Mousa would make dinner, but he preferred not to talk about that.

I did not believe Mousa's protests for a moment. He knew that his wife had a good job at Bashar Hospital, and that she enjoyed working and being around other people. In fact, he was always on the lookout for positions that would offer her a chance for more training or greater responsibility, and when they came up, he coached her on how to apply for them.

Their son liked to watch television in the evenings, but Hanan and Mousa did not care much for TV or the movies. "Why do I need films?" said Hanan. "My situation is a film."

Holiday Plans

As the end of the year approached, we were still not sure how much longer the hospital would stay open. Bruce, Ellen and Marcia had been planning to leave for a long time, and no replacements had been found for them. I wanted to stay for another six months, but unless our contract was renewed, it looked as if we would all be out of work in a few weeks. If we closed, it would not be for lack of patients. In our first year we had had almost 18,000 patient visits, the same census that one would see in the emergency room of a medium-sized American community hospital, and we had treated over 2,000 inpatients. About 85 percent of our patients were Palestinian. We had seen more than one hundred patients in our cardiac clinic, and another forty in the endocrinology clinic during its first two months of operation.

A couple of days before Christmas Bruce and Ellen returned from an expedition to Beirut with laboratory reagents, Christmas presents, suture material, and a week's worth of Beirut newspapers. The headlines in the papers, as Bruce pointed out, were not much different from those of a year ago. The Christmas turkey they bought had disappeared from the refrigerator of the Mayflower Hotel, but

fortunately Ellen found another one—a Hungarian turkey—in a Christian supermarket near Sidon.

I bought a few small gifts for friends at home. One unexpected find was a dusty copy of a children's book in English
entitled *Lenin at Christmas*. I bought Rima, our cleaning
woman, a new apron. She smiled and thanked me, but evidently did not understand my Arabic holiday greeting, because when the driver came to pick her up, she asked him if
I was celebrating my birthday.

Just before Christmas, we finally heard that the State Department had agreed to fund the hospital for another year,
and that we could go ahead and distribute Christmas bonuses to the staff. Our employees were paid in Lebanese
pounds, and in the year that the hospital had been open,
the pound had dropped in value from five to ten to the
dollar. We had tried to boost the employees' salaries with
periodic raises, but had been unable to keep up with the
pound's steady downward slide. When Bruce tried to start a
savings plan at the hospital, he learned that most of the
employees spent their paychecks almost as soon as they
cashed them. The few who had started savings accounts in
Sidon banks were beginning to realize that they would lose
money unless they converted their pounds into dollars.
Businessmen in Sidon bought or sold Lebanese pounds
whenever a piece of news suggested that the pound's value
might change substantially, but speculating in currency was
too risky and complicated for people with small incomes.

It is an Arab custom to visit friends and neighbors on
holidays, and as Christmas approached, many people
dropped by to see us at home. Mr. Ehssan, one of my cardiac
patients, called one day, bringing flowers and candy, like a
suitor from two generations ago. Mr. Ehssan was a soft-
spoken, distinguished-looking Palestinian gentleman in his
sixties. He had travelled widely around Europe and the
Arab world, and he was fluent in Arabic, English and Hebrew. I think he came to our hospital just for the conversation; he could have afforded to go to any cardiologist in
Sidon. Mr. Ehssan drove up in his shiny yellow Mercedes.
He was the first Palestinian who had ever come to see us
without a foreigner as an escort. But he was accustomed to

going where he pleased. He told me that he had once gone back to visit the home he had left behind in Palestine. He knocked on the door and asked the person who answered for a glass of water. Then he asked for a cup of coffee. He noticed that the new owners had changed the garden, but otherwise the house looked pretty much the same. Before he left he said to his host, "No offense, but this house you're living in used to be mine."

Mr. Ehssan's angina had been getting worse lately, and he had trouble working in the garden outside his house in Sidon. I suggested that he consult the cardiologist at Hariri Hospital, because he had exhausted the supply of anti-angina medications available in our pharmacy. The hospital was in Phalangist territory, and I did not expect him to drive there alone, but he did. I asked Mr. Ehssan what he thought would happen in Sidon when the Israelis withdrew. "I don't know," he said; "it's up to the Jewish."

Some of our hospital staff decided to visit us at home on Christmas Day. Most of them had never seen our house, and had not been to our neighborhood since the Israeli invasion, because to reach it they had to pass a checkpoint operated by some unpredictable soldiers from the South Lebanon Army. The soldiers had made anti-Palestinian comments to us in the past, but we had had no trouble with them for several months, and we decided that if people from the hospital came in the ambulance, with a Christian driver, we should have no problems.

First the ambulance brought a group of male employees. It returned about an hour later to pick them up and drop off our female visitors. We listened to music and served cookies, Pepsi and tea to each group. But just as the women's group was headed out the driveway, it was met by two jeeploads of soldiers who had decided that they, too, wanted to visit. The soldiers wore Israeli military uniforms, but said they were from the South Lebanon Army and wanted to look over the house for use as a possible military base. Why this inspection had to be carried out on Christmas Day, they did not say, but judging from the smirks on their faces, they knew we had company. Bruce told them they could come in if they left their guns outside and gave us their names and the same of their commanding officer. They would not agree to that, and after a few minutes they left, saying they would be back another time. Afterwards we realized that we would have to start hiding things that were popular with local militias, like our two-way radio transmitter. The next day I moved my journals, letters and notes to the hospital. I could not be sure they were safer there, but I did not know where else to put them. The soldiers came back once more a couple of days later, and once again we objected to their entering the house. We never saw them again.

After learning that the State Department would fund the hospital for another year, we decided to hold a Christmas party for our employees and their families—about 150 people. Marcia, Ellen and I bought and wrapped a present for each of the sixty children who were expected. The doctors discharged enough patients so that the party could be held in the women's ward, the largest room in the hospital. The beds were pushed aside, and the medical clerks hung streamers and balloons from the walls. Said, our pharmacist, brought a three-man electric band. A mystery guest wearing the mask and beard and red and white suit of Baba Noel, the Lebanese Santa Claus, danced around the room with the guests. Little girls in lace party dresses sat around tables that we had borrowed from the kindergarten downstairs, watching the dancing and eating cookies and meat pies. Their parents stood on the sidelines taking pictures of each other and clapping and shouting their encouragement when young unmarried adults danced sensual solos.

Toward the end of the afternoon we held a raffle: whoever came closest to guessing the number of (expired) tetracycline capsules in a giant jar would win the ten-speed bicycle that Mark had left behind. After the winner was announced, Baba Noel gave out presents to the children while Marcia, Ellen and I stood behind him scrambling for presents that were appropriate for their ages. The adults got their Christmas bonuses and their vacation pay.

The Christmas party was the first occasion when everyone on our staff had come together in one place. For the Americans at least, it would also be the last.

Withdrawal Pains

The talks between Israeli and Lebanese military representatives at Nakoura had been broken off many times because of disagreement over who would be responsible for policing South Lebanon after the Israelis withdrew. In early January 1985, the Nakoura talks were called off for good. The following week the Israeli cabinet voted to withdraw the army from South Lebanon in three stages. The first stage, which would involve the withdrawal of Israeli troops from Sidon, was to take place by February 18, and the third stage was to be completed by the end of the year.

Government officials in Beirut were surprised at the abruptness of Israel's announcement, but Sidon's political and religious leaders had been holding meetings for weeks to plan ways of working out security problems that might arise after the Israeli withdrawal. Their group was composed of Christian and Moslem politicians and clergymen, representatives from local militias, and Palestinian officials from the camps. They were determined to head off any provocation to fight with one another, although many opportunities would present themselves during the weeks that followed.

Their peacekeeping efforts were put to the test after Mustafa Saad, the Sunni Moslem leader of Sidon's Nassarite Popular Movement, was injured in an explosion. On the night of January 21, a one hundred kg. car bomb went off outside his apartment as he was holding a meeting with local Moslem leaders. Four people were killed and more than forty injured in the explosion. Mustafa Saad and his wife both suffered serious head injuries. Within hours they were airlifted to Beirut by helicopter, but his injuries left him permanently blinded.

The explosion was no doubt intended to foster a climate of suspicion and mistrust among Sidon's different political factions, but it seemed to have the opposite effect. The day after the bombing Christians joined Moslems in holding a general strike all over South Lebanon. Palestinians from Ein el-Hilweh streamed out of the camp to join Lebanese demonstrators holding a rally in front of Mustafa Saad's apartment. The funeral of Mustafa Saad's daughter, who died of her injuries two days after the blast, brought together 5000 mourners, including the leading Christian, Sunni and Shiite Moslem clergymen in South Lebanon.

The bomb blast was immediately blamed on members of the National Guard working with Israeli support. Suspicion centered on Mohammed al-Gharamti, known as Abu Arida, the National Guard Leader in charge of Sidon's port. Abu Arida had attempted to kill Mustafa Saad once before, in the days when he still worked for the PLO. Although the evidence against him was only circumstantial, Abu Arida decided that it was time for him to leave Sidon. Two days after the blast, according to a number of press accounts, he paid a farewell visit to IDF headquarters at Kfar Falous and then slipped away with twenty-five of his men from the port he had controlled for so many years.

After the Mustafa Saad episode, everyone was on the lookout for more "dirty tricks." Two attempts to bomb the UNRWA clinic in Sidon were foiled when men planting the devices on the roof of the building were spotted by neighbors. UNRWA schools in Ein el-Hilweh were closed for a day following a bomb scare. Our friend Nadim told us that our neighbors were keeping special watch on our house; as a Druze house in a Christian neighborhood occupied by foreigners, it could be the target for a bombing which could then be blamed on a number of different groups.

During the last two weeks of Israel's occupation of Sidon, it was impossible to do much more than stay home and wait for it all to be over. Sidon's main roads were closed for several hours each day while the Israeli army evacuated its heavy equipment from the hills above the city. Stores closed early, and a week before the Israelis were to leave the schools closed as well. There was intermittent gunfire around the city day and night, and masked men came out in every neighborhood as soon as it got dark. Some families from Ein el-Hilweh moved down to Tyre to stay with relatives until the situation improved. Members of the National Guard packed up and tried to slip out of town. Almost every day someone came to the hospital with a rumor that the Israelis were about to leave the city. It was impossible to know what to expect in the next few days, or even hours.

Few patients came to the hospital during the day. It was cold, windy and damp outside, and seemed even colder indoors. Since there was no bottled gas left in town, we had no heat at all. We sat in the conference room in our overcoats drinking tea and listening for news on the radio. Inside the pharmacy employees listened over our radio receiver as Druze and Christian soldiers in Iklim el-Kharrub traded idle threats and exchanged insults about each other's mothers. Downstairs, George, our afternoon driver, played backgammon with the guard by the front gate. George had started coming to the hospital early to get away from his home in the nearby Christian village of Darb es-Sin. Almost every day, Phalangists in his village clashed with masked men from the camp. Shots were exchanged, and each side accused the other of provoking a fight. George was a Palestinian Christian. He did not want to have to take sides in any battle. He had lost his house and his business during the Israeli invasion, and it looked as if he might soon be driven from his house again. Only a few weeks earlier he had danced and clowned as Baba Noel at our Christmas party, but now, aside from murmuring a brief hello to people he knew, he hardly spoke at all.

Since it was so difficult to get across town, I spent my nights near the hospital at the apartment of Barbara, Marcia's replacement. Barbara was a pediatric emergency room nurse from Seattle who had heard about our hospital from Marcia. She had recently worked at the Nong Samet refugee camp on the Cambodian border. After hearing Marcia's descriptions of the work we were doing she was interested enough in coming to take a semester of Arabic at home. She arrived as we were in the midst of disaster planning in the hospital, and with her emergency room background, she managed to fit in right away.

Barbara's apartment was on the road to Mieh Mieh near the northern edge of Ein el-Hilweh. There was a lot of gunfire around her apartment at night; according to local residents, armed elements were firing into Ein el-Hilweh from nearby buildings in an apparent attempt to provoke a battle. Their fire was not returned. I had trouble sleeping most of the time. I could not foresee any positive outcome in the days ahead, and in my sleep all the parts of the engine seemed to come apart, making separate sounds of damage. When I dozed off I dreamed of explosions, of watching one big weapon destroy another until the whole sky was black.

Almost every day there were stories of people who had been shot in the camp the previous night. Even Ali, a good-natured retarded boy who hung around the hospital, had a sense of foreboding. One night he came in to say, "Be prepared! I may come back tonight dead or wounded." But most of the people who came in during my night duty had medical problems that needed to be treated at a hospital in Sidon. They were afraid to go out on the road at night, and so were we. The streets of the city were empty, and if we saw another car on the road, we abruptly changed course to get away from it. When we took a woman with heavy vaginal bleeding to Bashar Hospital, we had to stop and walk the final one hundred yards to the emergency room because the hospital entrance was surrounded by barricades to deter car bombs. When we drove to the Old City late one night to take a woman in labor to the home of a local midwife, there was no one outside but a masked man, who said that he would escort her to the woman's house.

By the beginning of February, there were only 200 Israeli soldiers left around Sidon. Three thousand soldiers from the Lebanese Army waited north of the Awali River to move into the city as soon as the Israelis left. The Israeli troops who remained were in no mood to be friendly. By the beginning of February, attacks against them averaged six a day, double the number of the previous summer. And most of the attacks were coming not from the area they were leaving, but from the territory they were withdrawing to—the Shiite heartland of Jebel Amil and the villages around Tyre. The Westerners who got in their way met with verbal abuse, but local residents fared worse.

One day our ambulance was returning from Bashar Hospital when the driver found himself in a long line behind a checkpoint that Israeli soldiers had just established on the road. When he asked if the ambulance could turn around and use another road, the soldiers got angry and ordered him and our staff nurse out of the ambulance. They shot at the ground around the driver's feet, then turned and fired in the direction of a Lebanese woman watching from her balcony. Both the driver and the nurse were beaten and threatened by the soldiers before being allowed to proceed.

Meanwhile, soldiers from the South Lebanon Army were on a violent spree of their own. Since they would be leaving Sidon before the Israelis withdrew, they had no reason to act with restraint. On several occasions their armored personnel carriers stopped on the street and fired into Ein el-Hilweh at random. One afternoon I tried to pick up food at a supermarket in the middle of Sidon. It was only three o'clock, but most of the stores had already closed. The gates of the supermarket were down, but there were customers inside, so I entered. The owner said that soldiers from the South Lebanon Army had started firing in all directions from a tank around the corner. Someone had shot at them earlier, he said, and they were still furious. Every time I started down the aisle with a shopping cart, there was a hail of bullets outside, and I ran back to the meat counter with the other customers.

A Lebanese reporter darted in and out every few minutes to give us an eyewitness report on what the soldiers were doing. He was one of at least a dozen journalists who had come down from Beirut to see what would happen in Sidon after the Israelis left. He was investing too much enthusiasm, I felt, in covering this small event outside the supermarket. The soldiers used their tank to push down the sign in front of the gas station next door, and then moved further up the street and started knocking over the wall in front of a nearby house. I paid for my groceries and left.

Our new administrator, Violet, arrived in Sidon in the midst of these military adventures. Violet was a middle-aged Englishwoman who had agreed to come to Lebanon on short notice. She did not know much about the country but was keen to give it a try. She had asked at our New York office if there would be opportunities for sailing or horseback riding in Sidon. After seeing our house, she decided that a cleaning woman was needed every day, and since she was not accustomed to cooking for herself, she said, perhaps we should also engage a cook. In the hospital she looked very pale and thin-lipped. She never smiled; perhaps, I thought, she was having trouble unclenching her teeth.

By February 14 the South Lebanon Army had left Sidon. When they withdrew, said Sidon's deputy Nazih Bizri, they took along sixteen cars stolen from Sidon's port. According to the *New York Times*, Israeli General Ori Orr acknowledged that during the weeks leading up to their withdrawal one third of the soldiers from the SLA had deserted or had been killed or captured. The remaining troops moved to positions south and east of Sidon that were still behind Israeli lines. They were replaced at their checkpoints by members of the Lebanese Police. But the policemen had been told not to go near the checkpoints until experts came to look for mines, so they stood along the side of the road near the checkpoints with nothing much to do.

Most of the members of Israel's "National Guard" had slipped out of town. Hussein Akr turned up in West Beirut in early February, and was arrested by the Amal movement as soon as he was recognized. According to local news accounts he was executed on a deserted road south of Sidon three months later. "Captain Habli," a former member of the militia of Mustafa Saad who later joined the National Guard, was arrested following rumors that he had staged a mock funeral for himself to throw his enemies off the track. The following summer, in a luridly publicized ceremony, he was hanged in Sidon's central square.

The Israelis finally withdrew from Sidon on Saturday, February 16, two days ahead of their stated deadline. I heard the news when I stopped at Nijmi Square, near Sidon's Old City. People gathered on the street to share the news, and cars honked their horns as they drove by. Bruce and I got in the car and drove to the Awali River to join the crowds that had gathered there to welcome the Lebanese

Army. Some people danced, sang and ululated as they would at a wedding. One man sat on top of an armored personnel carrier and played a recorder. Soldiers from the Lebanese Army posed for pictures, or walked around with flowers stuck into the barrels of their guns. The Moslem Scouts gave out paper Lebanese flags to passing motorists. People waved at the soldiers when their convoy rumbled into Sidon, and some drivers got out of their cars to shake the soldiers' hands. Prayers of thanksgiving were broadcast from the loudspeakers of local mosques.

Lebanese military leaders denied Israel's claim that it had coordinated its troop withdrawal with the Lebanese Army. President Amin Gemayel and Prime Minister Rashid Karami got an enthusiastic welcome when they visited Sidon the day after the withdrawal, and, in a move that infuriated Israeli leaders, President Gemayel gave a speech calling for continued armed resistance to Israel's occupation of South Lebanon.

As the Lebanese Army moved into Sidon, Israeli planes streaked above the clouds and dropped leaflets warning the Lebanese not to tolerate the return of the PLO as a military force in South Lebanon. "Let us be good to each other," the leaflet concluded; "whoever does otherwise will be punished. May God be with us."

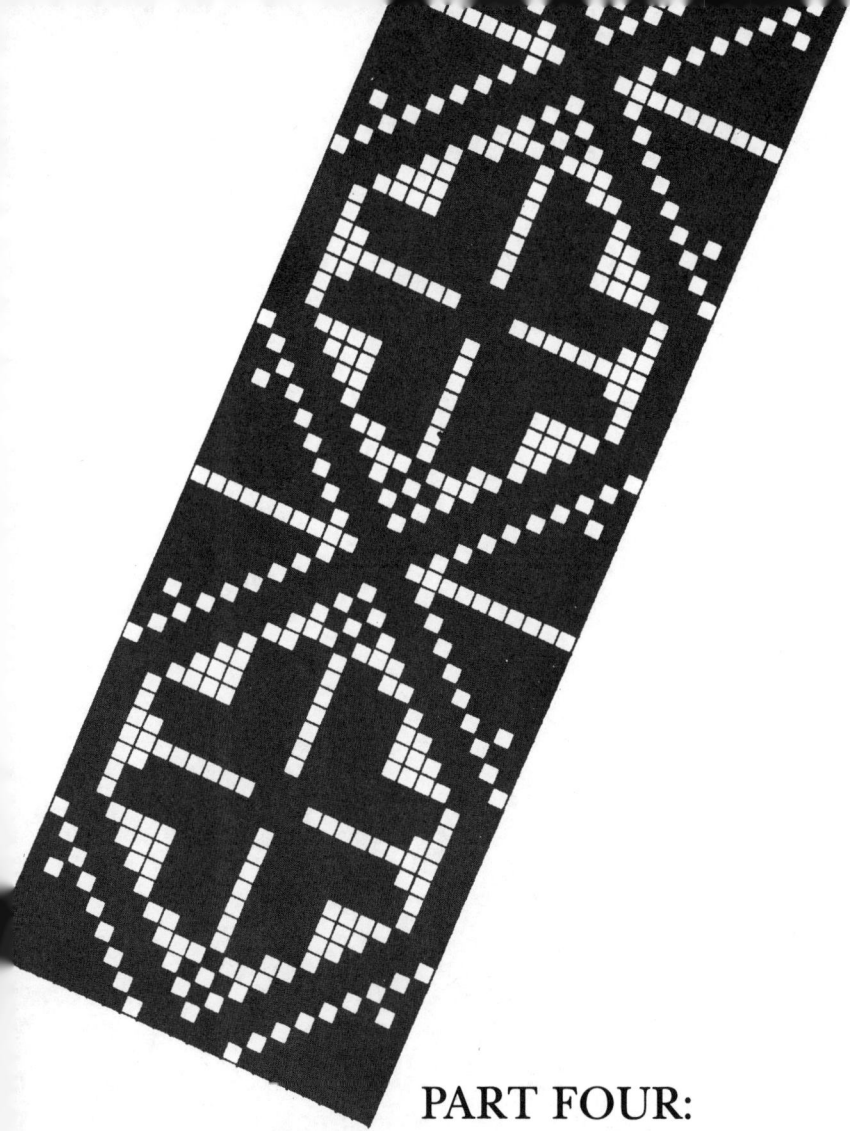

PART FOUR:
MARCH—JUNE 1985

Briefing

After the withdrawal of Israeli troops the Lebanese Army was responsible for the maintenance of order in Sidon, but in the nearby Christian town of Mieh Mieh there were signs that a clash between Christians and Palestinians could erupt at any time. In mid-March soldiers from the Christian Lebanese Forces occupied the hills above Sidon and fired down on the city for three weeks. Thousands of Christian and Moslem families fled from their homes to escape the shelling and sniping, and took shelter in schools and garages. A coalition of Moslem militias battled the Lebanese Forces while the PLO defended the area around the camps.

Our hospital was forced to close during the shelling, but we opened emergency clinics in three areas around Sidon to accommodate our scattered patient population.

In late April, the Lebanese Forces left the hills above Sidon and returned to East Beirut. Although most Christians in Sidon had been innocent bystanders in the fighting, thousands of Christian families fled to escape attacks by avenging Moslem and Druze militias. Their houses were looted, and many were burned.

In early May our hospital reopened. The beginning of the month of Ramadan in late May marked the outbreak of new battles around the Palestinian camps of Sabra, Shatila and Burj el-Barajneh in West Beirut, where Shiite Moslems battled Palestinians in what became known as the Camps War. The fighting lasted for a month and left more than 600 dead and 26,000 homeless. At issue was the military role which the PLO would play in South Lebanon in the months ahead.

Bowing to pressure from the U.S. State Department, the Interna-

tional Rescue Committee decided in May 1985 to stop its operation of our hospital, but agreed to keep it open until another sponsoring agency could be found. When I left Lebanon in June, the fate of the hospital was still uncertain.

Outside Agitators

The most tangible sign of our new freedom was the open coast road. For the first time in almost three years, people could go to Beirut whenever they wanted to. Some of our ambulance cases asked for new referrals to Beirut hospitals. Our translator Mansour drove to Beirut and back one morning just to see what it was like.

But the open road soon brought in a lot of unwelcome outsiders. Two days after the Israeli withdrawal, cars full of heavily-armed Shiite militiamen from Amal and Hezballah came down from Beirut to organize demonstrations. Some were angry at photographs of President Amin Gemayel drinking champagne to celebrate the Israeli withdrawal during a visit he had made to Sidon the day before, and they expressed their feelings by smashing liquor bottles in downtown supermarkets. By the time the demonstrators returned to Beirut that afternoon, most of the stores in town had closed, and broken whiskey bottles and beer cans were scattered on the sidewalks. The Sunni Moslems who made up the majority of Sidon's population were angry at this sudden religious invasion. Local leaders spoke out against it, and spokesmen from Amal and Hezballah later apologized for the excesses.

Other outsiders descended on Ein el-Hilweh: PLO organizers from Syria came trying to win converts to Abu Mousa, in a camp where most people backed Yasser Arafat; and undesirable elements from the PLO who had fled during the Israeli invasion returned to resume profitable careers in spying, theft and extortion. Our Palestinian staff did not expect armed conflict between different PLO factions in Ein el-Hilweh, since members of each had friends and neighbors in other factions, but they expected problems from the outsiders, most of whom had no personal ties to the camp. These new arrivals got a hostile reception; two weeks after the Israeli withdrawal, according to the *Daily Star,* residents in Ein el-Hilweh were mounting patrols to prevent PLO factions from reopening offices in the camp. But this resistance did not last long.

The daily routine which had been interrupted for the past few weeks returned to normal. Stores stayed open all day, and children went back to school. Dr. Ibrahim started coming to our cardiology clinics again. But the mood in the camp was somber. In the week after the Israelis left there was a military funeral almost every day for one of eleven PLO guerillas killed when the Israelis intercepted a patrol near the Awali river. Hearses carrying their coffins drove through the camp flying Palestinian flags and playing military songs from a loudspeaker, and cars filled with young men followed them. The masked men still came out at night. The Lebanese pound had sunk to fifteen to the dollar, and the price of most medicines had doubled. Our Lebanese friends were confident that there would be no fighting as long as local political and religious leaders continued to meet together to work out problems. But they knew that, given a strong provocation, heavy fighting could erupt at any time.

In early March the Lebanese Army and local political leaders managed to avert a battle around Mieh Mieh. A twelve-year-old Palestinian girl from the Mieh Mieh camp was brought to our emergency room late one afternoon by her neighbors with a gunshot wound in her chest. She had just been shot by a gunman from the Christian village of Mieh Mieh, where anti-Palestinian sentiment was strong. She was already unconscious and bleeding heavily. She soon lost her heartbeat, and nothing Dr. Refki and I did could save her. We pronounced her dead and cleaned up the room, but by the time we got downstairs the people who brought her had left—an ominous sign. The incident was sure to trigger a battle between angry Palestinians from the camps and Phalangists from the village of Mieh Mieh. The only way to stop it would be to contact a local leader with enough authority to act as an emergency peacekeeper.

It was already getting dark when my translator and I drove into Sidon vainly looking for representatives from UNRWA or the International Red Cross; I had hoped they would have more information about the shooting, since they could communicate with radios more sophisticated than ours. As we circled back into Ein el-Hilweh from the hills, we passed over a hundred armed men walking up to Mieh Mieh, and more of them were waiting in groups outside the hospital. Our headlights outlined women and children hurrying along the streets toward their homes or shelters. Everything was black; the lights had gone in the camp.

I drove again into Sidon, heading for the house of a Palestinian dignitary who knew leaders from all of Sidon's parties. I told him what had happened. He telephoned an official in the Lebanese Army and Dr. Nazih Bizri, a member of Parliament from Sidon and a well-known Sunni leader. Dr. Bizri was working on the problem already. He asked us to send the head of the Ein el-Hilweh camp committee to his house, and we did.

The Lebanese Army managed to intercede between the Palestinians and the Christians before a battle could begin. There was some sporadic shooting that night, but no prolonged gunfire. Dr. Bizri later blamed the shooting on outside provocation. A Christian friend who lived in Mieh Mieh told us that there were strangers in the village that day—probably Phalangist militiamen from East Beirut. Evidently some militant Christians in Mieh Mieh felt that coexistence between Christians and Moslems was impossible, and that renewed fighting was inevitable. A retired Palestinian official from UNRWA told me about a conversation he had had with the mayor of the village of Mieh Mieh; he had asked the mayor why the Christians in Mieh Mieh were so hostile to their Palestinian neighbors, who had never caused them any trouble. The mayor replied, "Sir, you have a good reputation. People like you. But how do I know that someday your son won't try to kill my son?"

Our Christian friend found that the village of Mieh Mieh did not return to normal after the shooting incident. Neighbors with whom she had always been friendly started to act secretive; though they liked her, they did not altogether trust her, because she was a foreigner, and therefore an outsider. Some hinted darkly about an upcoming battle; one neighbor said, "The camp [Mieh Mieh] will be in flames, and then it will be all over."

But I did not hear any of these gloomy accounts at the time. Our Christian neighbors in Bramieh were sure there would be no fighting since the Lebanese Army was securely established in key positions around Sidon. Members of Lebanon's Internal Security Force patrolled our neighborhood and often stopped to chat with the neighbors. As weeks went by I started to feel more optimistic too.

Meanwhile the Israeli Army was meeting with growing opposition in South Lebanon, and had imposed an "iron fist" policy, in the belief that brute force was the only way to stop the growing number of guerilla attacks. A dusk-to-dawn curfew was imposed, and travel on the roads was restricted. The new regulations were spelled out in leaflets dropped over the countryside by helicopters. Violators, the leaflets said, would be shot on sight. Israeli armored patrols raided Shiite villages which had gained local fame for their acts of resistance. When loudspeakers on village mosques warned of an approaching Israeli patrol, women and children barricaded the roads with burning tires and threw stones at the soldiers while the men from the village escaped to avoid arrest. Israeli troops rounded up hundreds of villagers, and dynamited houses and religious centers. Journalists were expelled from the area, and Red Cross workers and UNIFIL troops were prevented from entering villages to help civilians. But, as many had predicted, the iron fist policy only intensified Lebanese resistance, and left a large number of casualties on both sides. In the first month that the policy was put into operation, the average number of attacks against Israeli troops actually doubled, according to UN sources. At the end of March Israeli Defense Minister Yitzak Rabin announced that Israeli troops would withdraw from Lebanon by mid-May, not September, as originally planned.

The United States was drawn into the political consequences of Israel's actions, as it had been the summer before, when Lebanon sponsored a resolution in the UN Security Council in early March condemning Israel's "iron fist" policy. It was clear from the start that the U.S. would veto the resolution; Reginald Bartholomew, the U.S. Ambassador in Lebanon, said the U.S. favored a more "balanced" resolution condemning all acts of violence. The U.S. response to the Security Council resolution angered both Lebanese and Americans living in Lebanon. Students from the American University of Beirut held a protest march in front of a UN office in West Beirut, and Americans for Justice in the Middle East, a group centered in Beirut, later condemned the U.S. veto on Lebanese television and in newspaper ads.

The American government knew that the Security Council vote had serious implications for Americans in Lebanon; after the U.S. had vetoed the last Security Council resolution condemning Israeli practices in South Lebanon, the U.S. Embassy in Beirut was bombed. A few days before the vote was expected, American warships sailed toward Lebanon from the western Mediterranean, and on the day the U.S. vetoed the resolution, members of the U.S. Embassy staff were airlifted to Cyprus.

Several weeks earlier the State Department had advised our organization that Barbara and I should leave Sidon "until the situation clears up," but we intended to stay unless our lives as Americans were being threatened. None of our American or British friends were leaving. A colleague who had visited Washington told us that the State Department was very unhappy that we were still in Sidon; she thought that another attempt would soon be made to get us out. I had to admit that our hospital was a relic from another political era. We were representing the goodwill of a government that had changed its mind.

In early March I got ready to go on vacation. I had been waiting to go for weeks, but hesitated to leave when I felt a crisis was about to occur. With the Israeli withdrawal over it seemed like a good time to get away. I expected to wind up my job and return to the U.S. in another three months, and we had already found someone to replace me: Dr. Maher, a young Palestinian doctor from Tyre who had been working at Berbir Hospital. As I prepared to leave I turned over my responsibilities to the other doctors. There would not be much left for me to do at the hospital when I came back, and that was how I wanted it to be. My vacation was to be a rehearsal for my departure in June. I still had a few short-term medical projects in mind, but these involved working with other local agencies; arranging special surgery for some patients and helping a team from the American University Hospital in Beirut to bring a thalassemia screening and education program to South Lebanon. Once those plans were complete—*Inshallah*—I would be ready to go home.

It was a beautiful time of year. The winter snow in Lebanon lingers in the mountains, while in the towns and villages along the coast a stormy fall leads directly into a long spring, when grass grows over the fields, and wildflowers spring up everywhere. Women walked through the fields with big bags to pick *sliah* (greens that were used for cooking) and wildflowers for tea. By February some trees were already in blossom, and I could hear frogs and crickets outside my bedroom window. Some days were warm enough for people to bring the family canary out to get some sun. In March the popcorn and soft ice cream stands were back outside the stores. The air smelled of orange blossoms, and the grass in the field across from the hospital was so high that I could just see the ears of a goat twitching over it.

Mr. Latif, a patient in the men's ward, had gotten a touch of spring fever. Mr. Latif was a widower in his sixties who lived in Ein el-Hilweh with an unmarried daughter. We had hospitalized him many times over the winter. He had some medical problems—a chronic dry cough, swelling in his legs—but his perception of them was subject to marked seasonal variations. All winter long he told the doctors that he knew he was going to die soon. But he could not stay in the hospital, he said, because he had summoned his son back from the Gulf to see him before he died, and he wanted to be home when his son arrived.

I can not remember if his son finally came, but Mr. Latif perked up as the weather got warm. When nobody was looking he went over to the women's ward to chat with the female patients. He took a special interest in a young woman who obviously was not happy with his visits, but could not get away, being bedbound with arthritis. When the nurses led Mr. Latif back to his bed, he told them he was thinking of remarrying.

As I was sitting outside the hospital waiting for a ride home after my last day of work, I was spotted by Fatmeh Yusuf, who came over to greet me. She kissed me on both cheeks, as always, and presented me with a new pair of men's athletic socks—white cotton with blue stripes around the tops. She must have picked them up for one of her grandchildren, but decided on an impulse to give them to me instead. Of course I had to express my surprise and delight at getting such a gift, and not ask why.

I went to the office of Mr. Nidal, our local travel agent, to pick up my plane ticket, and stayed for a while to talk to him about "the situation"— especially the recent UN Security Council vote on Lebanon. I asked if he thought I would have any trouble at the Beirut airport because of my American passport. As I expected, he said no. Mr. Nidal was a friendly, helpful man, but I noticed that he rarely travelled anywhere himself.

A Short Vacation

I flew from Beirut to Cairo in mid-March and spent ten days in Egypt. While I was in Luxor I sat on the hotel terrace and wrote postcards to everyone in my address book to say that things were going well. I had seen a small news item in the *International Herald Tribune* about clashes between Christians and Moslems outside Sidon, but it sounded no more serious than other intermittent skirmishes over the past summer. I did not realize that these skirmishes were in my neighborhood, and were about to involve all of Sidon.

Dorothea and Peter, an American couple from Beirut, had invited me to join them in Tunisia. While I was there, in that tranquil and orderly country, the events in Sidon moved to the front page of Arab newspapers. We were driving to the Palm Sunday service at a little Anglican church in

Tunis when Peter told me that he had just read in the paper that Ein el-Hilweh had been attacked by the Lebanese Forces with mortar and rocket fire, and a thousand refugees had fled from the camp into Sidon. In front of the church I bought a paper and sat on a bench in the garden to read it as the church service started. The pastor's wife and another lady from the congregation came out to get me, and after a few minutes I went inside.

Although we had worried for months about a major clash in Sidon, no one could have imagined it would start this way. The news was especially painful because I was far away and without means of contacting anyone in Sidon for information. I would have to wait for days for a plane to Lebanon, and even when I got to Beirut, I might not be able to reach Sidon by car. At least we had tried to prepare our staff for this and had distributed emergency medical supplies. But that thought did not provide much consolation. Peter and Dorothea knew how I felt. Peter said, "Dorothea was asking me what I'd do if I were you, and she said she'd try to go back, but of course it's up to you."

I decided to fly to Istanbul, where the plane connections to Beirut were better. Besides, I had arranged to meet Barbara there for the last part of my vacation, and there was still a chance, though a slim one, that she would come. I shared a taxi to the airport with a husband and wife from the States who were in the middle of a trip through North Africa that was going to last for several months. They had already travelled through Morocco, Algeria and Tunisia, and were going next to Cairo. I asked if they had had any problems in their travels through Arab countries. None, they said, since they had stopped telling people that they were Americans. "When they ask us where we're from, we tell them we're Puerto Rican," they said. Not many Arabs have ever heard of Puerto Rico.

My flight to Istanbul from Tunis was on April Fool's day. At the Tunis airport, I was told that the computer had no record of my reservation for the flight. Nonetheless a supervisor managed to squeeze me onto the plane at the last minute. By then my unchecked suitcase had disappeared from behind the Tunis Air counter. No one could say what had happened to it.

In Istanbul, I was happy to learn that Barbara had come from Sidon after all. (My suitcase did not come from Tunis, though.) The fighting around Sidon had begun after she left, and now she wanted to go back as much as I did. She told me that our house in Bramieh, so often admired by military groups, had been taken over by the Lebanese Forces a couple of days after I left, and all of my belongings were gone. I listened to this news with some interest, as if I were hearing a story about someone else. For months I had packed and moved and hidden my belongings whenever the situation turned ominous. It was a meaningless ritual, and I knew it. But just before I left for vacation, I had moved all my belongings from a friend's place in town back to my house. My Christian neighbors were relieved that the Israeli withdrawal had taken place quietly, and they felt safe, they had said, knowing that the Lebanese Army was patrolling the neighborhood. We were all wrong, but my neighbors would suffer far more from this miscalculation than I .

Barbara said that Christian militiamen from the Lebanese Forces were firing down on the city from the windows of our house when she and Violet drove up to see what they could salvage. They were not allowed in my room, which was full of soldiers. When they returned the next day, a militiaman said that I should not come back to the neighborhood, and made a sign of cutting his throat. They had also made some predictable remarks about what kind of people would work with Palestinians. It sounded like they would destroy everything left in the house out of spite, even if they did not take it.

I opened my carry-on bag and looked at what I had bought in the *souks* in Egypt and Tunisia: a leather bag, a *jallabiyya,* and a 100 year-old set of lace underwear. It was all I had left. Thoughts floated through my head:

—I wonder if my father remembered to pay my travellers' insurance.

—This won't be covered by my insurance anyway, because it's an act of war (or is it an act of God?).

—If only I'd hidden my journals. What will those soldiers do with them?

—If only I'd left my medical files at the hospital.

—I wonder if they'll listen to my tapes. I don't think they'd like Dolly Parton.

—And we thought it was the Shiites we'd have to worry about.

—This will make me a better person.

I tried to picture all the things I had lost, believing that if I could do that, just mentally say goodbye to them, I would get over it sooner. I took a hot bath, rubbed some toothpaste over my teeth, and went to bed. It had been a long day.

The Shelling of Sidon

Barbara and I took the first plane back to Beirut. From reading accounts in local newspapers and talking to friends, we pieced together the story of what had happened in Sidon since we left. The Lebanese Forces had occupied the towns and villages in the hills above Sidon and were shelling the city, Mieh Mieh camp and Ein el-Hilweh. The fighting had taken everyone by surprise. Thousands of Lebanese, forced from their homes, had taken shelter in the city or left for other parts of Lebanon. Some Palestinians from Ein el-Hilweh had fled to Sidon, which was more protected than the camp, but most had gone to Ghaziyyah, a Shiite town south of Sidon which was out of range of the Christian guns. According to early news accounts, over 40 people had been killed in the first few days of fighting, and UNRWA sources reported that 40,000 Palestinians had fled from their homes. Militiamen from more than a half dozen Moslem groups were fighting the Lebanese Forces.

The battle had been instigated by a new leader from the Lebanese Forces in Beirut named Samir Geagea. A few days before the fighting began he had rebelled against the leadership of the Phalangist party, which had joined with Moslem groups in working on a Syrian-backed power-sharing plan. Geagea was a former AUB medical student, described as an intellectual and a mystic, and an expert at reaching the deepest fears of Maronite Christians, fears of a holocaust in which all Christians would be slaughtered by Moslems.

Soldiers from the Lebanese Forces (a coalition of Christian militias) had come to Sidon from East Beirut and joined local Phalangists, who claimed they were fighting to defend the Christian villages around Sidon. They could not control Sidon itself, a city that was 80 per cent Moslem, but they evidently hoped to force the city's Christians to join Christian communities in the mountains or in the southern border strip patrolled by the Israelis. The Christians in East Beirut looked upon Geagea as their savior, a worthy successor to Bashir Gemayel, but the rest of the country (including many Christians in South Lebanon) wondered what had prompted him to take such a suicidal step.

In Beirut, I picked up a pair of sneakers and some blue jeans from vendors selling their wares from station wagons parked along the street, and I bought a medical coat from a store near the American University. Friends gave me old clothes to wear. One does not look for work clothes in the stores of Hamra. We had no trouble finding a taxi going to Sidon. The one we chose filled up with passengers in just a few minutes. How many New Yorkers would be piling into a checker cab to go to White Plains if it were being shelled? Nobody seemed to mind, though. The driver turned on the radio to listen to the news, and when it was over, turned it off again.

It was a mild, breezy spring day. We had no stops on the road at all, and arrived in Sidon in little over half an hour. From the taxi, the road into town looked about the same as always; the stores were open and cars were out on the streets. But as we got closer, we could hear the sound of gunfire from the hills. Our eyes told us one thing, our ears another.

We spotted a British friend who worked for Oxfam and he advised us on how to get around. "Don't walk on the street," he said; "there are a lot of snipers. Try to stay in a car. If you walk in the street, watch what the people are signalling to you between buildings." Snipers on the hills were aiming at people in open areas, and shooting at cars and into the windows of buildings. Cars that had to go along open stretches drove very fast. At night people drove without headlights, but few people went out at night any more.

It was a while before I understood how radically our daily lives were going to change. The shelling and gunfire were usually distant and intermittent, except at night, so you did not have to worry about your personal safety every moment. Instead, you thought about how to get through the day: how to travel across the city without a car, for example, or where to buy food and cook it, or where to find a place quiet enough to work in and safe enough to sleep in. It was impossible to establish any kind of routine; these things had to be negotiated on a day to day basis.

First, Barbara and I needed a place to stay. She was homeless, like me; her apartment was close to the camp, so she could not return to it. Like the Lebanese and Palestinians, most of our American and European friends had left their apartments because of the shelling. They had to find places to stay in Sidon, or leave for Beirut. The safest place was on a lower floor of a building not directly exposed to the hills. Our friend from Oxfam offered to let us stay in his apartment, which was behind other buildings in the middle of town. It was a popular spot, we found; on some nights there were eight of us sleeping on his living room floor. But conditions were trying. There was no hot water, and since the electricity was off most of the time, food spoiled quickly and had to be bought almost every day. If you got home too early, you might not get into the apartment—there were not enough keys to go around. If you got back too late, the stores would be closed and you could not buy food.

At first I thought I could get used to it all. But then a day would come when I suddenly could not stand it any longer—eating stale peanuts for dinner, getting woken up over and over by the sound of exploding shells until I was ready to scream. Of course, I could always get in a taxi and to off to Beirut for a day or two. After a hot shower and a cold beer at the Mayflower Hotel, I felt ready to place long distance calls to distraught family members back home, and assure them that things were not as bad as they sounded on the news.

The few taxis still operating in Sidon would not venture onto exposed stretches of road, so we could not get to and from the camp unless we found someone to drive us there. Luckily, a friend gave us a lift on our first day. We were relieved to find that our staff was safe—but scattered. So far the hospital had not been seriously damaged, but it was closed because it was in an exposed area. Eight shells had landed around it that morning. The windows of the Lebanese pharmacy downstairs were blown out, and the metal gates were twisted from the impact of shrapnel. Most of our instruments and equipment had been moved to an office on the ground floor which was used by the Middle East Council of Churches as a center for the handicapped.

There seemed to be only two groups of people left in Sidon—displaced families and soldiers. The families that had fled from the villages around Sidon were squeezed into the apartments of relatives in town, or were living in construction sites, schools and garages. In the alleys between buildings women squatted in the dirt to wash their dishes with outdoor hoses. Children played in the street or ran in and out of guardhouses left empty by soldiers of the Lebanese Army. When shooting started up again, their mothers shouted for them to come inside. Men clustered in groups around their radios and listened to the news. On the hour, you could hear the theme song of Radio Monte Carlo played from a dozen balconies.

One day I ran into Rima, our cleaning woman, on the street, and she took me back to see her family. She and her children were living with another family in a two-car garage not far from our Oxfam apartment. Her oldest son had joined the *fedayeen* and had gone off to the hills to fight the Lebanese Forces. Rima's face was tired and lined, but it lit up with her old smile when she saw me. Seeing friends was the only form of entertainment left. Her daughter made coffee for us, and set the cups on cinder blocks on the floor. The garage was almost bare except for some mattresses and covers piled neatly in one corner and cups and food stacked along the wall. Rima asked how everyone from the hospital was doing and where we were staying. She invited me to stay for dinner, and asked if I wanted to come and live with her family in their garage. I wished I could offer her something in return, though she did not expect it. I thanked her and promised to visit her again.

Armed men walked along the streets in groups or drove by in beat-up trucks with machine guns and rocket launchers mounted on the back. You could not tell which militia they belonged to unless you spotted some sign of allegiance on them, like the picture of their political or spiritual leader that many wore around their necks—Ayatollah Khomeini, Musa Sadr, Yasser Arafat, Mustafa Saad. These older, more established militias were joined by others that had not been seen in town before. The National Syrian Socialist Party, a group supporting Lebanon's union with 'greater Syria,' was popular with young people because it had organized several suicide bomb attacks against the Israelis in South Lebanon. And Lebanese and Palestinian Sunni fundamentalists, identifiable by their black scarves or headbands, had formed their own militias, which operated out of several buildings around the city.

Business was dead in the Old City, but most merchants kept their stores open for half a day for lack of anything better to do. Some storeowners fortified their windows and doors with sandbags in imitation of the militia groups that had taken over nearby office buildings. The shelves in the supermarket I usually shopped at were half-empty, and the owner was no longer stocking fresh fruits and vegetables. He had moved his liquor to a back room after the day, two months earlier, when the Shiite militiamen from Amal and Hezballah had come to town on their smashing spree. But if you asked for alcohol in a whisper, it would brought out from the back in a brown paper bag. The owner seemed to be too depressed to mark up his prices in keeping with the fall of the Lebanese pound, and the prices were the lowest ever: you could get a bottle of champagne for less than five dollars—if you felt like drinking champagne.

The UNRWA medical department was coping as best it could. Two UNRWA doctors were working part-time in the Ein el-Hilweh clinic on their own initiative during the shelling. An UNRWA truck loaded with medicinies was being used as a mobile clinic. Every day the truck drove to areas where Palestinian refugees had gathered, and a doctor gave out medicines until that day's quota was gone. Most of the space in Sidon's UNRWA clinic was being used by refugee families. My friend Fatmeh Yusuf was staying in the clinic with part of her large family. Three of her grandchildren had been killed over the weekend, and one of them was still in the hospital. And Wissam, a heart patient of ours who had had an aortic valve replacement three months ago, was there with his family. He was growing a beard and looked very scruffy. I wondered if he was still taking his coumadin every day, but decided not to ask.

The Mayor's Committee

A few days after we got back to Sidon, Violet, Barbara and I went to a meeting organized by the mayor for all the organizations offering medical services in Sidon. The mayor wanted to discuss a plan for setting up emergency clinics around town. Many displaced families were living far from the established clinics, and they could not leave their neighborhoods to see a doctor because of the shelling.

The meeting was held at Bashar Hospital. The barricades outside the hospital, set up two months earlier to deter car bombs, had been removed, and the parking lot was open once again. But now the ground floor windows were packed with sandbags to withstand the shelling. The mayor was living in Bashar Hospital; he, too, had lost his home.

There was a big turnout for the meeting, and everybody was very cordial. A doctor from the Palestine Red Crescent Society was there, but no one from UNRWA; according to a representative from UNRWA's medical department, UN-RWA policy and procedures would not be affected by any decisions of the mayor's committee. For the benefit of the foreigners from voluntary organizations, the meeting was conducted in English. The mayor referred to a list of Sidon clinics and their services that we had put together for the meeting on Small Disasters the previous fall. One of his assistants held up a map dividing Sidon into emergency districts. Each clinic was to take over a district. We had been assigned an area not far from the UNRWA clinic. Everyone was in agreement with this plan. A subcommittee was appointed to meet daily. It consisted of an ICRC nurse, a Lebanese neurologist from *Secours Populaire* (a humanitarian organization with leftist sympathies), and myself (after a British representative from the Middle East Council of Churches declined to serve because she was leaving soon). Even though I sensed that foreigners were being appointed in the belief that we had all the money, I looked forward to being on the subcommittee. Still, my heart sank at the thought of how difficult it would be to come to these meetings every single day.

The second meeting was less amicable. The Lebanese neurologist insisted that we make a list of everyone's blood type in case of need. It was an absurd idea. How did he expect to identify blood donors in a population so scattered that people had trouble locating their own family members? Besides, the Lebanese Red Cross had already made a list of blood donors in town. Suddenly I realized that the Lebanese Red Cross had not been to the first meeting, though they had the largest and best organized system of clinics in Lebanon. I later learned that they had not been invited. Next the ICRC nurse announced that he no longer wished to be a member of the mayor's committee. The management of local clinics was not really any of his business. Of course, he said, in the event of a real emergency, the ICRC would be in contact with clinics and would provide any medical supplies that were needed.

"That's the ICRC for you," said the mayor, "always giving out umbrellas after the sun has started to shine again. You're only willing to help a person after he's dead, isn't that so? Ha ha!" The nurse retorted that he had gone out to visit clinics on the day the shelling began and had found them all closed, despite their administrators' promise that they would stay open during any crisis.

The mayor did not come to the third meeting, but representatives showed up from half a dozen clinics not on the subcommittee, probably because their administrators were afraid they were missing something. The ICRC nurse did not return. The representatives had come with lists of things they needed. Having been told by the mayor that every clinic with a lab should have a portable generator so that it could function during power cuts, these representatives had added requests for generators to their lists, which already included requests for walkie-talkies and more drugs. Everyone was pretending to be penniless and overburdened with patients, but no one had produced any statistics to show how many patients his clinic was actually seeing. When I asked why it was necessary to have a meeting every day, the others said, "Just for a few minutes! Just to see what's new."

The last committee meeting I went to was positively abject. Nobody showed up except a former engineer, who was working as a volunteer for the mayor, and a biochemist who represented the Islamic Foundation. He was in charge of giving out drugs on behalf of the mayor to all the local clinics, although, he said, the ICRC and the Lebanese Red Cross should be doing it, because they had plenty of drugs, and just did not want to share them with anyone. "How do you know what the Lebanese Red Cross is doing?" I asked. "They weren't even invited to these meetings."

"They're full of shit," he said. "This is an emergency; their drugs belong to everyone." I could see that there was no point in going to the mayor's committee meetings any more. A week or so later I got to the tail end of a meeting held in the Old City; it was announced that a central pharmacy had been set up where prescriptions for certain commonly-used drugs could be filled for free. The meeting was held in Arabic.

The shelling of Sidon in April 1985 left over 110 people dead and 430 wounded. Almost half of the casualties occured during the first week of fighting, because the shelling took everyone by surprise, and crowded areas were hit. After people had a chance to settle into shelters, the toll on their health was more psychological than physical.

I expected to see a flood of patients that month whose chronic illnesses had been exacerbated by stress. We were also afraid that we would see epidemics of pneumonia and diarrheal disease. But it did not happen. We treated over 2000 patients in our three emergency clinics during the shelling. With the exception of a few patients with minor injuries related to shelling, they had the same complaints as always: bronchitis, tonsillitis, viral syndromes, lacerations.

The ICRC worked with local organizations to insure that there was an adequate supply of food, fresh water and blankets. There were no serious shortages of medicines, as there had been the year before when the road to Beirut was closed. The real toll from the month of shelling was the breakdown of a working relationship between Christians and Moslems that prepared the way for the "cantonization" of the area around Sidon. In the weeks that followed, both Christian and Moslem leaders in Sidon worked to overcome the rancor and suspicion that had grown during the shelling, but they could not succeed. What happened in Sidon was no longer a local matter.

Return to Bramieh

Though I had resigned myself to losing my belongings, I still wanted to revisit the house to see if anything could be salvaged, and I knew that the longer I waited, the less chance I had of finding anything. I hoped at least to retrieve my journals and medical files. I decided to contact the priest from the Maronite church near our house to see if he could intercede with the Lebanese Forces on my behalf. I went to visit a Maronite nun named Soeur Ida, who administered a large clinic in town funded by Caritas, and asked her to help me contact the priest, whose name was Père Helou.

The entrance to the church next to the clinic was guarded by soldiers from the Lebanese Army. I met Soeur Ida in a stately reception room inside the church grounds. She was a short, trim woman about my age, serious and businesslike. Over coffee we traded news about how our respective organizations were coping with the situation. This had been the worst week of her life; she had been threatened a half dozen times by armed men since the shelling began. Though she had hoped to keep her clinic open, most of the doctors had fled, and I offered to help out part-time if it did remain open. Père Helou was still living in Bramieh, she said, and promised to try to contact him for me.

I saw Soeur Ida again the following week, but she had not been able to contact the priest. Once again we drank coffee in the reception room. Her comments were getting more political and more biting. She protested that all the press reports were about Palestinian refugees, and that nobody was talking about the displaced Lebanese. This was not, however, true of the English-language papers I was reading, which reported that both Christians and Moslems had been forced by the fighting to flee from their homes in the villages around Sidon. Soeur Ida also claimed that the Palestinian fighters of Ein el-Hilweh had cheated Christians in the neighboring village of Darbes-Sin by asking for a cease fire and then using it to occupy the village. She was angry at the religious polarization that grew worse every day. She had heard the *sheikh* of the mosque near her house in the Old City broadcasting talks every night on fallacies of the Christian religion. The exclusion of her clinic, one of the largest in the city, from meetings of the mayor's committee of medical clinics was also "part of the Islamicizing of the South," she said.

Finally a friend who worked with the Lebanese Red Cross arranged for a soldier from the Lebanese Army to drive me up to Bramieh in his car. Violet came along too. She had recovered most of her belongings during her first trip back to the house, but had not managed to find her electric blanket and wanted to try once again.

The road leading down the hill from our neighborhood into Sidon was on the front lines, so we drove along the sea and approached our neighborhood from the north in a roundabout way I had never used before. Just below our house the road had been sealed off by a roll of barbed wire, and soldiers from the Lebanese Forces had established a checkpoint nearby. Joseph, our escort from the Lebanese Army, told the soldiers that we worked for the Lebanese Red Cross. We waited while the militiamen radioed ahead for permission to let us pass.

Violet grew impatient at this delay, and had to be persuaded not to get out and walk. "If only we could speak to an *officer*," she said. After ten minutes we were allowed to proceed up the road. Joseph drove very slowly.

We were stopped again at a checkpoint near the Maronite church. I was surprised to see most of our neighbors still there, sitting on their porch chairs just like the old days. (Their houses were set back in the hill, out of the line of fire.) I saw Georgette, the owner of the little store across the street from our house, and walked over to talk to her. The other neighbors smiled and waved from their porches. Hearing that I was back to get my things, Georgette said, "It's too late, nothing is left." Most of the neighbors, she told me, had stayed in their houses during the shelling; only Nadim, whose views were too leftist for the Lebanese Forces, had gone. I wondered what was going to happen to them all after these militiamen left; didn't they wonder too?

Violet pointed out one of the soldiers at the checkpoint, the one, she said, who had threatened to kill me if I ever came back to the house. I kept talking to Georgette and did not look at him; I felt sure he was someone from Beirut who had never seen me before. Finally we were permitted to go into our house, for "five minutes only." The militiamen behind the trench along one side of the house gallantly offered to hold their fire while we were inside. Next to the name of the Druze owner by our doorbell someone had written in Arabic, "the Lebanese Forces in the South until victory," and "The forces of Geagea are in the South." Part of the living room wall had been blown away, and through the hole you could glimpse the sea. The floor was ankle deep in rubble, the rooms almost empty. Soldiers had dragged the living room furniture out under the trees to sit on, away from the firing. The rest of the furniture had disappeared, along with our new sterilizer and half a dozen electric fans from the hospital.

A big chubby soldier with curly hair followed me upstairs with his gun, and stood by the door as I looked in at what was left of my room. Clothes and papers were scattered all over the floor, and all the windows were broken. "Only five minutes," I thought, grabbing what I could recognize from the floor and heaping it on the bed. The curly-haired soldier puckered his lips and talked to me in Arabic while I scrambled around on my haunches, making me nervous enough to call out for Violet. She had not found her electric blanket, but had managed to retrieve two tins of Quaker Oats from the kitchen. Joseph came upstairs and clucked in amazement at the mess. He was surprised that most of my belongings had been stolen. I tied up what I had found in sheets and blankets and we headed out again.

The Lebanese Forces had taken all the appliances in the house, my jewelry, medical equipment and suitcases. Six-wheeled trucks had carted the contents of our house and of houses abandoned by their Moslem owners back to East Beirut for distribution. Still, I retrieved some of my clothes and medical files that day. My journals and our modest human rights files—accounts of patients who had been beaten and tortured in prison—had been stepped on but ignored. My photographs were gone, and someone had put a flame to newspaper pictures I had pinned to the door of Gandhi and Solzhenitsyn and Chekhov. Some of my books had been taken, but only because they were packed in one of the suitcases; thus I lost volume three of *Remembrance of Things Past.*

"*Leurs têtes sont vides,*" Joseph muttered as we took our leave of the militiamen. He dropped us off in Sidon and went on his way. I never saw him again, but I bought him a box of chocolates and left it with the Lebanese Red Cross.

Emergency Clinics

The Middle East Council of Churches had given us permission to use its physical therapy center downstairs as an emergency clinic. It stayed open all through the shelling, and some of our doctors and nurses slept there. The center was spacious, but grim and dark as a fallout shelter. There was no electricity, and very little light came in from the windows. The front entrance faced the surrounding hills, so was unsafe during the day. You had to climb up a ladder and get into the clinic through a rear window. Our doctors were determined to keep this emergency clinic open day and night. It was a point of pride to them, a sign of continuity for the people left in the camp. Although most of the Palestinians had fled from the camp, the PLO fighters remained, and about 300 families stayed behind in spite of the shelling, including many older people. (Explaining why his parents refused to leave their home, one man said, "They don't want to make the same mistake they made in Palestine.") Most clinics around the camp were still open, and the Palestine Red Crescent Society had moved medical teams into both Ein el-Hilweh and Mieh Mieh. Their clinic in Ein el-Hilweh had a surgeon and two ambulances on call 24 hours a day to treat and transport the wounded.

Off-duty members of our staff stopped in to see what the others were doing. Violet came by every morning with a bunch of carrots; she had taken it upon herself to feed the mule and the horse in front of the Government Hospital. When the horse was hit by a piece of shrapnel, she sent a nurse out to dress the wound. The horse died anyway; fortunately the nurse did not. Violet stayed with Dr. Mazen and his family during the shelling.

We saw only about ten patients a day at the Ein el-Hilweh clinic. Some were combatants: a young man, temporarily blinded by a flash of light, was brought in by friends; a religious fighter came in complaining of abdominal pain, but giggled with embarrassment when I started to examine his abdomen and hurriedly left. Most of the other patients had minor complaints.

The clinic was a friendly place at night. Somebody always managed to bring food for dinner and a radio to listen to. At first we ate the emergency rations stored upstairs in the hospital, but after they ran out the food started looking like something you might eat on a boat that had been at sea for several weeks: stale bread, canned beans, and hard-boiled eggs. After dinner some people stayed up and talked, and others went off to sleep on exercise mats in the physical therapy room—the men in one room, the women in another.

The shelling was heavy at night. I flinched whenever I heard a loud explosion or a dull thud nearby, but everyone else, even the younger women, could tell the difference between a shell that was being launched and one that was landing. They laughed when they saw me wince and said "outgoing!"

One day I found everyone sitting in a circle around the radio listening to a man's solemn chanting, which I mistakenly referred to as music. It was a religious leader reading from the Koran. One of the medical clerks looked as if she were about to cry. A sniper's bullet had narrowly missed her a few days earlier. Her family had left their house with nothing more than the clothes they were wearing and had gone to stay with relatives in Sidon, but now that part of the city was being shelled, and they were thinking of moving again. Twice before she had lost all her belongings in bombing raids. She was twenty-one years old. I asked if the chanting made them sad. "No," she said. "It gives us peace and self-confidence."

I wished I could feel that way. The Christians continued their shelling even on Easter Day. When Easter hymns were broadcast on the radio, I turned it off.

Dr. Refki came in to start his shift one day as we were eating lunch. Before sitting down, he walked around the clinic, looking in all the rooms and out all the windows. I thought perhaps he had not been to the clinic before, but when I asked what he was doing, he said, "The bullets come from this side [pointing to the north], and the bombs from that side [pointing east]. I just want to know where to sit." Later in the day we learned that the latest shelling had just killed three of his nephews, who had gone into the camp with their mother to take a bath and get some clean clothes.

The next day Dr. Refki came back to the clinic so that we could pay our respects. When he entered, we all stood up.

He walked around and shook the hand of each of us as we murmured our condolences, and then left without a word.

A few days after the shelling began we got ready to move our medical staff and equipment to other locations around Sidon. Our doctors thought we should establish satellite clinics to treat patients in the areas where they were living, and after meeting with representatives from UNRWA and the mayor's office, we decided where the clinics should be.

Violet arranged for us to use an empty Lebanese school in the village of Ghaziyyah, south of Sidon. On the day we moved there we loaded medicines and supplies for the clinic into the ambulance before dawn, when gunfire was at a minimum, and by noon we had unpacked enough supplies to start seeing patients.

The building in Ghaziyyah was roomy and bright, and had everything we needed except electricity. Later we bought a portable generator so that we could operate a laboratory. The Ghaziyyah clinic was the busiest of our satellite clinics; it stayed open seven days a week, and we treated over a hundred patients a day. We had both Lebanese and Palestinian patients, but 80 per cent were Palestinians; most of them had taken shelter in schools in the neighborhood. We took patients who were seriously ill by ambulance to one of the hospitals in Sidon, but most had the same ailments we had treated them for in the past: minor infections, gastroenteritis, and complaints related to living under stress— headaches, insomnia, palpitations, fatigue.

At the mayor's request, we opened a third clinic in downtown Sidon. It was in an unused medical suite on the second floor of an office building. But someone from the mayor's office had also promised the suite to a displaced family. We surprised each other when we both moved in with our belongings on the same day, and traded polite smiles and angry calls to the mayor's office. But the mayor could only suggest that we make the best of it, and so we did. Some of our old patients found us at the clinic we shared with the refugee family, but not many; in spite of a modest advertising campaign, we never saw more than twenty patients a day there. Considering our crowded circumstances, it was probably just as well. We spent most of the time talking about the situation and listening to news through the failing batteries of a small transistor radio.

The logistics at our emergency clinics were formidable. Every morning our ambulance drivers picked up about twenty members of the hospital staff from shelters all over town and dropped them off at one of our three emergency clinics. The drivers had to remember where the people were sleeping who were not living with their families, and who had the day off. Between shifts they delivered messages and supplies and carried patients between clinics, and when each shift was over, they took the staff members home. Record-keeping was another problem. The medical clerks still collected statistics on our patients by age, sex, nationality and diagnosis, but the doctors had to record information on index cards, because the patients' charts were back in the hospital at Ein el-Hilweh.

Every week our doctors worked in two or sometimes three different clinics. It was impossible to make out a doctors' schedule that was equitable. In the clinic at Ghaziyyah, a doctor might see thirty or forty patients in a morning, but in the other clinics he might see only a handful. On the other hand, Ghaziyyah was a safe spot to work in, while Ein el-Hilweh could be shelled at any time. Some clinics were a half-hour's drive from where the doctor lived, others only a block away. Finally, I gave the schedule to the doctors and let them make it out themselves, but some were still dissatisfied.

Dr. Jawad objected to my insistence that each doctor take a day off every week. "We are not in the time of off these days," he said crossly. I noticed that he had been wearing the same clothes for almost a week: a jacket, sweater, shirt and trousers in four different patterns of plaid. His wife had had a cerebellar stroke just before the shelling began, and was still confined to bed in a house far from town. In addition to the hours he spent with us, Dr. Jawad still worked at the Maroof Saad clinic every day; he was the only doctor there.

Though he kept it to himself for a long time, Dr. Jawad bore me a grudge for making him take those days off; months later he still looked back on them as a punishment, a sign that I lacked confidence in him. I discovered this by accident one day, and we talked the matter over. After our conversation he apparently decided that the incident represented a temporary lapse of judgment on my part, but nothing that he should take personally.

Living Among the Shells

Shortly after our return to Sidon a couple who were leaving for a while offered to let us stay in their apartment. They had been working in Lebanon for several months on agricultural and reconstruction projects for the Mennonite Central Committee. They liked Lebanon, and hoped to continue their projects after the fighting in Sidon stopped. But the husband was American, and they had to admit that it was no longer safe for him to stay. They planned to go to Cyprus for a couple of weeks to decide what to do. With the exception of the ICRC staff, which did not mingle much with anyone else, most of the foreigners working for voluntary organizations in Sidon were women. The men who remained were Canadian or British.

Our new apartment was in a house set among fruit trees on a hill above Ein el-Hilweh, on the way to the Mieh Mieh camp. There was no such thing as a safe place to stay, but I was homeless, and Barbara still could not return to her apartment, so we decided to move in. We were tired of living out of shopping bags and sleeping on the floor.

The apartment was quiet and roomy before, and had become even more so for having recently been looted. The stove and refrigerator were gone, but most of the other furniture was still there. Barbara brought a small gas range and a cardboard box of food and condiments from the kitchen of her apartment. There was no electricity, but at least we had solar-heated water and a toilet that flushed.

The house was in a Moslem neighborhood, but a couple of nonmilitary Christian families had stayed on; if they were going to get killed, one of them said, they wanted to die in their own homes. A Lebanese Moslem family living next door offered us the use of their basement as a bomb shelter. A family of Palestinian refugee squatters had moved into another apartment in the house. We introduced ourselves to the others when we moved in, and were all on good terms.

We ate dinner on our terrace the first night by the light of a gas lantern. It was a decent meal for a change: a roast chicken we had bought in town, fresh peppers and tomatoes, and a bottle of Châteauneuf du Pape that I had brought from Beirut. It was relatively quiet when we went to bed, but just before dawn I was wakened by the sound of explosions shaking the house. Rockets were whizzing past our window, and clouds of smoke arose among the trees outside. The birds did not stop singing even when the shells landed; did that mean there was no cause for alarm? Barbara was sound asleep. I went to the window and looked at the clouds of smoke. I really should wake her up, I thought. Finally an explosion came louder and closer, and I shouted her name. She woke up as alarmed and confused as I was. At first we moved a mattress into the hall away from the windows, but the house continued to shake from the impact of the shells, so we grabbed our pocketbooks and headed for the shelter next door.

A half-dozen older men sat in the shelter playing cards by the light of a gas lamp. They were relaxed and talkative; they seemed to have been there for some time. They made a space for us on a mattress in one corner, gave us a couple of blankets, and then resumed their game. They left about an hour later, after the 6 o'clock news, and we went back to the apartment and got ready for work.

The shelling continued intermittently for most of the two weeks we spent in the apartment. We did not have to take refuge in the shelter again, but we slept with our passports and flashlights at hand just in case.

A few days later I sat down to go through some papers. Machine gun fire erupted every now and then from the barracks of the Lebanese Army across the street. The soldiers of the Lebanese Army were almost the only noncombatants left in town, so I did not think anything serious was happening, but I still felt jittery. Violet had just given me a copy of the new life insurance policy sent to us from our New York office for me to initial and return. It came with a note saying that it was, unfortunately, less generous than our previous policy had been. In fact it would scarcely have covered the cost of flying out my remains. It was shorter than most insurance policies, and the benefits were easier to understand.

Loss of life	$15,000
Loss of both hands or both feet or sight of both eyes	$15,000
Loss of one hand and one foot	$15,000
Loss of one arm or leg	$7,500
Loss of one hand or one foot or the sight of one eye	$7,500

And so forth, through another half dozen permutations. No compensation was provided for depression or mental anguish that might occur in the line of duty; in fact, "mental and nervous disorders or rest cures" were excluded from the policy, as was "self-destruction or any attempt thereat while sane." Of course, acts of "declared or undeclared war" were also excluded.

I had never given much thought to life insurance before and was disappointed to see that such a small value had been assigned to me and my lost limbs. But it was a generous policy by Lebanese standards. It would have to do. I initialled the policy and sent it back to Violet.

Beirut Clashes

In late April Barbara and I drove to Beirut for the day. A few hours after we arrived, street fights broke out between Amal and the Murabitun, the once-powerful Sunni Moslem militia based in West Beirut. (Most of West Beirut's residents were Sunni Moslems.) As usual, it was a fight over territory, which Amal was to win.

We spent most of the day trapped inside the Mayflower Hotel. A couple of hours after the shooting stopped we went for a short walk around West Beirut. Burned cars with smashed windshields were parked along the road. Groups of armed men hung out on street corners. A few vendors were selling wilted vegetables, but all stores were closed. We walked to the Commadore Hotel, the home of many Beirut-based foreign journalists, and looked at news on the telex. A story was just coming out with the headline "Lebanese Government Falls." I felt exhausted. I wanted to find a dark, quiet place where I could be alone.

But when we got back to the hotel, an American friend called, and we went to see her. She was a teacher at AUB who had lived in Lebanon on and off for many years. She told of a recent brush with armed elements in West Beirut: she was walking home one evening when she noticed a car coming toward her signalling with its lights to another car driving alongside her. Suddenly the second car pulled up in front of her, and four armed men got out. Her whole body went cold. She put her arms out to show that she was not going to resist, but to her surprise the men walked past her and into a nearby building. "I'm probably the only person here who has volunteered to be kidnapped," she said.

Later that evening we met Daniel, a translator at our hospital, and his brother, who had just come from the U.S. for a visit. Daniel wanted to ride back to Sidon the next day in our car so that we could protect him, as he put it; Amal had surrounded the Palestinian camps in West Beirut, and there were reports that new checkpoints had been set up along the coast road. Six Palestinian men had been found bound and beheaded in Sidon the day before. Why? By whom?

The next morning Daniel came to our hotel, and we left early to minimize the chance of meeting problems on the road, but I was very worried. If Daniel were pulled from our car, I would never have forgiven myself. How could we know that the road was safe? We could only say that it was safer for us than for him. We rolled up the windows and locked the doors and agreed to speak only English at checkpoints. (Members of the staff who travelled with us tried to get by with showing their hospital ID cards at checkpoints, be-cause it did not specify nationality.) We stopped at a taxi stand to ask if there had been any problems on the road to Sidon. "Nothing so far today," they said. We were lucky; no one stopped us at all.

Later that day I was talking about the situation with a Lebanese friend and mentioned how hopeless things seemed now that the government had fallen. "Oh, that doesn't mean anything," he said. "They'll put something together; just wait and see."

Withdrawal of the Lebanese Forces

Three weeks after the shelling had begun, and just as the municipality of Sidon had started to erect ten-foot high earthen walls to shield open areas from snipers, the Leba-nese Forces suddenly announced that they were going to withdraw. The departure of the Lebanese Forces coincided with the Israelis' phased withdrawal from the nearby town of Jezzine. Had the Lebanese Forces stayed longer, they risked being cut off from the Christian port of Jiyyah, north of Sidon, their only escape route back to East Beirut.

As the Lebanese Forces sailed off from Jiyyah, Moslem militiamen from a half dozen factions advanced up the hills towards Jezzine, now being defended by soldiers from the South Lebanon Army. Thousands of Christians fled from their homes, and every Christian village along the way fell to the Moslems. Shiite and Druze militiamen sacked aban-doned Christian villages north of Sidon, PLO groups over-ran the Christian villages of Mieh Mieh and Darb es-Sin, and men from the *Nasiriyyun*, the local Sunni militia of Mustafa Saad, occupied the empty Christian houses in Si-don.

I was in Beirut when the Druze announced that the coast road would be closed for two days while their militia took control of Christian villages north of the Awali River. Chris-tian Sidon was being dismantled. I hated having to sit and wait until it was over. When things got bad, it was always easier to keep working, to concentrate on getting through the next few days or weeks. But an ugly event like this exhausted my small reserves of optimism. The future seemed to hold nothing but a choice among horrors worse than what existed already: kidnapping, bombing, murder, massacres, betrayal.

I remembered a conversation I'd once had with an older woman who was brought into the emergency room semiconscious after an apparent drug overdose. As she was lowered onto the stretcher she opened her eyes and looked at me. "Do you know where you are right now?" I asked.

"Yes," she said; "at the very end."

I went to visit an American friend in an apartment near the Italian Embassy. She felt as gloomy as I did. She was planning to leave Lebanon soon; she wanted her next assignment to be in a place that was "pretty, quiet, and safe." Back at my hotel, I got Barbara's tape recorder out of the stored luggage room, put on a tape and played it over and over until I fell asleep. When I woke up, I felt a little better. The still, small voice came back. I knew I could keep going, but I didn't know why.

As soon as the coast road opened again, I took a taxi back to Sidon. There was no one left in the Christian villages north of the Awali except a few militiamen. Every house and every store had been smashed and looted. Abandoned cars had been burned, and some had been flattened by tanks. In one village a dead mule lay beside the road, and a living-room set, with brocade upholstery, stood outside an empty gas station. All windows in the houses were broken, and doors swung open and shut, showing rooms with broken, overturned furniture. Militiamen were still poking into some houses, and you could hear broken glass crunching under their boots. One militiaman wore a sombrero, another sat in the middle of the road in a bentwood rocker. The scene made me think of a giant corpse teeming with flies and worms.

In Sidon homes and stores had been set on fire in the Christian villages in the hills: Abra, Mieh Mieh and Darb es-Sin. A pall of smoke covered the horizon between the sky and the sea. Jubilant militiamen shot their guns in the air as soldiers from the Lebanese Army looked on. Cars and trucks packed with loot and looters came down from the hills with lamps and tables and knickknacks sticking out of their trunks, and stopped along the way to drop off passengers. Our downstairs neighbors acquired a large number of couches, tables and chairs, and stacked them neatly in a corner of the garage.

Behind the looters came the journalists. A British reporter stopped by our house on his way back to Beirut. He was so excited he could barely sit still. He had just been to the village of Abra, and was on his way to Mieh Mieh. "The Palestinians are really going to look bad in this one!" he said. Sure enough, there were widespread reports in the press of Palestinians burning Mieh Mieh and Darb es-Sin. The mood in our hospital was gloomy. While the looting was in progress in Darb es-Sin, two planes from the Lebanese Army flew over Sidon just before sunset and strafed Ein el-Hilweh. People ran into the nearest buildings, and moments later ambulance sirens were wailing. Daniel said, "This is a punishment and a warning for the PLO." Everyone understood why men from the PLO were bent on revenge: parts of the Palestinian camp of Mieh Mieh had been burned twice by the Phalangists since the Israeli invasion, twenty Palestinian men had been kidnapped from a Phalangist checkpoint south of Ein el-Hilweh in the same period of time, and a cemetery near the camp had been leveled and turned into a football field. But they knew that looting and burning would provoke more acts of revenge, and they were the ones who would suffer for it eventually.

A couple of days later I went back to our house in Bramieh with Violet to see if anything more could be salvaged now that the Lebanese Forces were gone. For the first time in a month, we were able to drive up along the Jezzine Road, which had been the main battle line in Sidon. Some houses had been gutted during the fighting, and all had been abandoned by their owners and looted. Every single building along the road had been damaged by shells and machine gun fire. The main street in our old neighborhood was quiet and deserted. The Phalangist emblems stencilled on walls had been X'd out. Every house had been broken into, and all the neighbors were gone. The green and white religious flag of the Moslem militias flew over the Maronite church. It read, "There is no God but Allah, and Mohammed is his prophet."

From the outside, our house looked the same. The Sunni militia of Mustafa Saad had crossed out the graffiti left by Geagea's men, and written under it: "The party of the *Nasiriyyun.*" Inside, there was more destruction than before. Another shell had come through the outside wall. All the remaining furniture had been smashed. The smell of feces emanated from my bedroom. I managed to pick up some more papers from the floor. Violet took pictures of the damage and retrieved some linen.

Barbara decided to move back to her apartment at the foot of the Mieh Mieh road, and invited me to come along. The electricity came back on as we unpacked, so we played new tapes that we had bought in Beirut. Listening to Billie Holiday restored a certain feeling of well-being and even sophistication that might otherwise have been supplied by a hot shower with water pressure, a well-cooked meal, or a group of handsome men to mill around in, none of which, of course, was forthcoming. The next day we returned to our hospital, to the relief of all the staff. Some of the upstairs windows were broken, and the water tank on the roof was full of holes, but we got them fixed after a few days. Patients started coming in as soon as they saw that we were back.

When the Lebanese Forces were gone, thousands of Moslems drove to Sidon—Moslems who had fled to Beirut during the shelling, and displaced families from Beirut looking for a place to live. The Christian villages north of Sidon, looted only a few days earlier, were now quickly occupied by Shiite squatters from the outskirts of Beirut and a few Palestinians; but at the same time religious leaders in Sidon were trying to arrange for the return of Christian families who had fled to Jezzine. Christians were welcome to return as long as no one in their families was a member of a Christian militia. But few Christians dared to come back.

One of our Christian friends, a Lebanese nurse who worked for UNRWA, sent word that she intended to stay with her husband in a Christian village in the mountains for a few months until the situation settled down. Moslem friends had prevented her house from being looted and had moved her furniture to a safe place for storage, but her house was in Salhiyyah, a Christian village in the hills above Sidon, and it was not safe for her to return. Moslem militias were battling the South Lebanon Army nearby, and her village was still a volatile area.

I met a young Lebanese Moslem on the street who used to work for us as a driver. He had always been careless with money, and was getting into desperate financial straits around the time the shelling began. We had not heard from him for a month, but when I saw him that day he was in good spirits: he had just come into possession of a small dress shop in Abra, a village above Sidon where many Christians had lived. His inventory was low just now, he said, but he expected to be getting more things soon. I congratulated him, not very enthusiastically, on his good fortune.

Not long afterwards I visited Rima, our cleaning woman, in her house in Ein el-Hilweh. We talked as her daughter made coffee. On a nearby table was a pile of "red letters"—letters from prisoners which the ICRC distributed to their families. Rima's husband had been in prison for almost three years. On another table was a handful of unused bullets arranged in a geometric design. A lifesize poster of Yasser Arafat, popularly known as Abu Ammar, looked down on us from the wall.

Rima's oldest son had joined the *fedayeen* during the shelling and fought the Lebanese Forces around Mieh Mieh. Though still a teenager, he had decided, as the man of the house, that his mother should not work as a cleaning woman any more. She would still do our laundry, she said, if we brought it to her, but she would not go out of the house to work. She wanted to give me a present, a little plastic model of a child and a priest in a box, with an inscription that read, "For Your First Communion." I realized with a sinking heart that this was Christian loot brought back by her son. "Thank you," I said, "but I'm not Maronite." She went back to her room and emerged with a lucite paper-weight with an artificial rose inside; it was an advertisement for an American drug for arthritis. She showed me other new things she had gotten—all trinkets not really worth keeping, much less hauling off: ashtrays, plastic flowers, cheap framed pictures. But to her, there were all beautiful.

Just before I left, Rima's son came back for a visit. He smiled and shook my hand with the hand that was not holding his machine gun.

Spring Lull

The UNRWA schools reopened ten days after the Lebanese Forces withdrew from Sidon, and a few days later construction work resumed on some of the big office and apartment buildings going up around town. Traffic was heavy, and shoppers were out on the streets again. But as Shafik, our night nurse, observed, "The situation is on a question mark." Only a handful of Christians had returned to Sidon. The private schools were still closed, because many of the teachers were Christian, and people whose homes were destroyed during the shelling still had no place to live. The Maroof Saad Foundation tried to match refugee families with homes formerly occupied by Christians who were unlikely to return, but their system was cumbersome, and some of the available buildings were expropriated by officials on the Foundation's payroll for their own use.

New buildings were going up in Ein el-Hilweh. One day Abu Karim took me to see his new mosque. The members of the mosque had raised the money to build it, and new Korans had been contributed by the PLO. The Palestine Red Crescent Society was operating two temporary clinics in Ein el-Hilweh while a larger clinic was being built nearby, which would have its own laboratory and pharmacy and stay open twenty-four hours a day. When the PRCS returned to Ein el-Hilweh after the Israeli withdrawal, its doctors had trouble finding space for a new clinic; people in the camp knew that PLO political and military offices would come next, and soon the Israelis would be bombing the camp again. They were right. But the PRCS had gained a foothold in Ein el-Hilweh and Mieh Mieh during the month that Sidon was shelled. We knew their medical staff; they were capable and well-organized. Within a few days of the Lebanese Forces' withdrawal, the PRCS clinics in Ein el-Hilweh were treating 150 patients a day, and a new clinic was planned for the Mieh Mieh camp.

There were fewer militiamen on the streets. No battles were being fought around town, so prolonged gunfire usually signalled an emotional response to an important event, like a wedding, a visit from an out-of-town leader, or a lunar eclipse. The news of the return to Lebanon of Sunni leader Mustafa Saad, Sidon's local hero, inspired an evening rooftop concert of rocket and machine gun fire which lasted until a car went through the streets with a loudspeaker asking militias to stop the shooting. I wondered how a man who had been blinded in a car bomb explosion would react to hearing this welcoming chorus of artillery. A picture in the newspaper showed him getting off the plane in Beirut wearing dark glasses, surrounded by bodyguards and well-wishers. "He's taking it very well," said a member of his family.

Barbara and I were getting used to our new neighbors. An Islamic militia had recently moved into the house across the street. A few days after the Lebanese Forces withdrew, a van had pulled up in front of the house, and a group of men got out and went inside. Before long, black and green religious flags with words from the Koran were raised over the roof. Only a few weeks earlier, before the shelling started in Sidon, the owner of the house, a Christian woman, had tried to persuade Violet to rent it; she knew that it would be seized sooner or later if it stayed empty. The house was one of several military centers Sunni Moslem fundamentalists established around Sidon that spring. Some of the men in the house across from us were Lebanese and others were Palestinians from the camps; among the latter I recognized one of our former nurses.

When I was working in the kitchen I could watch our new neighbors from the window. On some mornings a group of them left their house as soon as it was light and walked to a nearby playing field to carry out military exercises. About twenty soldiers would assemble on the porch before walking down the street in single file. They were heavily armed, but did not wear military uniforms. As they walked along, each would wheel around and look in all directions every few steps. At the playing field they spread out in a line, walked and crouched and aimed their guns at imaginary targets in the distance. Their drills continued during Ramadan, when they had to fast during the day. They were a disciplined group, and seemed to take no part in the petty crimes and factional fighting that other militias engaged in. Their efforts were directed against one enemy: the Israelis remaining in Lebanon and their supporters in the South Lebanon Army.

Every morning I passed their house on my way to the hospital. Sometimes a soldier was out sweeping the sidewalk or sitting on the porch cleaning his gun. Late in the afternoon some of them came out to play volleyball. What did they think of their two American neighbors? I asked people at the hospital who knew them if they objected to our presence. "Don't worry," they said, "they won't bother you."

Still, I could never be sure if they knew, or cared, what we were doing. I never went near the kitchen window if I was wearing shorts, and I felt a little guilty every time I reached into the refrigerator for a beer. But we got used to each other. During the day we heard many long religious and political speeches broadcast from the mosque next to their house, and on some evenings as they sat on their porch after dinner they heard the Talking Heads. I did not want to offend any political or religious group, but I did not want to feel that I had to hide from anyone, either; had I felt that way, I would have left.

A few days after we moved back into the hospital, Violet joined Barbara and me for dinner at a seaside restaurant south of town. We were relieved that our hospital and staff were still intact after the shelling, and we thought a small celebration was in order. Before we sat down Violet took the precaution of giving our table a thorough spraying with a can of insect repellent that she carried. Then she sprang some unexpected news: at the strong urging of both UN-RWA and the State Department, our organization had decided to pull out of Lebanon. Barbara and I would have to leave by the end of the following month, and if no other organization could be found to take it over, the hospital would close. Violet did not say what her future held in store, but evidently she expected to stay on in a caretaker role. State Department funds earmarked for Lebanon would be used for "reconstruction work" after the war was over, she said.

I was surprised and saddened to hear that the hospital would be abandoned on such short notice. Only six months earlier we had been told that our project was to be funded for another year, and we had expected that UNRWA would take it over after that. We were seeing almost 100 patients a day. Our clinics were busier than ever, and we still had four adult patients waiting for open heart surgery that our organization had agreed to pay for. The closing did not affect my work—I had planned to leave in June anyway—but Barbara had intended to stay for the rest of the year. UNRWA, it seemed, was not enthusiastic about taking over the hospital, and Violet was looking for another sponsor. But it would not be easy; although the cost of medical equipment and services in Lebanon was only a fraction of what it would be in the U.S., our budget was higher—over $200,000 a year—than most other organizations could afford. We agreed not to pass this gloomy news on to the staff until Violet had talked to other organizations; we did not want them to get demoralized and drift away if there was still a chance that the hospital could be kept open. But we could not keep them waiting for long.

Spring Travels

The Israelis withdrew from the city of Tyre at the end of

April, and afterwards confined most of their movements to a narrow strip of land near the Lebanese border. Some soldiers from Maj. Gen. Lahad's South Lebanon Army went to the border strip with the Israeli troops. Others remained in Jezzine, where 25,000 displaced Lebanese Christians had taken refuge, and battled with a coalition of Moslem militias. But this was beyond the sight and hearing of Sidon; it was easy to forget that fighting was still going on only fifteen miles away.

The prospect of travelling on roads free of Israeli and Phalangist checkpoints for the first time in three years brought out a wanderlust among the unmarried Palestinian men on our staff. Within a few weeks of the Lebanese Forces' withdrawal, four of them had bought new or second-hand cars. Those who could not afford their own wanted us to take them on trips in our car, and we did. Barbara and I went to Tyre and up through the Shouf Mountains with Daniel and his friend Tareq, one of the medical clerks. Daniel had been our translator at the hospital ever since Bilal and Mansour left for other jobs, and he was our guide for these trips. Daniel had an innate cheerfulness that always boosted our spirits. He had learned in school, he said, that taking a hot shower helps to give one self-confidence, and this advice became a standing joke in the hospital, especially during the weeks when we were under attack from the Lebanese Forces.

Daniel had been studying business and office practice at an UNRWA-sponsored training school at the time of the Israeli invasion. The first time he was arrested he was released after a few days and allowed to return to school. A few months later he was hailing a taxi in Ein el-Hilweh when a car full of men from the National Guard drove by and picked him up instead. They took him to the _Saraya_, Sidon's municipal headquarters, and told the Israelis that Daniel had a gun in his house. When Daniel denied the story, an Israeli soldier punched him in the face and knocked out two of his teeth. Later the soldier summoned him back into his office. He offered to release Daniel if he would agree to work as an informer. When he refused, the soldier filled out some papers and said, "This is your visa application for Ansar."

Daniel spent a year in Ansar. In spite of the lack of hot showers, he regained his self-confidence as he got used to prison life. People enjoyed his company because he was friendly and outgoing. Israeli soldiers liked him because he said good morning in Hebrew when they came to count the prisoners. But they did not like the way he smiled and rolled up his eyes when his prison ID picture was taken.

Some Israeli soldiers made friends among the prisoners. Although they risked disciplinary action if they were caught talking with prisoners, they lingered by the fences at the end of the day to talk about politics or their families or their hopes for the future. A few were trying to recruit informers, but most seemed lonely, and those who got to know the prisoners no longer believed their government's claim that all of them had worked with the PLO. Some prisoners gave the soldiers things they had made—carved medallions, painted combs made from wooden packing crates, pieces of beaded jewelry—in return for cigarettes and food, or as keepsakes for them or their girlfriends. A soldier who befriended Daniel gave him his address and telephone number in Israel before he left, and told Daniel to try to call him sometime when he had a chance. Daniel liked the soldier, but he threw the address away, fearing that anyone who found it would accuse him of being a spy.

Daniel knew people everywhere we went on our travels. Some were old friends from Ansar. One, a fisherman from Tyre, came up to Sidon to visit him after the prisoner exchange, and stayed at his house for three days. When we drove to Tyre we found him at the port, and he took us out on his boat. When it seemed safer not to be Palestinian, Daniel chose an identity which better suited the occasion. At a local photography store where he went to order copies of some pictures I had taken of a political demonstration, he took the precaution of using a Christian name. On our out-of-town travels, he wore a necklace with pictures of Amal leader Nabih Berri and Druze leader Walid Jumblatt on opposite sides. As we neared a checkpoint he would put the appropriate picture in front, and then sit back looking relaxed, his arms over the seat, and say, "Do you want to see my I.D. card?" "No, no," they usually said, and waved us on.

In mid-May I decided to visit Syria for a few days. It was easy to reach from Lebanon, and many Lebanese and Palestinians (women, mostly) who had relatives there made the trip often. The simplest way to go was to reserve a place in a group taxi, called a *service.* The taxi left early in the morning, and the trip from Sidon or Beirut to Damascus took about four or five hours, depending on how much traffic there was at the border. Daniel helped me reserve a seat with a taxi company in Sidon, and also gave me a letter addressed to him, using one of his false names, for me to give to the driver in Damascus, saying that I had safely arrived. For years Palestinians traveling through areas in Lebanon where there was a risk of getting kidnapped had used a similar system; the traveler would send back a small personal item, like a pen or a comb, with the driver on his return trip to signify that he had reached his destination safely.

In the taxi the next morning I found myself sitting next to one of my patients, an ample, smiling Palestinian woman in her fifties. As soon as I settled into my seat, she took out her medications to show me—some digoxin tablets and two other kinds of tablets, each in a bottle labelled "digoxin." One kind was for her pressure, she said, and one was for her heart. I could not say for sure what medication she was taking, since UNRWA doctors gave out whatever generic medicines they had on hand each month, not necessarily the exact brand the patient was accustomed to. But my patient seemed sure of her regimen, so after she showed me the pills, I said what she wanted me to say: "Fine, fine. Very good."

The *service* made a few halts near the Syrian border to pick up bargains that passengers wanted to stock up on. My patient insisted on stopping at a store which had a good price on giant boxes of Kleenex. We stopped for a cup of coffee, and we stopped again so that everyone could buy bread. On the Syrian side of the border we had to stop several times for routine police checks.

I spent about three days in Damascus shipping and walking around. In the Christian quarter one afternoon I saw two nuns from Mother Theresa's order. I had spent some time working with Mother Theresa's nuns in a clinic in Calcutta. I have always had mixed feelings about them; I find them exasperatingly naive, but sweet and plucky. The two nuns I saw had been in Syria for only three weeks. One spoke no Arabic yet, but the other had helped set up a mission in East Beirut five years ago. I asked how she liked Damascus. "We like it wherever we are," she said. Atta girl! She invited me to visit them. They were off to visit the poor somewhere nearby. "God bless you!" I said, and we went our separate ways.

When you are ready to return to Sidon, you go to the *garage* (taxi station) for Lebanon and sit in a cab bound for Sidon until it fills up. If the driver cannot find enough riders, you can get a place in a cab going to Beirut, and take another taxi from there. The taxi I got into filled up after an hour or so. It was not in good condition; on the way back to Sidon we got a flat tire, and after the driver put on a spare, the engine refused to start. We were on the outside shoulder of a narrow road in the Shouf Mountains at the time, and I was afraid that a speeding car might come around and knock us off the side. A Druze military procession passed enroute to a funeral. After the driver got the engine started, we heard the sound of automatic weapons fire nearby. There were no other cars on the road. He stepped on the gas. Finally we passed a vendor at a roadside vegetable stand. Our driver stuck his head out the window and, giving a characteristic twist of the hand that looks like an attempt to unscrew a large light bulb, said, "*fi shi?*" ("Anything going on?"). No, he said, the gunfire was only a ceremonial outburst related to the funeral. After that we slowed down a little, and everyone started talking again.

One is aware right away of having crossed the border from Syria to Lebanon. The roads become narrow and rutted. Stone walls around houses and fields have been knocked over, and power lines are down. Whole villages have been gutted with no attempt to rebuild them. There is litter everywhere; my fellow-passengers added to it as soon as they finished their sandwiches. And yet the wash is hanging on the clotheslines, people sit in front of their houses talking to neighbors, and roadside produce stands are well-stocked with fruits and vegetables.

An old Lebanese *hajji* sitting in the back of the taxi with me talked on and on about something that was bothering her. I could not understand everything she was saying, but I knew that the correct response was to sigh and shake my head and say "What can we do?" The passenger in the front seat was a Lebanese man on leave from a job in Saudi Arabia, a nosy, patronizing fellow. At the border he insisted on looking at my passport and residence permit after I showed them to the immigration official. Then he asked how old I was, and whether I was married. One tires of this when one is tired already. His comment when we heard gunfire in the distance was "Don't worry; every day, anybody dead."

The Revolted South

I got back from Damascus late in the afternoon, in time to see a film called "Resistance Fighters of the South" (translated on the billboards as "The Revolted South"). It had come to Sidon for one week, and this was its last day. It was a locally-made melodrama about the resistance of Shiite villagers in southern Lebanon to the Israeli occupation, and it starred a real-life Resistance fighter named Ali. According to the *Daily Star*, it had played to packed houses in Beirut, and had audiences standing up and cheering. I went to see it with Daniel who, though he had already seen it earlier in the week and did not think it was very good, was willing to see it again, so he could explain it to me.

The movie opened with the scenes from Beirut before the civil war, showing beach clubs, yacht clubs, jewelry stores, and people driving expensive foreign cars. Then it shifted to views of devastated streets along the Green Line between East and West Beirut, with gutted buildings as far as the eye

could see. This was followed by scenes, without commen-
tary, of battles fought by the Israelis in the Sinai and during
the 1982 invasion of Lebanon.

After this silent introduction, the story began, and we
were introduced to Ali, the young and handsome Resistance
fighter, and his wife, Fatmeh. Ali was leading a group from
his village in guerrilla attacks against the Israelis, and the
Israelis were determined to track him down and crush the
Resistance. The Israeli officer in charge, portrayed as brutal, stupid, and single-minded, was assisted by a Lebanese
Christian informer, but toward the end of the movie this
informer turned out to be a double agent who would se-
cretly help Ali.

The plot was very simple. While Ali was away planning
the next ambush, Fatmeh was captured by Israelis and
beaten ("Where is Ali?" they asked her). She escaped, but
then Ali was captured after being wounded in battle. He was
beaten in captivity (but no worse, it seemed, than his wife
had been) and left in a hospital room. The Christian double
agent helped Ali escape, but Ali was weak and confused
and, after staggering along a deserted road, he collapsed in
a village churchyard, still swathed in bandages. A nun and a
priest found him and nursed him back to health. He finally
managed to return to his village, but by then Fatmeh had
been killed, another martyr to the cause.

In the end, Ali and his men succeeded in surrounding an
Israeli military outpost. Ali shouted *"Allah akbar!"* and led
the final assault as music from "Die Valkyrie" played in the
background. Ali confronted the odious Israeli officer,
forced his mouth open with both hands, and stepped on his
face, causing the officer to make terrible gagging noises and
finally die. As the officer made his final guttural sounds, Ali
hurled a hand grenade at the Israeli flag, still flying over the
smoking ruins. Then he mounted the hill, took out a Lebanese flag, which he had stored folded up in his shirt for this
occasion, and raised it on the flagpole. Having done this, he
posed for about thirty seconds in profile looking up at the
flag. Here the audience was supposed to cheer. They did the
first time, I was told, but on this day there were only a half-

dozen people in the audience. Nobody said a word, and the pause seemed awfully long.

Daniel and I traded remarks during the film about what was "true." It was not true, we agreed, that the Lebanese resistance would end if leaders like Ali were captured and imprisoned. But neither was it true that the Israelis would ever find one of their command posts surrounded by the likes of Ali and his men; the best these Resistance fighters could hope for with their style of fighting was to shoot one or two soldiers every once in a while in an ambush or to blow up an Israeli military vehicle with a roadside bomb.

This was a low-budget film; the only real props were the weapons. After a shooting scene, actors would simply fall on the ground and play dead until the camera stopped rolling. The plot was sometimes interrupted by silent footage showing ruined buildings and people playing dead as a child's voice, squeaky and high-pitched, sang a song called "Where is My Family?" Daniel thought that this was a nice touch. "Many orphans in Ein el-Hilweh said this after the invasion," he said, "and an organization came and took them away to Switzerland." He also liked the scene where Ali was nursed back to health by the nun. At one point, as she bent over his bed, her crucifix touched the medallion around his neck which said "Allah." "Very nice!" he said, as the camera showed this in closeup.

But Daniel was not carried away by the film's message. When Ali raised the Lebanese flag at the end, he said, "Really, there are many flags he could have put up." Was Ali really fighting on behalf of all the Lebanese? The answer was both yes and no. It was an ethnic film, after all; Ali was a poor, pious Moslem villager, and the film was about the courage and unity of the Shiites in the South. The message I got was this: "We are leading the fight against the Israelis. We are the ones making sacrifices to rid our country of this occupying army. If the rest of you (Christians, Palestinians, Druze) want to join us, we will fight together, but if you don't, the credit and the power will be ours."

The Camps War

Ramadan was supposed to begin at the first sign of the crescent moon; a religious committee in each Moslem country watched for it, and their proclamation marked the beginning of the fast. But there was some confusion about when Ramadan started in 1985. In Syria, Moslems started fasting a day before the Lebanese expected Ramadan to begin. One mosque near our hospital announced that people should begin fasting until the matter was settled, but most people, hearing nothing official on the radio, went ahead with their usual daily routine, and there were two or three weddings in the camp that day. (Moslem couples usually do not marry during Ramadan). With the beginning of Ramadan came news of a new disaster as violent and shocking as the shelling of Sidon had been, but far more devastating in its toll of dead and wounded. It was the Camps War.

For weeks there had been reports of increasing tension between the Amal movement and the PLO in the three largest refugee areas in West Beirut—Sabra, Shatila and Burj el-Barajneh. Amal had surrounded the Beirut camps in mid-April, after clashing with the Murabitun, the Sunni Moslem militia friendly with the PLO, and new Amal checkpoints were established south of Sidon at that time. Then, just before Ramadan began, Amal militiamen arrested ten men from the PLO in Ein el-Hilweh, and the next day five of their men were arrested in turn. But nobody expected the prolonged and brutal fighting that ensued; the battles lasted for a month, and left more than 600 people dead and 26,000 homeless. That the fighting occurred during a holy month was nothing new for Lebanon, but all the same it was cause for sorrow to Moslem observers on both sides.

According to newspaper accounts, the fighting began after an argument about the treatment of a Palestinian taken into custody by Amal. It soon grew into a fierce battle during which the camps were surrounded by Amal militiamen and Lebanese soldiers from the army's Sixth Brigade. Families escaping from the camps fled to nearby shelters and to Druze-held areas of West Beirut. The Druze gave their passive support to the Palestinian side, and allowed the PLO to fire on Amal positions from their territory in the Shouf Mountains.

After overrunning part of Sabra, Amal militiamen optimistically predicted an early victory. But soon they found that the camps were connected by an elaborate system of underground tunnels, allowing defenders to emerge and shoot at them from all directions. A long war of attrition began: Amal destroyed the water towers in the camps and tried to starve the people left inside. The ICRC was not allowed to transport the wounded or evacuate the dead. Amal militiamen captured Gaza Hospital, where hundreds of Palestinians had taken refuge, and destroyed it. They surrounded the American University Hospital and shot Palestinians who were brought to the emergency room by ambulance. (I spoke with a relative of one of the victims and with a doctor at AUH who had witnessed these events.)

Barbara and I drove to Beirut a few days after the Camps War started with seven units of 0 positive blood in an ice chest for one of our open-heart patients. Three of our patients were hospitalized at AUH waiting for open-heart surgery, but all elective surgery, we learned, had been cancelled because of the fighting. No one knew whether it was more dangerous for our patients to stay in the hospital or leave. They stayed, but the brother of one was kidnapped from inside the hospital when he came to donate blood. His father, knowing what had happened, decided not to tell his ill son; but he sat in his son's hospital room for three days, afraid to go out in the hallway.

We ate lunch in a coffee shop near the hospital. Cars were racing back and forth from the hospital at top speed, and machine gun fire erupted outside every few minutes. After a particularly long outburst, the owner, seeing that I had almost choked on my cheeseburger, came over to reassure me that the gunfire was just a twenty-one-gun salute for an Amal soldier who had died.

After the first few days we started seeing Palestinians who had fled to Sidon to escape the fighting. One man came in to our hospital after having been severely beaten. He and his friends had been stopped on the street in West Beirut by a group of Amal militiamen. His friends were shot, but he escaped with a beating because he knew someone from Amal. Two Palestinians told me of going to look for relatives who had been arrested and finding their mutilated corpses with the eyes gouged out. Even Palestinians living outside the camps in Beirut's southern suburbs had to flee from their homes. An old woman who had lived for twenty-three years in a Shiite suburb south of Beirut and always gotten along with her neighbors was now suddenly told by them, "We want to kill all the Palestinians. If you stay, we will kill you too." All houses known to be owned by Palestinians were looted and burned.

An editorial in the *Daily Star* was at a loss to explain why the fighting was so brutal, and why it had started so suddenly. Amal claimed that Arafat had smuggled more and more arms into the camps during recent weeks (nobody denied this), and that this constituted a threat to Amal, which did not want to see the PLO gain control of South Lebanon once again. A Shiite friend of ours said that Arafat had boasted that the PLO would soon stage a comeback in South Lebanon. Amal's growing frustration with the PLO was understandable, but that did not explain the savagery of the fighting, which reminded many of the Phalangist massacres at Sabra and Shatila in September 1982.

Our hospital staff was gloomy and apprehensive. One day some nurses were in the conference room listening to a tape we had heard many times before. It was a popular song from the Resistance called *Narfoud Nahna Mout*, "We Refuse to Die." Someone brought in a newspaper which was being distributed at Amal checkpoints around Sidon. The headline read:

AMAL BLOCKS ABU AMMAR'S PLANS TO RETURN TO SOUTH LEBANON. CLASHES NOW BECAUSE OF WHAT HAPPENED BEFORE THE INVASION. AMAL: THE LIBERATION OF SOUTH LEBANON WILL BE THE BEGINNING OF THE LIBERATION OF PALESTINE.

One nurse took the newspaper and started to redesign the faces of the Amal leaders in the photographs. "Nabih Geagea," he muttered, "Walid Hobeika." To him all Lebanese leaders were the same. The Lebanese Forces had been gone from Sidon for only three weeks, but already another militia was lining up to shoot at them. Amal declared that the fighting would continue until PLO fighters surrendered their heavy weapons. The hospital staff was proud that all factions of the PLO had united to fight against Amal. "Why should we give up our arms?" they said. "If we do, we'll all be killed." And who could say that was not true? Who had enough authority to guarantee their safety?

Would the fighting spread to Ein el-Hilweh? For the first time, our male patients who carried guns refused to leave them with the guard at the door of the hospital. An official from Fateh listened on his walkie-talkie while one of the doctors examined his young son. Then a seventeen-year-old kid from Fateh limped in. He was from the Burj el-Barajneh camp in Beirut, but had come to Sidon recently. He said that his superior had beaten him on the soles of his feet and all over his trunk as a punishment for threatening to start a fight with Amal. His body was covered with welts and bruises, and he looked exhausted.

From time to time, as in the old days, you could hear bursts of machine gun fire in the distance, followed by the sound of a car driving away very fast. "We'd better start sleeping with our passports and our flashlights again," said Barbara. Dr. Refki and his wife went to the *Saraya* to get their passports renewed. Dr. Zuhdi was afraid to drive home through the Shiite suburb of Harat Saida, so he spent the night at the hospital.

Outside our hospital window, giant earthen barricades were being erected to protect the lower part of the camp if there were attacks by snipers in the hills. Ein el-Hilweh should have been safe from any large-scale battles with Amal, because Sidon's Shiite population was relatively small; most Shiites lived several miles away in the town of Ghaziyyah. Besides, the supply of arms in the camp had grown during the previous month's shelling. Some people claimed that there were Katyusha rockets in the camp, though nobody had actually seen one. Still, even those who said that the PLO had enough arms to finish off any Shiite opposition in twenty minutes jumped whenever they heard a gun go off outside.

One afternoon I watched a military drill for children being held on the street below our hospital. The children ranged in age from about six to twelve and were dressed in camouflage uniforms. As they stood in line, their adult in-structor shouted to put their right foot forward, but some were too small to know their right foot from their left, so another instructor went around and pulled out the right foot of the little ones. When they were all lined up correctly, they raised their arms and shouted in unison *"Thowra! Tho-wra!"* ("Revolution!") and marched off. *"Coulu Abu Ammar."* ("They're all for Abu Ammar"), said one of the nurses, and smiled. To him, the sight of these uniformed children was cute, and a bit absurd, but not unusual. But I could not bear to look at it.

"Don't worry about the childhood of our people," said Abu Karim. He told me about a conversation he had just had with his son. When Abu Karim returned home from Ansar, his fourteen-year-old son said he wanted a gun so he could fight the Israelis. Abu Karim persuaded him to forget about fighting and stay in school. He was a good student, and his father wanted him to study engineering.

Then in April 1985 Abu Karim's wife was shot in the back by a sniper from the Lebanese Forces firing into the win-dow of the house. It was some time before she could be evacuated to a hospital. After that his son said he was going to join the PLO. This time Abu Karim gave him a different answer.

"Finish your school first," he said, "so as to be a high rank with the PLO, and not a small soldier."

After an opening round of self-righteousness, the Amal leadership began getting defensive when unpleasant re-ports of atrocities appeared in the foreign press. Nabih Berri acknowledged that "some excesses had occurred." Newsmen were denied access to areas around the fighting, and the photographs which appeared in local newspapers were ludicrously self-serving: grim-faced Amal militiamen yanking feeble-minded patients out of a home for the aged in Sabra; a militiaman from Amal taking time off from the fighting to pray with his machine gun at his side. He was wearing a black T-shirt with a skull and crossbones design which was fashionable with all the militias at the time. It read:

> Airborne
> Mess with the best
> Die like the rest

More than two weeks after fighting began, the ICRC was allowed into Sabra and Shatila to evacuate all the wounded it could carry. They were taken to a hospital in Druze-held territory in the Shouf; from there they could choose to go to larger hospitals in Syria or Sidon for treatment. President Gemayel met with Syria's President Assad to try to arrange for a ceasefire, but neither leader publicly condemned the fighting.

On June 20, after a month of fighting, a Syrian-sponsored accord was signed by representatives from Amal and a coalition of Syrian-backed PLO factions. Under the terms of the accord, the Palestinians in the Beirut camps were allowed to keep their light weapons; they would surrender their heavier arms at some future date. The war had done little to alter the political status quo, and it was hard to feel anything but a sense of dread about what would happen next.

Last Visits

One morning in late May Daniel's brother woke him up to say goodbye. In a couple of hours he would be on a flight back to the U.S. He had gone to the States to study, and had married and settled there. He had come to Lebanon the month before to visit his family for the first time in six years. He had been planning the trip for a long time, but had wanted to wait until the Israelis left Sidon. His timing could not have been worse. He arrived in Ein el-Hilweh in early April. A few days later, the shelling of Sidon began. He went to Beirut to stay with relatives, but as soon as he arrived Amal started battling with the Murabitun on the streets outside their apartment. Then, just as he was planning to return to the States, the Camps War broke out. He postponed his departure, because he risked getting killed or kidnapped on the road near the Beirut airport. But finally he could wait no longer. He got an old friend of his from the Lebanese Army to drive him to the airport. Daniel's brother wept as he said goodbye. "I'll never come back here again," he said.

The Palestinians I knew were shaken by the shelling of Ein el-Hilweh and the Camps War, and they expected more trouble in the months ahead—perhaps a major battle in Ein el-Hilweh. They talked about papers that were said to have been found in the homes of Phalangist officials in Mieh Mieh and Darb es-Sin, outlining plans for the bulldozing of Ein el-Hilweh and the extermination of its inhabitants. Most people I talked to had thought of leaving Lebanon. Those with technical training could try to get a job in one of the oil-rich Arab countries. Others could apply for a passport and try to make contact with relatives who had left for other countries years ago. People felt better having up-to-date passports, even if there was no place to go.

One day I went to see Sonia, a woman in her early twenties, who had been our first adult patient to undergo open-heart surgery. The surgery had gone well, and four other adult patients had felt confident enough to follow her example. Her family had been talking about the Camps War. Arabs had given birth to civilization, her mother said; why were they killing each other now? When I mentioned that I had visited Syria, she raised her hands and looked up at the sky, imploring Allah to rain bombs down on President Assad for what he had done to the Palestinian people. After the shelling of Ein el-Hilweh Sonia had decided to leave the camp for good. She was living in a small house near an orange grove south of Sidon with her husband and children. It was quieter there, she said, and she felt safer.

Before leaving Lebanon I visited a member of our staff whose wife had just given birth to their second child. Barbara has told him about the protest demonstrations in the U.S. during the sixties and seventies. He seemed surprised to hear about them. "You can have demonstrations, and your government allows it?" he asked. The people in the camp had held many demonstrations against the Israelis in the past; now the time had come, he felt, to demonstrate against their own leadership. He was giving some thought to how that could be done. He had also thought about leaving. The Camps War was on his mind, and he knew that our hospital might soon close. He considered taking his family to Germany; he had worked there several years before, and taught himself German. But then he decided to stay. "I feel that no matter where I am, if my people aren't strong, I can't be strong," he said, "so it's better to stay here with my people."

One day I went with Daniel to pay a visit to his family. They lived in the middle of the camp in a house rebuilt after the Israeli invasion with funds sent by his brother who worked in the Gulf.

Daniel's mother was a woman in her fifties with a warm smile and kind, loving eyes. She had married when she was very young, and had never learned to read and write. Like many of the older ladies in the camp, she supported Abu Ammar. She used to go to every speech he gave in Ein el-Hilweh. After the Israeli invasion, in August 1982, she went to the IDF headquarters to get permission to travel to Beirut. She told the Israeli officer that she was going for medical treatment at AUH.

"You're going so that you can say goodbye to the PLO," the officer said. She admitted it was true. He gave her permission anyway. She went to Beirut and stayed to watch Abu Ammar sail away with the PLO fighters. She only wished that she had had a chance to kiss him goodbye.

Whenever Daniel's mother went to the mosque, she prayed to Allah to keep Abu Ammar in good health. "Abu Ammar will bring us peace," she said. "He is the only leader who represents all the Palestinian people." She was sure that he would be able to negotiate for the Palestinians through diplomatic channels. Many times she took her son aside and said, "Promise me you'll never join a military group."

Daniel's father backed one of the radical factions of the PLO. When his wife started talking about Abu Ammar, he said (referring to the large sums of PLO money coming into the camp), "Abu Ammar is buying us and selling us." Not long before he had berated Daniel for not joining the PLO. He could not understand why his son did not feel the way he did; hadn't they both suffered in Ansar? "Why won't you fight the Israelis?" he said. "The PLO will give you the best future, the most self-respect."

Daniel had his own political views, and he did not want to work for the PLO. He was hoping to go to college in the U.S., though he knew that it would be hard for him to leave home. "I feel that Ein el-Hilweh is my country, " he said.

Barbara and I went to see Hanan one day after she had moved into an apartment in Sidon that had belonged to a Christian family. The owner had fled the country after the shelling began, and a relative of his invited her to stay in it as long as she liked—better her, he said, than squatters or gangsters. But she also got a permit from the *Nasiriyyun*, the organization that was trying to match homeless families with empty houses and apartments, and she insisted on paying rent.

Hanan's new apartment was roomy and clean, but she had almost no furniture. She was living with her son and two girls who had been separated from their parents during the fighting in Sabra and Shatila. She had not seen Mousa for two weeks; he was trapped in Beirut by the Camps War. They had had to abandon their apartment in the Shiite southern suburbs.

When I went outside to buy some Pepsi, I found myself surrounded by a half-dozen militiamen from a checkpoint maintained by the *Nasiriyyun*. They let me pass after I showed them my ID card, but then, seeing Barbara out on Hanan's balcony, some of them decided to pay a visit. They walked in the door and made themselves at home, and Hanan prepared coffee for then. After inspecting the apartment, Corporal Khaled, their leader, offered to get Hanan more furniture, but she politely declined.

Later that evening, Corporal Khaled came back. He liked Hanan's apartment and had decided that he wanted it for himself. She had three days to get out, he said. She showed him the papers that authorized her to stay in the apartment, but he refused to look at them. "I don't care what the papers say," he said, "I want this apartment, and I'm taking it."

A soldier who had come with him told Hanan to ignore him; he was drunk. The soldiers were unhappy with him too; they had not been paid for several weeks, and were not getting much to eat. Hanan locked her door after the soldiers left. A few minutes later her water was turned off. She did not dare to go outside.

The next morning I went with Hanan to speak to an official in the *Nasiriyyun*, the organization that had issued her permit and was also affiliated with Corporal Khaled's militia. The official smiled and shook his head—Corporal Khaled was a well-known troublemaker. Before the Israeli invasion he had worked with one of the PLO factions. When the PLO left he stayed behind and joined the South Lebanon Army. When the SLA withdrew from Sidon he signed up with the *Nasiriyyun*.

Corporal Khaled visited Hanan again that night and tore up the special letter we had obtained from the *Nasiriyyun*. The next day she started to ask around for other apartments. But they were not easy to find; one of our nurses had lost her house and been living in a schoolroom with her family for several weeks.

Finally a male friend of Hanan's decided to speak to Corporal Khaled himself. He found him that night on the Corniche, sitting in a car and watching the families make their evening promenade by the sea. He informed the Corporal that the PLO had taken an interest in Hanan's case. Corporal Khaled changed his mind about her apartment after that. He was later transferred to another part of town.

My last days at the hospital were sad and trying. The staff and my patients had known for several weeks that I was leaving, but at my last endocrine clinic, Dr. Fadi, our consulting endocrinologist, seemed taken aback by the news. "You're leaving and not coming back? Take me with you! I can't stay here, " he said. We had had similar conversations many times before. Dr. Fadi was an excellent clinician and a kind, compassionate man. But he had a superstition about

Americans shared by many Lebanese I had met, a belief that Americans in Lebanon, even in their dwindling numbers, exercised a kind of stabilizing influence. News of more kidnappings, massacres and bombings was greeted with a sigh and a shake of the head. But an American leaving! That was something serious, that was a bad omen. (This faith in outsiders still working in Lebanon also extended to representatives of other Western countries, but it was most pronounced, I felt, toward Americans.)

Behind their disappointment lurked a half-spoken reproach: how dare you leave! You're supposed to help us! Americans, it was true, had played an active part in Lebanon's development for over a hundred years, long before the country gained its independence. Many Christian and Moslem families still sent their children to one of the prestigious evangelical schools founded by American missionaries, and the American University of Beirut was a national institution; in fact, one could argue that it was the only national institution left in the country. It was not surprising that the Lebanese felt ambivalent about Americans—our government showed a similar ambivalence about our role in their country—but the confidence my Lebanese friends had in our ability to help was as exaggerated as their resentment at our interference, and part of the same vicious circle.

Rally for Mustafa Saad

On June 6, the third anniversary of its invasion of Lebanon, Israel announced that its uniformed troops had completed their withdrawal from the country. Prime Minister Peres said that there would be no Israeli Army unit on Lebanese soil after that date. Since the beginning of "Operation Peace for Galilee," 654 Israeli troops and security personnel had been killed and almost 6000 wounded; the number of dead included twenty-one who had committed suicide while on duty in Lebanon. Another 140 Israeli soldiers had gone to prison for refusing to serve in Lebanon. The casualties on the other side were much higher; according to Lebanese government figures (statistics furnished by hospitals, police and civil defense workers) over 19,000 Lebanese and Palestinians were killed during Israel's invasion and three-year occupation of South Lebanon.

Israel retained control of a twelve-mile deep strip along the Lebanese border; it was patrolled by Israel's proxy militia and by several hundred Israeli troops. In an article in the Jerusalem *Post* that appeared the day after Israel's announced withdrawal, the paper's defense correspondent, Hirsh Goodman, wrote, "There will be no formal end to Israel's presence in Lebanon."

A week later I went with a Palestinian friend to a rally for Mustafa Saad and the Resistance. The Camps War was then in its third week, with no sign of an agreement that could lead to a cease-fire. The rally was held in a open area between apartment buildings in the middle of town. Folding chairs were set up around a wooden platform on one side of the grounds. By the time we got there, most of the seats had been taken, and many people were watching from apartment balconies. Militiamen from the *Nasiriyyun*, Mustafa Saad's Nassarite Popular Movement, stood around the stage, some with flowers in their gun barrels.

The rally started with long repetitive speeches by local officials extolling the bravery of the people of South Lebanon during the Israeli occupation and the shelling from the Lebanese Forces. The speakers urged Lebanese and Palestinians to fight together against the Israelis. Between speeches, musicians played political songs, cheered and applauded by the crowd. A group of about twenty Palestinians near us broke into their own songs whenever the official singing stopped. A Shiite sang a song taken from a poem by the Palestinian poet, Mahmoud Darwish. But the most popular song was so well-known that everybody sang along, and then the musician was asked to repeat it. The refrain went:

> I will fight with the Resistance with
> the Palestinians
> I will not recognize Israel
> I will not recognize Israel

> I will fight with the Resistance to the last drop
> of my blood.

Most Lebanese at the rally were Sunni Moslems, like the Palestinians. Shaken by the Camps War, the Palestinians longed for their support, and for the moment, the two groups could sing together. But the Palestinians knew that their allies could change their minds, and their songs, at any time.

Mustafa Saad was a Sunni Moslem who had studied in the Soviet Union and married a Russian woman. One of his sisters was married to a Palestinian, and many men in his militia were Palestinians. In theory, he backed the Palestinian cause, but his militiamen and PLO often got in each other's way. A couple of weeks earlier, soldiers from the *Nasiriyyun* had gotten into a heated argument with a group of PLO factions at the entrance to Ein el-Hilweh over the placement of a checkpoint. Leaders from both sides shouted at each other while their men fired machine guns into the air and cars sped off in every direction. We were in the middle of a cardiology conference at the time, and dove for cover as our patients fled from the building. Fortunately, no one was injured, but tension was high, especially on the Palestinian side. The truce between the two sides was shaky.

The rally had been in progress for over an hour before Mustafa Saad, the man everybody wanted to see, finally arrived. On the night he was injured in a car bomb explosion outside his apartment the previous January, 300 people had stood in line outside Bashar Hospital to donate blood for him and his family. The bombing was attributed to Israeli agents, and Mustafa Saad shared this view. In an article in the *New Statesman* on May 17, 1985, he provided an account of several ominous encounters with Israeli military officers in the months before he was injured, and pointed out that the Israelis did not seem interested in allowing him to get adequate medical treatment on the night of the explosion; Israeli soldiers argued with UNIFIL soldiers for three hours before allowing a U.N. helicopter to transport him and his wife to Beirut.

Those who knew Mustafa Saad admitted that he was not the charismatic figure his father had been, but he had always been a respected leader and arbitrator, and after the explosion he became a hero, a symbol of the Lebanese Resistance. There were posters of him everywhere in town. In one, taken from an old photograph, he was dressed in a sportjacket, smiling shyly. He used to be a handsome fellow. Another poster showed him after the explosion, a man with a scarred face wearing dark glasses, a corner of his upper lip twisted in a grimace.

At last Mustafa Saad arrived with his entourage. A brass band played, and his soldiers made the crowd (many of whom, like myself, had managed to stand up on folding chairs) sit down. Everyone cheered as he was led to a chair in the front row. After a moment the program resumed. I expected him to give a speech, but he never did while we were there. Just before we left I walked behind the stage and stood on a cinder block to see him at close range. His face was shiny from scar tissue, and his upper lip was slightly twisted. People stopped by from time to time to say a few words to him, but he sat impassively, smoking one cigarette after another, his arms held stiffly at his sides.

Last Trip to Bramieh

The day before I left Lebanon for the U.S. I decided to visit our old house in Bramieh one last time. I had heard that some Christian families had returned to their houses in Sidon; I hoped that a few of my Christian neighbors were among them, so that I could say goodbye.

Although the house was only a five-minute drive from the center to town, I had not been there for over a month, and I knew no one who could tell me what the neighborhood was like. Ghassan, a Shiite friend, offered to go with me at first, but then changed his mind and said I should not go either. An old Christian teacher of his, who lived high in the hills in a town called Majdalyun, had also decided to pay a last visit to his house, which had been almost destroyed during the previous month's fighting. He got a permit to visit the area from the *Nasiriyyun,* but Ghassan had argued against his going—no permit could guarantee his safety. What he did was a form of suicide; he never came back. Ghassan had pursued the matter as far as he could, only to be told in the end, "Forget it; he's dead."

I changed my mind about going when I heard this story, but then, after hearing that a Palestinian nurse in our hospital had recently driven through the neighborhood with no trouble, I decided to go after all. At the checkpoint closest to our neighborhood the Sunni militiamen said that things were quiet on the road, as far as they knew. I was driving, and had brought along Daniel, our translator. The street that ran past the big Druze villas was silent and empty. A bulldozer was parked beside the road, with big piles of earth around it. "They must be fixing the road," I thought. Closer to the house, we saw a fat old man sitting in a chair alongside the road. He rose and asked where we were going; I explained, and he waved us on.

I drove very slowly. The Maronite Church at the end of the road was gone, and so were the houses on either side of it where our Christian neighbors had lived. I looked around. I realized that all the houses were gone, except for the Druze-owned ones. I turned the car around without stopping. We headed back, but now the fat old man stood in the middle of the road holding a machine gun and waving us to a stop. We had driven into a military area and would have to be detained, he said. We had been set up. I pulled off the road as he ordered, and waited.

He summoned the officer in charge—a young man, clean-cut, well-dressed, and heavily armed. He began a long, serious conversation with Daniel. The fat man searched the car. I showed him my identity papers, but realized suddenly I had nothing to prove that I had ever lived in the house down the street. The officer in charge took my camera and ordered Daniel to step on the film. I tried to explain what we were doing, but the officer said he did not want to hear from me.

For the first time in all the months we had worked together, Daniel got desperate. He begged and wailed and pounded his chest, trying to talk us out of being "detained."

The officer said he thought at first that we were Christian; if we were, he would have shot us on the spot. But, he added, Americans and Palestinians were almost as bad. "You Palestinians are so stubborn," he said to Daniel. "You should know better than to come up here." And since I was an American, he said, I was probably a spy. Finally he said to Daniel, "Well, I'll let you go this time, but if I ever see you here again, I'll kill you." He spoke very slowly, and repeated his threat again before he let us leave.

Later I heard that the PSP, the Druze militia, had blown up the Christian houses because they felt that all the land around the Druze houses belonged to them—the Christians never had a right to live there in the first place. Never mind that Christian families had been living in the neighborhood for almost a hundred years. The Druze wanted no Christians to return, and they did not want empty houses to be taken over by Moslem squatters, either. My Christian neighbors were gone without a trace. I will never know what happened to them. And they were the ones who were always trying to protect us.

Beirut Airport

I bought my ticket to New York from Mr. Nidal, the travel agent who did not like to travel. My sadness at leaving was mixed with a dread of going to the Beirut airport. On May 28 the Chairman of the American University Hospital had been kidnapped on the street in West Beirut. Two French journalists were kidnapped the day before that. A professor of agriculture from AUB was kidnapped near the Beirut airport on June 9 after returning from the United States. Two days later, a Jordanian plane was hijacked in Beirut; the hijackers threatened to hold the passengers until all Palestinians left West Beirut. The following day a Palestinian in Cyprus retaliated by hijacking a Lebanese plane.

Barbara drove me to the airport and stayed to talk until it was time for me to get on the plane. We had no problems on the road, and the airport looked as it had when I left for vacation three months earlier: passengers crowded into lines at the counter of Middle East Airlines, the Lebanese-owned company which was almost the only one flying in and out of Beirut airport. The nearby counters which had once been used by other international carriers stood dusty and empty. No one searched my bags, and my overweight luggage was overlooked for a small fee. The airlines officials were friendly and cheerful.

Our flight was late in taking off. We had waited on the runway for an hour before the pilot announced that there was a delay in loading the baggage. I did not believe him, but when I looked out the window, I saw nothing suspicious. Another hour went by before the plane took off. As soon as we were aloft, stewardesses came round and served champagne to all the passengers.

It was not until I reached New York that I heard about the TWA plane that had been hijacked between Athens and Rome. Earlier that day, and again the next, it had landed in Beirut, where one of the American passengers was shot and killed, and thirty-nine American passengers were held hostage in Lebanon for the next two weeks.

Soon after I returned home I visited my father, who lived outside of Pittsburgh. The passage of time had done nothing to change his views about the Arab mind. Although he never discussed the matter with me, I later learned that he had tried to convince his Congressman that I should be rescued from Lebanon by helicopter.

An American friend from Lebanon persuaded me to volunteer to be interviewed by a Pittsburgh newspaper. Coming in the wake of the TWA hostage crisis, the subject of the interview, a plea for sympathy for the victims of war in Lebanon, was considered unusual enough to merit a front-page story. My father was so pleased that he brought up every copy of the paper at the newsstand. I doubt that I succeeded in winning him over, but he never brought up the subject of Lebanon again.

Postscript: December 1987

One day Daniel went to visit a cousin who lived in a village in the foothills of the Shouf Mountains north of Sidon. His cousin had a guest—a young soldier—who stared at Daniel for some time and finally said, "I know I've seen you somewhere before, but I can't remember where or when."

"I went to Bramieh with an American doctor a couple of months ago, and you threatened to kill me if I ever went back."

"Yes, now I remember! Well, I'm sorry."

"Never mind," said Daniel.

I returned to Lebanon for a two-week visit in November 1985. In the Beirut airport I went to the Lost and Found Department and located the suitcase that I had lost in Tunisia the previous spring. Hassan, the Middle East Airlines employee who worked in Lost and Found, was a bit hurt when I expressed some surprise at finding the bag. Why shouldn't it be there? he replied. My name and address were on it. Did I think that Lost and Found wasn't doing its job because a war was going on?

In the months since I had lost the suitcase, hundreds of people had been killed and kidnapped in battles near the Beirut airport. Some had been buried in mass graves; nobody was sure how many had died. But Hassan had a ledger where telexes about each lost bag had been stamped with the date received, and stapled to the page in neat rows. He took me to a hangar where hundreds of suitcases were stored in containers waiting to be claimed. There were no lights on in the hangar, but in the darkness Hassan unlocked one of the containers and dove inside with a cigarette lighter to retrieve my suitcase. The bag was locked, and I had lost the key, but the customs agent at the airport waved me past, and the bellboy at the Mayflower Hotel opened it for me with a sledgehammer.

Construction was going on all over Sidon, and in Ein el-Hilweh, where space was limited, buildings were spreading upwards instead of out. The Upper Street was being paved at last. People gathered outside the doors of their houses to watch as workmen rolled out a line of asphalt along the street.

On the day I visited our hospital Violet was in Beirut getting her hair done, but the rest of the staff was there. Nobody was sure how much longer the hospital would stay open, and people talked about looking for work elsewhere. Most of the doctors had thought of going abroad for more training, or finding a job somewhere in the Gulf.

Dr. Jawad seemed tired and discouraged. He still had not been able to organize his life into an orderly routine. After Ein el-Hilweh was shelled the previous spring, he had closed his clinic and moved his family to an apartment in Sidon. But his wife missed the camp, so after a while they moved back to their old house. He did not expect the hospital to stay open much longer, and talked of going to Saudi Arabia to work. But he was already in his forties, with a large family to support. It wouldn't be easy for him to make such a move and start over once again.

When I visited Dr. Jawad, the Lower Street around his house was being dug up while sewer lines were put in. There were huge mounds of earth along the sides of the street, and it was impossible to reach his house by car. Dr. Jawad was rattled by this upheaval and the dirt and the noise that went with it. Perhaps that was why he sounded gloomy that day. As he thought over his prospects, he did not feel that he had much to show for all his years of work as a doctor. "Really," he said, "if I had been a merchant, I think my situation would be better than it is now." Yet he had always hoped that his oldest son would go to medical school, and was very pleased when his son was accepted at the American University of Beirut. Another son was enrolled in a university overseas, and he hoped that his oldest daughter would study nursing.

Hanan listened as I read over some episodes from the story of her life which I had written down. She did not see why I was interested in them, but decided that she liked the way it all sounded.

"Really," she said, "I don't know the impossible." I was not so sure. Hanan had just told me her latest idea: to emigrate with her family to join one of her relatives, a wealthy doctor. The only problem was that he had left many years ago, and she did not know exactly where he lived. It seemed that at first he had gone to the United States, but now he was somewhere in South America. She wanted me to help her find him. She had just renewed her passport, she said, and was ready to leave at any time.

A few months after I left Lebanon, the Maroof Saad Foundation agreed to take over our hospital, but to stay open it had to make deep cuts in hospital services and staff salaries. Some members of our original staff still work there today.

Sidon was calm in November 1985, but in Ein el-Hilweh people worried about the pressure building up among the PLO factions in the camp. There had been two gruesome executions over the summer in an ongoing power struggle between Fateh and the Syrian-backed PLO faction led by Abu Musa. A battle had almost broken out a few days earlier after a succession of speakers at a rally had condemned the leadership of Yasser Arafat. Armed men were refusing to surrender their guns at the entrance to the hospital; a couple of days earlier, a man had threatened to blow up the hospital because he did not like the way his wife had been treated. Referring to the general feeling of helplessness these rivalries were generating around them, one of the medical clerks sadly recalled an Arab proverb: "When the elephants fight, the grass will be trampled." Meanwhile, Israeli reconnaisance planes flew overhead almost every day; people expected bombing raids to begin again soon.

They were right. Over the next two years the Ein el-Hilweh camp, already crowded with refugees who had lost their homes in the Camps War, became a frequent target of Israeli air raids. No justification had to be given for the raids, which were also carried out over Tripoli, the Shouf Mountains and the Bekaa valley; they were always described as being directed at "terrorist bases". But civilians were frequently killed and homes destroyed. According to eyewitness accounts, the heaviest losses in some raids occurred when planes returned to bomb an area as rescue attempts were under way. A raid which struck residential areas of Ein el-Hilweh on May 6 and 8, 1987 killed fifteen people, wounded fifty, and destroyed twenty houses, according to western relief sources. Most of the victims were women and children. On September 6, 1987 an air raid on a guerilla base near Ein el-Hilweh killed fifty-six and left one hundred and ninety wounded. Israeli Chief of Staff Dom Shomrom told the Knesset Foreign Affairs and Defense Committee that "no civilians were killed in the raid, unless by chance one happened to be inside the PLO base at the time." But according to UNRWA nine women were killed, and twenty-one of the wounded were women and children. Lebanese civilians were also killed in the raid.

The purpose of these air raids were seldom questioned. A few western reporters pointed out that Israel usually chose Palestinian targets even though most attacks against their troops in South Lebanon were conducted by pro-Iranian Lebanese fundamentalist militias. But one Israeli wondered aloud why the air raids had to take place at all. Naftali Ben-Moshe wrote in *Al Hamishmar* on May 12, 1987, "I find myself continually wondering just what good these IDF air raids against terrorist targets in and around the densely populated southern Lebanese refugee camps do for our defense—and what ethical justification they have. For every child killed in an air raid, ten new terrorists spring up. Is this the way to make Israel safe?"

Meanwhile, guerilla attacks continued in South Lebanon against Israeli soldiers and their allied militia, the South Lebanon Army, which occupied a six-mile deep "security zone" along Israel's border with Lebanon. Critics charged that Israel's continued presence on Lebanese soil served as a magnet which drew Moslem fundamentalist fighters to the area, but Israel insisted that the security zone was essential to protect its northern border.

Jerusalem *Post* reporter David Rudge writing in May 1987 noted that not a single Israeli civilian had been killed in an attack emanating from Lebanon in the two years that Israel had occupied the security zone. But during that same period of time, according to Financial *Times* reporter Nora Boustany, at least one hundred civilians had died in South Lebanon as a result of retaliatory attacks by Israel; this number does not include Palestinians and Lebanese killed in Israeli air raids on Palestinian camps. UN Secretary General Javier Pérez de Cuéllar called on Israel to withdraw from South Lebanon and allow UNIFIL troops to deploy south to Lebanon's border, as called for in its original mandate. But UNIFIL's future was put in question when the United States, the nation which had brought it into being, balked at paying its share of UNIFIL's $140 million budget; congressional leaders claimed the force was ineffective. (However, Congress has allocated $18.7 million for UNIFIL for 1988.)

Political alliances in Lebanon were undergoing another seasonal change. Amal and the PLO stopped fighting for a while during the summer of 1985, and some of the Palestinian families who had fled from their homes in Beirut's southern suburbs during the Camps War moved back again. However in the spring of 1986 fighting began again over the issue of the movement of men and weapons into Palestinian camps in Beirut and South Lebanon. The early battles had been confined to the camps in West Beirut—Sabra, Shatila and Burj el-Barajneh. But in October 1986 fighting started around the Rashadieh camp in Tyre, where there was a PLO presence. Amal laid siege to the camp and overran the unarmed camps of El Buss and Burj el-Shemali, burning homes and taking more than a thousand men into custody. In response PLO fighters in Sidon took over a number of Christian villages held by Amal to force Amal to stop the siege of Rashadieh. Then the Shatila and Burj el-Barajneh camps were attacked. (Sabra was destroyed during the first Camps War and was never rebuilt.)

The siege of the Beirut camps continued during the winter of 1986-7 and attracted worldwide attention when starving Palestinians inside the camps asked Moslem religious leaders for permission to eat human flesh. The arrival of a large contingent of Syrian troops in West Beirut in February 1987 brought a halt to the fighting, which had caused some nine hundred deaths. But hundreds of Palestinian men remained in the custody of Amal, and movement in and out of the Beirut camps was restricted. According to an UNRWA report quoted in *Al Fajr* in June 1987, more than half of the homes in the Tyre and Beirut camps were damaged or destroyed, but as of December of 1987 UNRWA had not been permitted to rebuild them. As winter approached more than 35,000 Palestinians displaced by the camps wars were still living in shelters, according to UNRWA. The fighting also damaged homes in the Shiite southern suburbs and displaced some 4,000 Christians from the village of Maghdushi near Ein el-Hilweh. Iranian negotiators worked on an agreement that would end the camps war, and high-level talks were held between Amal and PLO leaders, but there was no reason to believe that long-term solution could be found.

The battles fought around West Beirut were not confined to the camps. In November 1985 Amal militiamen turned against their usual allies, the Druze, in a bitter three-day battle for control of West Beirut. Because it allegedly began over an argument about lowering the Lebanese flag, it became known as the "flag war." Over sixty people were killed and 350 were wounded in the fighting, according to the *Daily Star*, and another 300 were kidnapped. As I drove through a Druze-held area north of Sidon one evening with some Palestinian friends, we saw trucks filled with Druze soldiers heading toward Beirut to join in the fighting. The soldiers at the Druze checkpoint were in a festive mood. When they saw that there were Palestinians in our car, one of them said, "Welcome! If you don't have a gun, we'll give you one."

But a few weeks later the two sides were sufficiently reconciled to join the leader of the Lebanese Forces in signing a series of accords worked out under Syrian sponsorship, including a peace treaty and a constitution giving Moslems and Christians an equal share of power in the government. Shiite leader Nabih Berri announced that the signing of the pact, which followed months of negotiations, meant that the war was over and a new era was beginning for Lebanon. But less than two weeks later President Gemayel, under pressure from Maronite leaders, unexpectedly rejected the accord.

Moslem ministers responded by refusing to hold any Cabinet meetings with the President. Rashid Karami, the Sunni Moslem Prime Minister, resigned in May 1987, citing his disillusionment with President Gemayel. A month later he was killed by a bomb which had been placed under his seat in a helicopter. More violence is expected in 1988, when a new Lebanese president will be elected.

The deadlock over government reforms and concern over the growing lawlessness of Lebanon's militias helped to undermine the economy. Between 1985 and 1987 the Lebanese pound lost eighty percent of its purchasing power. Upper class families with money invested overseas were protected from the pound's rapid decline, as were militias that got money and weapons from other countries. But middle class families were hit hard. By August 1987 the minimum monthly wage had dropped to sixteen dollars. In a survey conducted by *Le Commerce Du Levant*, an economic weekly published in Beirut, fifty percent of those responding said they spent all their income to buy food, and twenty percent said they had gone into debt to feed their families. Teachers reported that children were fainting from hunger in school, and people scavenged for food in garbage cans. Dr. Salim al-Hoss, Lebanon's acting Prime Minister, declared that "the militias are sucking the people's blood," while some militias showed their concern by expanding their humanitarian and social services to include public transportation, scholarships and subsidies for children's schoolbooks.

As of December 1987 nineteen foreigners, including eight Americans, were still held hostage in Lebanon. More than six thousand Lebanese and Palestinians have been abducted since the start of Lebanon's civil war, according to the International Committee of the Red Cross. Their families are rarely able to learn of their whereabouts, and militia leaders have provided Amnesty International with little information about them. The governments of Israel and Syria have not been helpful either. The Israeli Attorney General, responding to inquiries about prisoners held in Khiam, the prison run by the South Lebanon Army in Israel's security zone, said Israel was not responsible for the behavior of SLA soldiers; he offered no comment about allegations that torture of detainees in Khiam "sometimes took place in the presence of, or under the supervision of, members of the IDF or the Israeli security service," according to Amnesty's 1987 annual report.

The government of Syria did not respond to appeals made by Amnesty International concerning Lebanese prisoners transferred to Damascus for interrogation. Amnesty describes the torture of prisoners held in Syrian jails as "routine." In December 1986 Syrian troops and members of local pro-Syrian militias, responding to an attack in which fifteen Syrian soldiers were slain, killed an estimated two hundred Moslems in a thirty-six hour operation in the northern Lebanese city of Tripoli. According to witnesses and rescue workers, most of the vicitims were shot in the head. Many of them had been roused from sleep, including women and children. The event received little news coverage at the time. The London *Times* reported that many of the victims were later buried in mass graves. When asked about the incident, a Syrian government spokesman described it as an act of self-defense.

"You were working in *Lebanon*? But there's nothing left over there . . . is there?"

The news reports from Lebanon always sound the same: fighting breaks out again between rival militias. A bomb concealed in a car or a handbag or a suitcase or a box of candy explodes in a crowded area, killing and injuring scores of people. More dead bodies are uncovered somewhere, another camps war begins. Lebanon has almost faded from our consciousness: we do not understand what is happening there, and except for trying to recover our hostages, why should we care?

It does not seem likely that the Lebanese will be able to resolve their differences by themselves. Their president travels to foreign capitals seeking support from Yasser Arafat and Muammar Khadaffi, then tells a Maronite audience in New York that Christians and Moslems could live together in peace if foreign nations would stop meddling in their affairs. Lebanese political leaders are deadlocked, and even if they could agree on a program of political reforms, their militias would not be eager to surrender their weapons. There is not much reason to believe that countries supplying arms and money to Lebanese militias are interested in seeing an end to the fighting, either, for Lebanon has become the chessboard where neighboring states plot ways to block or outmaneuver each other. The conflict in Lebanon now reflects all the rivalries and unsolved problems in the region, particularly the long Iran-Iraq war and the Palestinians' need for a homeland.

There is an urgent need for humanitarian aid in Lebanon. The need cannot be measured merely by a look at the numbers, though they are staggering: more than 120,000 people have been killed in Lebanon and 150,000 seriously injured since the start of the civil war. According to the information office of Caritas, a Catholic relief agency, there are 50,000 orphans in Lebanon, and more than 625,000 Lebanese have been displaced from their homes. But it is more difficult to describe the war's terrible psychological impact. The Lebanese people have been betrayed by their leaders, and Lebanese society has been unravelled by a war which all sides have lost. Thousands of families have been uprooted from their homes and villages and have little hope of ever returning to them. The partitioning of Lebanon into religious and ethnic enclaves has made its people prisoners in their own country. There is no way they can escape from the stress caused by economic hardship and the constant threat of violence. The trust and tolerance that bound their society together is gone, and will take generations to restore. Life will not return to "normal" when the war comes to an end; Lebanon has changed forever, and no one can predict what will happen to it now.

Financial support is needed for reconstruction, food, clean water and public health projects in Lebanon. But just as important is the need for compassion and sympathy for the victims of the war. We must also listen to the grievances of the Lebanese and Palestinians, even though we may not agree with them. To do otherwise will increase the anger and bitterness in a younger generation which already feels it has nothing to lose, and will invite acts of violence and desperation for years to come.

Glossary

AUB: American University of Beirut

AUH: American University Hospital

Abu Ammar: Yasser Arafat

Amal: Shiite Moslem militia which grew out of the "Movement of the Disinherited," a social welfare organization begun by Imam Musa Sadr, spiritual leader of Lebanon's Shiites.

Druze: Islamic sect founded in Egypt in the late tenth century. Forced to flee because of religious persecution, the Druze settled in what is now Syria, Lebanon and Israel. In Lebanon the Druze make up about five per cent of the population.

Fedayeen: guerilla fighters

Hezballah: The "Party of God," a pro-Iranian Moslem fundamentalist militia.

ICRC: International Committee of the Red Cross

IDF: Israeli Defense Force—the Israeli army.

Lebanese Forces: Militia formed by Bashir Gemayel during Lebanon's civil war which incorporated the Phalangist militia and other Christian militias.

Maronite: Christian sect of Aramaic origin whose members fled to northern Labanon to escape religious persecution during the Byzantine Empire. They are the largest Christian sect in Labanon, making up about 25 per cent of the country's population.

Murabitun: Sunni Moslem militia based in West Beirut.

NSSP: National Syrian Socialist Party, a leftist Lebanese organization which advocates a merger of Syria and Lebanon.

Nasiriyyun: Nasserite Popular movement, a leftist coalition of Sunni Moslems in Sidon held by Mustafa Saad, who has his own militia and directs a social welfare program named after his father, Maroof Saad, a former mayor of Sidon assassinated in 1975.

National Guard: Group of Lebanese and Palestinian informers armed by Israel in South Lebanon.

PLO: Palestine Liberation Organization.

PRCS: Palestine Red Crescent Society, a network of medical clinics, hospitals, health care training and rehabilitation services affiliated with the PLO.

PSP: Progressive Socialist Party; political party founded by Druze leader Kamal Jumblatt. Since his assassination in 1977 the party and its associated militia have been led by his son Walid.

Palestinian: Resident, or descendent of a resident, of the area known as Palestine, who fled during the fighting that surrounded the creation of the state of Israel in 1948. Most Palestinians are Sunni Moslems.

Phalangist: Party founded by Christian leader Pierre Gemayel. Its constituents are primarily Maronite Christians. Its allied militia was later incorporated into the Lebanese Forces by Pierre's son Bashir.

Shiite: The largest minority sect of Islam, with about 80 million followers worldwide. Their name derives from *Shi'at Ali*, or followers of Ali. They broke away in the seventh century after the assassination of Ali, the son-in-law of the prophet Mohammed. They believe that Ali's descendants and a line of twelve *imams* (leaders) are the Prophet's lawful successors. Shiites are now the largest religious sect in Lebanon, comprising more than 30 percent of the population.

Souk: Marketplace

South Lebanon Army: Lebanese militia trained, outfitted and paid by Israel, which patrols Israeli-held territory in South Lebanon.

Sunni: Orthodox Moslem sect which regards the first four caliphs, religious leaders who were disciples of the prophet Mohammed, as his legitimate successors. They believe that he Koran and the hadith, the texts which record the sayings and deeds of Mohammed, form the *sunna* or beaten path. They comprise about 20 per cent of Lebanon's population.

Tal Zaatar: Palestinian camp in an industrial suburb of East Beirut which fell to Christian militias after a long siege in 1976.

Tawheed: Islamic Unification Movement; fundamentalist Sunni Moslem group and militia based in Tripoli.

UNIFIL: United Nations Interim Force in Lebanon, a peacekeeping force of about 5000 troops drawn from several countries which has patrolled a portion of South Lebanon since 1978.

UNRWA: United Nations Relief and Works Agency for Palestine Refugees in the Near East.

Acknowledgements

The people I knew in Sidon and Ein el-Hilweh will be surprised to find themselves in a book. Though only some of them are mentioned in these pages, they all contributed to it. This does not mean that they will be pleased with the result. They may feel that I have left out many important details, and they will wonder why I have included some stories and not others. I cannot give them a satisfactory answer. Many stories are still waiting to be told, and others can tell them better than I.

I want to express my thanks to friends and colleagues from Lebanon who commented on an early draft of this book: Sylvia Anderson, Kay Mc Divitt, David Huie, Marcia Stone and Barbara Pizacani, members of IRC's Lebanon medical team, and Dorothea Franck and Marilyn Raschka, editors of the newsletter of Americans for Justice in the Middle East, the voice of Beirut's uprooted American community. Ann Lesch, Trudy Rubin, Gail Pressberg, Ellen Siegel and Linda Butler provided valuable suggestions, and Salah Taamari offered general comments and literary advice. I owe special thanks to Abu Ahmad, Ibn Mohammed and Ibn Mahmoud, who gave careful answers to questions which arose long after I had left Lebanon, and to Nancy Brooks and Jane Kronenberger, whose wise comments prompted me to rewrite several chapters of this book.

James Fine, formerly of the University of Pennsylvania's Middle East Research Institute, and Marwan Bishara and the staff of Claremont Research and Publications provided me with access to much-needed source material. Robert Gallagher of UNRWA, James Graham of Amnesty International and Khatmeh Osseiran of Save Lebanon located some of the facts and figures which appear in these pages. Lenore Davis at the Johns Hopkins School of Hygiene and Public

Health helped me arrange my academic year so that I would have time to work on this book.

Mary Anne Caruso, Deborah Ruggeri and the staff of TOPS sent the manuscript on many trips through the word processor. Esther Cohen, Sandy Kadet and the staff of Adama Books have been delightful to work with. I would also like to express my gratitude to Larimer Richards, Larry Stern and Alfred Hyslop for their unwavering support.

This book does not do justice to the many voluntary agencies still working in Lebanon with limited budgets, low profiles and modest expectations. God bless them all.

Bibliography

Abu-Lughod, Janet. "The Demographic War for Palestine." *The Link*, 19: (December) 1986.

Advisory Committee on Human Rights in Lebanon, American Friends Service Committee. *Lebanon: Toward Legal Order and Respect for Human Rights*. Philadelphia: August 1983.

Amnesty International Reports 1984-1987. London: Amnesty International Publications.

Ball, George W. *Error and Betrayal in Lebanon*. Washington: Foundation for Middle East Peace, 1984.

Bryce, Jennifer. *Cries of Children in Lebanon*. UNICEF, Beirut, 1986.

Carter, Jimmy. *Keeping Faith: Memoirs of a President*. New York: Bantam Books, 1983.

Clifton, Tony and Leroy, Catherine. *God Cried*. London: Quartet Books Limited, 1983.

Cobban, Helena. *The Palestine Liberation Organization*. Cambridge University Press (Cambridge Middle East Library), 1987.

Gilmour, David. *Lebanon, The Fractured Country*. New York: St. Martin's Press, 1983.

Hirst, David. *The Gun and The Olive Branch: The Roots of Violence in the Middle East*. Norfolk: The Thetford Press Ltd. Second Edition, 1984.

Khalidi, Walid. *Conflict and Violence in Lebanon: Confrontation in the Middle East*. Cambridge: Center for International Affairs, 1978.

Nazzal, Nafez. *The Palestinian Exodus from Galilee 1948*. Beirut: The Institute for Palestine Studies, 1978.

Randal, Jonathan. *Going All the Way: Christian Warlords, Israeli Adventurers, and the War in Lebanon*. New York: The Viking Press, 1983.

Said, Edward W. *The Question of Palestine*. New York: Times Books, 1979.

Said, Edward et al. *A Profile of the Palestine People*. From the International Conference on the Question of Palestine, Geneva. Distribuited by the Palestine Human Rights Campaign, 1983.

Schenker, Hillel (ed.) After Lebanon: The Israeli-Palestinian Connection. New York: The Pilgrim Press, 1983.

Schiff, Ze'ev and Ya'ari, Ehud. *Israel's Lebanon War*. New York: Simon and Schuster, 1984.

Stevens, Janet. *The Israeli Use of U.S. Weapons in Lebanon*. Belmont: AAUG Press, 1983.

Timerman, Jacobo. *The Longest War: Israel in Lebanon*. New York: Alfred A. Knopf, 1982.

Weir, Ben and Carol with Dennis Benson. *Hostage Bound Hostage Free*. Philadelphia: The Westminster Press, 1987.

Wright, Robin. *Sacred Rage: The Wrath of Militant Islam*. New York: Linden Press, Simon and Schuster, 1985.

Yermiya, Dov. *My War Diary*. Boston: South End Press, 1984.

Information about UNRWA comes from the following sources:

Lilienfield, Lawrence et al. "UNRWA and the Health of Palestinian Refugees." *The New England Journal of Medicine*. 315: 595-600 (August 28), 1986.

Viorst, Milton. *UNRWA and Peace in the Middle East*. Washington: The Middle East Institute, 1984.

UNRWA Publications:

UNRWA's Emergency Operation in Lebanon: 1982-83. June 1984.

UNRWA: A Survey of United Nations Assistance to Palestine Refugees. March 1986.

UNRWA: Past, Present and Future. June 1986.

Guide to UNRWA. January 1987.

References

The articles below provide further details of some of the incidents referred to in the preceding pages. The division into distinct subjects is somewhat arbitrary, since articles often cover a number of subjects. I have tried to put each article into the category that best describes its primary theme.

The Shouf War and Aftermath:
1. Robert Fisk, "Ceasefire Agreed in Lebanon War," *London Times,* September 26, 1983.
2. Rebecca Trounson, "Flood of Refugees Creates Problems for Lebanese City, "*Boston Globe,* October 6, 1983.
3. William Claiborne, "Refugees Flooding Sidon," *Washington Post,* October, 8, 1983.
4. Lynda Shuster, "In Lebanon, Blockade of a Village Leaves Legacy of Bitterness," *Wall Street Journal,* January 6, 1984.
5. "117 Bodies Found in Lebanese Village Recaptured from Christians," *New York Times,* February 17, 1984.

Deir el Kamar:
1. Timothy Mc Nulty, "Village Faces 'Fight to the Death,'" *Chicago Tribune,* October 4, 1983.
2. Trudy Rubin, "Caught Between Warfare and Politics," *Christian Science Monitor,* October, 5, 1983.
3. Ihsan Hijazi, "Druze Forces to Lift Their Siege of Christian Town," *New York Times,* December 5, 1983.
4. Joseph Treaster, "Thousands of Christians Set Free as Druze End 3 Month Siege," *New York Times,* December 5, 1983.

Ansar Prison Camp:
1. David Shipler, "Defiance and Despair at Israeli Prison in Lebanon," *New York Times,* October 2, 1983.
2. Yeshaiahu Ben Porat and Eitan Hagger, "A Yellow Field Turned Trap for Israel," *Yediot Aharanot,* September 21, 1983, translated in *Al Fajr,* September 30, 1983.
3. Chaim Carney, "Amnesty Cites Israel for Arrests in Lebanon," *Jerusalem Post,* October 26, 1983.
4. David Shipler, "Palestinians and Israelis Welcome Their Prisoners Freed in Exchange," *New York Times,* November 25, 1983.
5. Edward Walsh, "Israeli Joyfully Welcomes 6 Home After PLO Swap," *Wahington Post,* November 25, 1983.
6. "IDF Releases All Ansar Prisoners," *Jerusalem Post,* November 25, 1983.
7. "Red Cross Reports Israel Reneged," *New York Times,* December 14, 1983.
8. "Israel Won't Release Additional Terrorist," *Jeruslem Post,* December 14, 1983.
9. UPI, "Lebanon Residents Say Israel Reopened Prison Camp," *Boston Globe,* January 3, 1984.

10. John Richardson, "Ansar: Israel's Grim Legacy to the History of Mass Detention," *Al Fajr*, December 30, 1983.

11. "Israel Still Holding 480 in Camps 'Closed' Last Year," *Toronto Star*, May 29, 1984.

12. "Ansar Escapees Hold Press Conference," *Al Fajr*, July 13, 1984.

13. "Israel is Accused of Jail Torture," *Toronto Star*, October 30, 1984.

14. Gershom von Schwartze, "From Berlin to Tel Aviv and Back," *Chotam*, April 11, 1986, reprinted in *Israel and Palestine*, September 1986.

Other Detention Centers in South Lebanon and Israel:

1. Marvine Howe, "Israel Said to Have Several Detention Camps," *New York Times*, August 27, 1982.

2. Orly Rappman, Every Ansarit Had Sombody at Ansar," *Ha'ir*, reprinted in *Al Fajr*, February 15, 1984. A description of the women's prison at Nabatieh.

3. "Red Cross Complains About Israel," *Jewish Telegraphic Agency*, June 11, 1984.

4. "Humanitarian and Legal Rights Denied 136 Prisoners in Israel," *Amnesty Action*, Amnesty International USA, June 1984.

5. Jeanne Butterfield and Salim Madi, "One Third of the Country Is 'One Big Prison,'" *The Guardian* (US), March 13, 1985.

6. Bernard Gwertzman, "U.S. Accuses Israel of Violating Pact on Shiite Captives," *New York Times*, April 4, 1985.

7. UPI, "Israel Frees 752 Prisoners in Lebanon," *Washington Post*, April 4, 1985.

8. Hugh Pope, "Lebanese Allege Abuses at Hands of Israeli Jailers," *Philadelphia Inquirer*, April 5, 1985.

9. Thomas Friedman, "1000 Prisoners Are Moved to Israel," *New York Times*, April 3, 1985.

10. Christopher Walker, "Peres Denies Breach of International Law in Transferring Prisoners," *London Times*, April 6, 1985.

11. Jim Muir, "Relief Officials Allege Torture in South Lebanon Jail," *Christian Science Monitor*, April 15, 1985.

12. Michael Addams, "Jerusalem Silent on 121 Missing POW's," *The Guardian*, April 16, 1985.

13. Thomas Friedman, "Legacy of War," *New York Times*, May 26, 1985.

14. "Israelis Assert Moving Shiites Was Not Illegal," *Washington Post*, June 20, 1985.

15. Dan Fisher, "Atlit Prison: An Israeli Fixture," *Los Angeles Times*, June 24, 1985.

Israel's 'North Bank':

1. William Claiborne, "Israel Razing Houses in Southern Lebanon," *Washington Post*, October 5, 1983.

2. Timothy J. McNulty, "South Lebanon Becomes Israel's 'North Bank,'" *Chicago Tribune*, October 5, 1983.

3. "IDF May Stay in Lebanon for Years, Peres Warns," *Jerusalem Post*, October 3, 1983.

4. Ya'acov Friedler, "Cease-Fire in Lebanon Restores Israeli Trade," *Jerusalem Post*, October 6, 1983.

5. David Zucchino, "In Lebanon, West Bank Tactics," *Philadelphia Inquirer*, October 9, 1983.

6. David Richardson, "Unease in Lebanon," *Jerusalem Post*, October 25, 1983.

7. Terence Smith, "At Least 39 Die as Truck Bomb Rips Israeli Post in Lebanon; Jets Strike Palestinian Sites," *New York Times*, November 5, 1983.

8. Christopher Walker, "Angry Israelis Press for Partition of Lebanon," *London Times,* November 7, 1983.

9. Menahem Horowitz, "Shiites on Strike," *Jerusalem Post,* November 9, 1983.

10. Menahem Horowitz, "Awali Traffic Now Requires IDF Permits," *Jerusalem Post,* November 18, 1983.

11. David B. Ottaway, "Israeli Security Steps in South Lebanon Curb Economy, Spur Opposition," *Washington Post,* December 3, 1983.

12. (Reuters), "Arrests Lead to Strike at Port," *The Guardian,* December 30, 1983.

13. Alan Cowell, "Israel Shuts off South Lebanon from the North," *New York Times,* December 31, 1983.

14. (Reuters), "Beirut Protest Israeli Actions to U.S.," *Washington Post,* January 1, 1984.

15. "No Winners at the Awali," (editorial) *Jerusalem Post,* January 1, 1984.

16. David B. Wilson, "Israel and the Litani," *Boston Globe,* January 22, 1984.

17. (Reuters), "Civilians Hurt as Israelis Fire in Sidon Streets," *The Guardian,* February 2, 1984.

18. Alan Copps, "South Lebanon Strike over Israeli Killings," *Daily Telegraph,* March 31, 1984.

19. "Ex-Coordinator of West Bank Takes Over in South Lebanon," *Jerusalem Post,* March 26, 1984.

20. (Reuters), "Radical Israelis Plan Settlement in South Lebanon," *Toronto Star,* December 29, 1984.

The National Guard:

1. Thomas Friedman, "For Israelis, Beirut Now Seems Only a Sideshow," *New York Times,* October 9, 1983.

2. Robert Fisk, "Israelis Set Up New Militias," *London Times,* October 13, 1983.

3. Ellen Powel, "Home Guard Defense," *Jerusalem Post,* October 20, 1983.

4. David Hirst, "Israel's Strange Partners in the Occupied Zone," *The Guardian,* August 14, 1984.

5. "Abdallah Nassers' Bullet-Ridden Body Found on Road." *Washington Post,* November 26, 1984.

6. (Reuters), "Two Palestinian Members of National Guard Found Slain," *Washington Post,* January 18, 1985.

The South Lebanon Army:

1. "Pro-Israel Militia to Lose Chief," *Chicago Tribune,* October 13, 1983.

2. Judith Miller, "Israel to Cut Reliance on Haddad Troops," *New York Times,* November 6, 1983.

3. "Major Saad Haddad, 47, Israel's Christian Ally in South Lebanon," (obituary) *New York Times,* January 15, 1984.

4. Hirsh Goodman, "Haddad's Death Opens Path to Lebanese Army," *Jerusalem Post,* January 15, 1984.

5. Joshua Brilliant, "A New Army Takes Shape," *Jerusalem Post,* March 23, 1984.

6. (Reuters), "Retired General Takes Over Israei-Backed South Lebanon Militia," *New York Times,* April 5, 1984.

7. Hirsh Goodman, "Lohad, Israel's Man in South Lebanon," *Jerusalem Post,* April 4, 1984.

8. Loren Jenkins, "Frail Force Key to Israeli Plans," *Washington Post,* August 14, 1984.

9. "Thirteen Muslim Villagers Slain by Militiamen," *Los Angeles Times,* September 21, 1984.

10. "SLA Groomed to Act As Israel's Seeing-Eye Dog," *Toronto Star,* September 21, 1984.

11. Hirsh Goodman, "Massacre Was 'A Private Act of Revenge,'" *London Times,* September 23, 1984.

12. "No Reason For Us to Be Here," *Ha'aretz*, translated in *Al Fajr*, October 12, 1984.

13. "Lahd Drops All Charges Against Sohmor Accused," *Daily Star*, October 13, 1984.

14. Menachem Horowitz, "Premier Takes First Tour of Lebanon, Lauds SLA," *Jerusalem Post*, November 9, 1984.

15. Mary Curtius, "Israel Losing Its Lebanese Militia as Withdrawal Nears," *Christian Science Monitor*, February 14, 1985.

16. "Israel's Ally in Lebanon Sees 'A Long War,'" *Los Angeles Times*, June 5, 1985.

17. "Incognito Israeli Troops Join SLA Militia as Withdrawal Hopes Fade," *London Times*, June 6, 1985.

18. Hirsh Goodman, "IDF Stays as SLA Melts," *Jerusalem Post*, June 7, 1985.

19. "The Burden of the SLA (editorial)," *Jerusalem Post*, July 8, 1985.

20. Nora Boustany, "Lebanese Charge Israeli-Backed Militia Tortured, Robbed Them," *Washington Post*, March 1, 1986.

21. Joel Greenberg, "Israel Likely to Increase Military Aid to South Lebanon Militia," *Christian Science Monitor*, September 22, 1986.

UNIFIL:

1. "Norway Takes on Israel," *Al Fajr*, November 18, 1983.

2. "U.N. Complains to IDF About 'Wild' Lebanese Militiamen," *Jerusalem Post*, February 10, 1984.

3. Alan Cowell, "After 5 Years, U.N. Lebanon Force Has Air of Permanance," *New York Times*, February 28, 1984.

4. (Reuters), "Israel Bars a U.N. Role at its Northern Border," *New York Times*, March 20, 1984.

5. "Bewitched and Bewildered," (editorial) *Jerusalem Post*, March 20, 1984.

6. "UNIFIL Under Orders to Shun South Lebanon Army," *Jerusalem Post*, July 19, 1984.

7. (Reuters), Associated Press, "Fistfight Erupts as UN Troops Defy Israelis," *Toronto Star*, February 15, 1985.

8. Christopher Walker, "French Fury Grows over Rabin Slur," *London Times*, February 28, 1985.

9. Dan Fisher, "UN Role: Trying to Shield Lebanese from Violence," *Los Angeles Times*, March 14, 1985.

10. David Landau, "Israel Is Unhappy Over UNIFIL Plan," *Jerusalem Post*, March 29, 1985.

11. Robin Lustig, "Lebanon's UN Peacekeeping Force Faces Axe," *The Observer*, April 21, 1985.

12. "29 Soldiers of UN Seized by Militia in South Lebanon," *New York Times*, June 6, 1985.

13. "Unfortunate Incident," *Jerusalem Post*, June 9, 1985.

14. "Kidnapped UN Soldiers Accuse Israelis," *London Times*, June 13, 1985.

15. Robert Fisk, "UN Troops Caught in South Lebanon's Bitter Crossfire," *London Times*, December 19, 1985.

16. Curtis Wilkie, "Timor Göksel: A Middle East Reporter's Best Friend," *Boston Globe*, July 25, 1986.

17. David Rudge, "'Iron Fist' To Meet Attacks Against UNIFIL, Says Amal," *Jerusalem Post*, August 25, 1987.

The Lebanese Forces in South Lebanon and Israel, 1984-5:

1. Bradley Graham, "Christian Militia Says Understanding with Israel Set," *Washington Post*, January 28, 1984.

2. Robert Fisk, "Israelis Call on Christian Extremist to Help Fight

South Lebanon Guerillas," *London Times,* February 4, 1984.

3. David Bernstein, "Phalange to Close All Barracks South of Awali," *Jerusalem Post,* February 15, 1984.

4. Nicholas B. Tatro, "Lebanese Militia Plans Israel Office," *Philadelphia Inquirer,* May 9, 1984.

5. Edward Grossman, "Lebanese Christians Open Jerusalem Liason Bureau," *Jerusalem Post,* May 18, 1984.

6. "Fears of Religious Division Haunt South Lebanon," *Le Monde,* translated in *Manchester Guardian,* October 14, 1984.

7. David Hirst, "The Blood-Stained Legacy of an Invasion," *The Guardian,* April 2, 1985.

8. Christopher Walker, "Christian Militia Role in Sidon Battlefield Points to New Amity with Israel," *London Times,* April 3, 1985.

David and Captain Albert:

1. David Zucchino, "Israel in Lebanon: A Heavy Price for Both Sides," *Philadelphia Inquirer,* June 27, 1984.

2. "A Disturbing Incident," *Middle East International,* July 27, 1984.

3. David Hirst, "The Borderline Between Caprice and Cruelty," *The Guardian,* August 13, 1984. Provides a sketch of Captain Albert.

Events in Ein el-Hilweh, May 1984:

1. J. Michael Kennedy, "Israel Destroys Homes in Refugee Camp Sweep," *Los Angeles Times,* May 26, 1984.

2. Associated Press, "Woman Reported Slain in a Palestinian Camp," *New York Times,* May 18, 1984.

3. David Lennon, "Israel Denies Camp Shootings," *Financial Times,* May 18, 1984.

4. Hugh Orgel, "Israeli Planes Bomb Terrorist Base and Training Center in Lebanon," *Jewish Telegraphic Agency.* Records IDF's version of Israeli searches in Ein el-Hilweh and subsequent demonstrations and shooting.

5. Menahem Horowitz, "Violence at Ein el-Hilweh Camp After Israeli Arms Searches," *Jerusalem Post,* May 17, 1984.

6. "Palestinian Mother Killed by Militia," *London Times,* May 18, 1984.

7. J. Michael Kennedy, "Palestinian Woman in Refugee Camp Killed in Second Day of Violence," *Los Angeles Times,* May 18, 1984.

8. Reuters, "Woman Killed in Palestinian Camp," *The Guardian,* May 18, 1984.

9. Norman Kempster, "Israel Lists Arms Uncovered in Palestinian Sweep," *Los Angeles Times,* May 19, 1984.

10. Timothy J. McNulty, "Bloody Struggle for Dominance Rekindles Terror in Refugee Camp," *Chicago Tribune,* May 21, 1984.

11. Edward Walsh, "Israel Limits Reporters Access in South Lebanon," *Washington Post,* May 21, 1984.

12. "Ein el-Hilweh Quiet; IDF Attacked," *Jerusalem Post,* May 21, 1984.

13. "Refugee Casualty Toll 60," *The Guardian, May 22, 1984.*

Bater:

1. Alan Copps, "Israeli Blockade Traps Drivers up to 6 Days," *Daily Telegraph,* April 9, 1984.

2. "Israel Blocks Fuel Supply to Lebanon," *The Guardian,* June 6, 1984.

3. David Zucchino, "Israel Controls and Exploits Passage into South Lebanon," *Philadelphia Inquirer,* June 7, 1984.

4. John Kifner, "South Lebanon: A Trauma for All Sides," *New York Times,* July 22, 1984.

5. John Kifner, "Israelis Seal Road to South Lebanon," *New York Times,* August 21, 1984.

266

6. James Ferron, "Shamir Defends Moves in Lebanon," *New York Times,* August 29, 1984.

7. Agence France Presse, "Refugee Aid Blocked by Israelis," *London Times,* October 11, 1984.

UN Security Council Vote and Aftermath, August-September 1984:

1. "Lebanon Says U.S. Not Restraining Israelis," *Boston Globe,* August 19, 1984.

2. Nora Boustany and David Lennon, "Lebanon Plans UN Protest at Israeli Actions in the South," *Financial Times,* August 23, 1984.

3. David Hirst, "Karami Tells U.S., 'Go to the Devil,'" *The Guardian,* September 8, 1984.

4. John Kifner, "23 Die, Including 2 Americans, In Terrorist Car Bomb Attack on the U.S. Embassy at Beirut," *New York Times,* September 21, 1984.

5. "There is No Doubt Among the Lebanese About Why Embassy Was Bombed," *Los Angeles Times,* September 23, 1984.

6. "U.S. Intensifies Pressure for Israeli Pullout," *Financial Times,* September 25, 1984.

Israeli Occupation and the Resistance: June 1984-March 1985:

1. "PLO Again Makes Inroads into Lebanese Political Life," *Lebanon News,* June 10, 1984.

2. "Muslim Sheikh from Sidon Forced to Leave South Lebanon," *Philadelphia Inquirer,* July 18, 1984.

3. "South Lebanon Strikes to Protest Sheikh's Expulsion," *Al Fajr,* July 20, 1984.

4. John Kifner, "Rival Leftist Militias Battle in Beirut," *New York Times,* July 30, 1984. Mentions death of Mohammed Mabrouki.

5. "IDF Issues Directive Forbidding Display of Photos of Foreign Leaders," *Jewish Telegraphic Agency,* August 10, 19984.

6. Loren Jenkins, "Growing Lebanese Resistance to Occupation Confronts Israel," *Washinton Post,* August 11, 1984.

7. Robert Fisk, "Turn of the Tide, But Not Only Israel Will Suffer," *London Times,* September 24, 1984. Refers to the expulsion of four western journalists from South Lebanon on the orders of the IDF.

8. Loren Jenkins, "Arafat's Guerillas Resume Using Beirut Camps as Base," *Washington Post,* September 29, 1984.

9. Reuters, "Sniping Recurs in Beirut; Protests Continue in Sidon," *Washington Post,* November 30, 1984.

10. Menahem Horowitz, "Trade with Lebanon Drops Following Threats and Violence," *Jerusalem Post,* November 7, 1984.

11. "Attacks Increase As Lebanese Resistance Tallies Strikes," *Al Fajr,* November 30, 1984.

12. Menahem Horowitz, "IDF Captures 8 Terrorists," *Jerusalem Post,* January 1, 1985.

13. John Kifner, "Israelis Raid Moslem Villages in Lebanon's South," *New York Times,* February 7, 1985.

14. Reuters, "Anti-Israeli Strike Paralyzes Towns, Roads in South Lebanon," *Toronto Star,* February 8, 1985.

15. Thomas Friedman, "Lebanese Attacks Against Israelis and Their Agents Are up Sharply," *New York Times,* February 12, 1985.

16. Thomas Friedman, "Israelis Press for Quicker Pullout from Lebanon Than Is Planned," *New York Times,* February 20, 1985.

17. "They Shot at Those Who Had Surrendered," Al Ittihad, *Ha'aretz,* February 28, 1985. Translated in *Al Fajr,* March 1, 1985.

Nakoura Talks and Preparations For Israel's Withdrawal for South Lebanon:
1. "Cabinet Unanimously Approves Rabin's Plans for Negotiating a Political-Military Solution in South Lebanon," *Jewish Telegraphic Agency,* September 29, 1984.
2. Thomas Friedman, "U.S. Declines to Take Mideast Mediator Role," *New York Times,* November 2, 1984.
3. Thomas Friedman, "Lebanese Meet with Israel About a Pullout," *New York Times,* November 9, 1984.
4. "UN Fear for Palestinians After Israeli Pullout," *London Times,* November 17, 1984.
5. UPI, "Lebanese Clashes Threaten Troop Deployment," *Boston Globe,* December 3, 1984.
6. Charles P. Wallace, "Israeli Talks on Lebanon Pullout Close to Collapse," *Los Angeles Times,* January 7, 1985.
7. Thomas Friedman, "Israel Announces 3 Stage Plan to Leave Lebanon," *New York Times,* January 15, 1985.
8. Christopher Walker, "South Lebanon Fears Revenge Bloodbath When Israelis Withdraw," *London Times,* January 15, 1985.
9. Robert Fisk, "UN Plans Secret Move into Sidon," *London Times,* January 28, 1985.
10. John Kifner, "Fear Enters Lebanese City as Israelis Leave," *New York Times,* January 30, 1985. Refers to presence of Lebanese Forces near Jezzine.
11. John Kifner, "Israeli Pullout: New Attacks Are Feared," *New York Times,* January 31, 1985.
12. Reuters, "Israel Warns 35 Nations of Massacres," *Philadelphia Inquirer,* January 31, 1985.

13. Hirsh Goodman, "The Beginning of the End," *Jerusalem Post,* February 1, 1985.
14. Robert Fisk, "Gun Battles Break Out in Sidon," *London Times,* February 2, 1985.
15. Tom Masland, "Resentful Charges Follow Withdrawing Israelis," *Philadelphia Inquirer,* February 16, 1985.
16. Thomas Friedman, "Israel Completes a Step in Pullout in South Lebanon," *New York Times,* February 17, 1985.
17. Andrew Tarnowski, Reuters, "The Streets Resound with Jubilation," *Philadelphia Inquirer,* February 17, 1985.
18. Jonathan Randal, "Gemayel, in Sidon, Praises 'Resistance,'" *Washington Post,* February 17, 1985.
19. "Gemayel and Army Get Big Welcome," *The Guardian, February 18, 1985.*
20. John Kifner, "Sidon Erupts in Celebration After Pullout," New York Times, February 17, 1985.
21. John Kifner, "Shiite Radicals Throng to Sidon for a Big Rally," *New York Times,* February 19, 1985.

Foreboding in Mieh Mieh:
1. Robert Fisk, "Sinister Change on a Windy Hill," *London Times,* February 13, 1985.
2. Tom Masland, "Israel's Pullout Raises Fear in a Lebanese Village," *Philadelphia Inquirer,* February 17, 1985.
3. Stephen Handleman, "Small Village Tells Real Tragedy of Lebanon," *Toronto Star,* February 22, 1985.

Mustafa Saad Bombing and Aftermath:
1. John Kifner, "Key Sunni Is Hurt in South Lebanon," *New York Times,* January 22, 1985.
2. Nora Boustany, "Car Bomb in Sidon Injures Sunni Leader," *Washington Post,* January 22, 1985.

3. Edward Walsh, "Bomb Reflects Sidon's Fears," *Washington Post,* January 23, 1985.

4. Christopher Walker, "Sidon Bombing Protests Overshadow Progress in Israel Pullout Talks," *London Times,* January 23, 1985.

5. Hirsh Goodman, "Many May Have Wished Death of Sunni Leader," *Jerusalem Post,* January 23, 1985.

6. Associated Press, Reuters, "Strike Paralyzes Sidon in Wake of Car Bomb," *Jerusalem Post,* January 23, 1985.

7. Reuters, "Pro-Israeli Militia Leader Leaves Sidon Suddenly," *Jerusalem Post,* January 25, 1985.

8. Robert Fisk, "Collaborators Flee Sidon," *London Times,* January 25, 1985.

9. Reuters, "Unity at Muslim Funeral," *The Guardian,* January 26, 1985.

10. John Kifner, "Amid Sidon's Joy, A Settling of Scores Begins," *New York Times,* February 18, 1985.

11. Mustafa Saad, "Another Way to Control Lebanon," *New Statesman,* May 17, 1985.

Israel's 'Iron Fist' Policy:

1. Robert Fisk, "Villages Raided by Israeli Troop in 'Iron Fist' Roundup of Guerillas," *London Times,* February 21, 1985.

2. Reuters, "Ex-Mayor Said to Die in Raid by Israelis," *New York Times,* February 23, 1985.

3. Associated Press, "Israeli Tank Units Raid 7 Villages in South Lebanon; 20 Are Dead," *Washington Post,* February 24, 1985.

4. John Kifner, "Israel Force Raids Lebanese Village," *New York Times,* March 3, 1985.

5. Nora Boustany, "An Israeli Checkpoint: A Violent Slice of War," *Washington Post,* March 4, 1985.

6. Menachem Horowitz, "IDF Imposes New Restrictions on Lebanon South of Litani," *Jerusalem Post,* March 4, 1985.

7. Ihsan Hijazi, "Blast in Lebanon Kills 15 in Mosque," *New York Times,* March 5, 1985.

8. Reuters, "Israelis Reportedly Storm South Lebanon Hospital," *Los Angeles Times,* March 5, 1985.

9. Reuters, "Israelis Deny Abuses," *New York Times,* March 9, 1985.

10. David Hirst, "Israel's Fistful of Wrath," *The Guardian,* March 6, 1985.

11. "Feeding a Golem," (editorial), *Jerusalem Post,* March 6, 1985.

12. John Kifner, "Car Bomb Hits an Israeli Convoy in Southern Lebanon, Killing 12," *New York Times,* March 11, 1985.

13. Nora Boustany, "Israeli Raid Kills 34 in Town in South Lebanon," *Washington Post,* March 12, 1985.

14. Julie Flint, "Israelis Show Zrariye Their Iron Fists," *The Guardian,* March 13, 1985.

15. Ian Black, "Jerusalem Plans to Speed Up Withdrawal," *The Guardian,* March 14, 1985.

16. Ihsan Hijazi, "Israelis Kill 21 in Lebanon Sweep; 2 Members of CBS News Crew Die," *New York Times,* March 22, 1985.

17. "Complete Withdrawal in 10 Weeks, Says Peres," *Jerusalem Post,* March 18, 1985.

18. Christopher Walker, "UN Spells out High Cost of Israel's Iron Fist Policy," *London Times,* March 21, 1985.

19. Thomas Friedman, "The Israelis' Iron Fist," *New York Times,* March 23, 1985.

20. Julie Flint, "Grieving Lebanese Give Details of Atrocities of Israeli Raiders," *The Guardian,* March 23, 1985.

21. "IDF's 'Iron Fist' Kills 70 Guerillas," *Jerusalem Post*, March 29, 1985.
22. Thomas Friedman, "Israel's Troops Are Leaving, but the 'Lebanon Problem' Persists," *New York Times*, March 31, 1985.
23. Menachem Horowitz, "Hundreds of Shiias Flee South Lebanon Villages," *Jerusalem Post*, April 1, 1985.
24. "Timely Withdrawal," (editorial), *Jerusalem Post*, April 26, 1985.
25. "Israeli Soldiers in Lebanon," *Al Fajr*, May 10, 1985. Translations of interviews from several Israeli newspapers with soldiers who had participated in 'Iron Fist' operations.

Revolt of the Lebanese Forces and the Shelling of Sidon:
1. John Kifner, "Christian Forces in Lebanon Rise Against Leader," *New York Times*, March 14, 1985.
2. UPI, "Militia Rebels, Army Clash in South Lebanon," *Los Angeles Times*, March 19, 1985.
3. Ihsan Hijazi, "Christian-Moslem Fighting Paralyzes Lebanese Port," *New York Times*, March 20, 1985.
4. William Claiborne, "Sectarian Battle Flares in Lebanon," *Washington Post*, March 20, 1985.
5. Charles P. Wallace, "Strife Ends Dancing in Port City's Streets," Los Angeles Times, March 21, 1985.
6. Julie Flint, "Struggle for Sidon Cuts off Families," *The Guardian*, March 21, 1985.
7. Associated Press, "Lebanese Christian Guns Said to Kill 40 in Sidon," *New York Times*, March 31, 1985.
8. "PLO Returns to Southern Lebanon," *Philadelphia Inquirer*, March 30, 1985.
9. Nora Boustany, "Sectarian Fighting Numbs Sidon," *Washington Post*, April 1, 1985.
10. Robert Fisk, "36 Killed as Phalangists Shell Sidon," *London Times*, April 1, 1985.

11. Robert Fisk, "Phalangist Group to Quit Sidon Hills," *London Times*, April 23, 1985,.
12. Christian Villages Set Ablaze in Muslim Raid Near Sidon," *Philadelphia Inquirer*, April 26, 1985.
13. Robert Fisk, "50,000 Christians Flee to Safety of Southern Lebanon," *London Times*, April 26, 1985.
14. Ihsan Hijazi, "Palestinian and Moslem Militias Capture, Loot and Burn Lebanese Christian Towns," *New York Times*, April 27, 1985.
15. Ihsan Hijazi, "As Lebanon's Christians Yield Towns, Druze Seize Coast Highway," *New York Times*, April 27, 1985.
16. Edward Blanche, Associated Press, "Lebanese Forces Replace Leader," *Washington Post*, May 10. 1985.

Israel's 'Security Zone':
1. "Isreal's Christian Buffer Zone," *Newsweek*, December 26, 1983.
2. Joshua Brilliant, "Token Force In Lebanon 'Indefinitely,'" *Jerusalem Post*, February 8, 1985.
3. "The Illusion of the Security Belt," *Al Fajr*, May 7, 1985. Translations of articles from *Al Hamishmar* and *Ha'aretz*, April 24, 1985.
4. "IDF Using Iron Fist in Buffer Zone," *Jerusalem Post*, May 31, 1985.
5. John Kifner, "Pullout Nearing an End, Some Isrealis Not Expected Home," *New York Times*, June 1, 1985.
6. "Israel Says Pullout Has Ended," *Philadelphia Inquirer*, June 7, 1985.
7. Thomas Friedman, "Some Israelis Stay Behind in Lebanon," *New York Times*, June 7, 1985.
8. Ze'ev Shiff, "The Making of a Security Zone," *Ha'aretz*, June 11, 1985.
9. Edward Walsh, "Israeli 'Security Zone' Angers Shiites," *Washington Post*, June 27, 1985.

10. Thomas Friedman, "The Choice in Lebanon. Israel Is Debating Its Security Zone," *New York Times,* July 10, 1985.

11. Gideon Samet, "Lebanon—Chapter Two," *Ha'aretz,* March 12, 1986.

12. Augustus R. Norton, "Defuse Southern Lebanon Now," *New York Times,* April 11, 1986.

13. Julie Flint, "Israel's Open Secret is a Closed Land," *The Observer,* June 8, 1986.

14. David Rudge, "Desertions Force SLA to Begin Recruitment Drive," *Jersualem Post,* December 29, 1986.

15. David Rudge, "Israel As Guardian," "Uniform Aims," *Jerusalem Post,* May 29, 1987.

16. Nora Boustany, "Lebanon 'Martyrs' Step Up Attacks," *Financial Times,* June 10, 1987.

17. Thomas Friedman, "Shiites' Raids Goad Israel to Respond," *New York Times,* September 29, 1987.

The Camps Wars:

1. Nora Boustany, "Shiites Battle Palestinians in Beirut," *Washington Post,* May 21, 1984.

2. Robert Fisk, "Shia Militia Attack PLO in Beirut Camps to Stifle Arafat's Influence," *London Times,* May 21, 1985.

3. Nora Boustany, "Beirut Car Bomb Kills 60; Fighting in Camp Spreads," *Washington Post,* May 23, 1985.

4. Tom Masland, "Palestinians Are Reported Summarily Executed in Beirut," *Philadelphia Inquirer,* May 25, 1985.

5. "Palestinian Toll Is Reported High in Beirut Slayings," *New York Times,* May 27, 1985.

6. John Bulloch, "Syria to Blame for an Arab Tragedy," *Daily Telegraph,* May 28, 1985.

7. Nora Boustany and Tony Walker, "Palestinians Seek Refuge from a Storm of Killing," *Financial Times,* May 28, 1985.

8. Richard Johns, "Brutal Logic of Beirut Bloodshed," *Financial Times,* May 29, 1985.

9. "Deafening Silence," (editorial), *Wall Street Journal,* May 30, 1985.

10. Tony Walker, "Gemayel Asks Syria for Help to End Bloodshed in Beirut," *Financial Times,* May 30, 1985.

11. "Gemayel and Assad Agree on Plans to End Lebanon Conflict," *Financial Times,* June 1, 1985.

12. "It Was Harder Than They Thought," *The Economist,* June 2, 1985.

13. "Palestinians Face More Carnage in Fight to the Finish," *London Times,* June 2, 1985.

14. "Shatila Refugees Bury Casualties," *Washington Post,* June 7, 1985.

15. "Arabs Turn Down 'Massacre' Inquiry," *London Times,* June 10, 1985.

16. Jonathan Randal, "Beirut Cease-Fire Pact Seen as Retreat for Syria," *Washington Post,* June 19, 1985.

17. "Beirut Cease-Fire Permits Rescue of the Wounded," *New York Times,* June 20, 1985.

18. "Amnesty Wants Probe of Beirut Camp Events," *Jerusalem Post,* July 21, 1985.

19. Ihsan Hijazi, "Lebanese in South Report Blocking Palestinian Arms," *New York Times,* July 21, 1985.

20. Nora Boustany, "Factions Battle for Beirut Camps; Concern Mounts That Shiite-Palestinian Conflict May Spread," *Wahington Post,* April 1, 1986.

21. Nora Boustany, "Fighting Intensifies in Beirut," *Washington Post,* June 1, 1986.

22. "Siege and Starvation: The Story of Three Palestinian Refugee Camps in Lebanon." *Palestine Human Rights,* Special Report, March 1987. Pro-

vides detailed chronology of 1986-87 camps war.

23. Nora Boustany, "Syrians Enter Beirut Camp; Refugees Decribe Horrors," *Washington Post*, April 8, 1987.

24. Godfrey Jansen, "The Victors and the Losers in the War of the Camps," *Middle East International*, April 17, 1987.

25. Zahra al-Bahr, "The Frozen Siege of Chatila," *Middle East International*, June 12, 1987.

26. "Turmoil Continues Five Years After Invasion of Lebanon," *Al Fajr*, June 14, 1987.

Israeli Air Raids in South Lebanon, 1986-7:

1. Dan Fisher, "Israeli Jets Strike Palestinian Camps in Lebanon," *Los Angeles Times*, March 28, 1986.

2. Thomas Friedman, "Israel's New Tactic," *New York Times*, September 26, 1986.

3. Nora Boustany, "Israeli Jets Hit Bases in North Lebanon," *Washington Post*, October 7, 1986.

4. Ian Black, "Israel in New Lebanon Attack," *The Guardian*, February 14, 1987.

5. Naftali Ben-Moshe, "Our Planes Attacked Terrorist Bases in Lebanon," *Al Hamishmar*, May 12, 1987.

6. "Lebanon's Latest Accord," (editorial), *Jerusalem Post*, May 29, 1987.

7. Joshua Brilliant, "Shomron Raps Air Raid Critic," *Jerusalem Post*, September 9, 1987.

8. "UNRWA Provides Relief for Civilian Survivors of Air Raid in Lebanon," *UNRWA press release*, September 14, 1987.

The Lebanese Economy:

1. Joyce Starr, "Lebanese Economy: Costs of War," *Christian Science Monitor*, January 5, 1984.

2. Roger Cohen, "War's Winners," *Wall Street Journal*, March 27, 1984.

3. Ihsan Hijazi, "Lebanon is Fearful of Shortages," *New York Times*, August 17, 1987.

4. Robin Mannock, "Inflation Puts Squeeze on Lebanon's Education," *Boston Globe*, October 11, 1987.

5. Ihsan Hijazi, "Lebanon's Militias Providing Social Services," *New York Times*, October 18, 1987.

6. Nora Boustany, "Lebanese Cope with Economic Crisis," *Washington Post*, October 26, 1987.

7. Robin Mannock, "Lebanon Stunned by Currency's Free Fall; Strike to Begin Today," *Boston Globe*, November 5, 1987.

Hostages/Casualties/Human Rights:

1. Robin Wright, "The Search for the Missing Is Lebanon's Next Agony," *Christian Science Monitor*, July 15, 1984.

2. "Beirut Publishes List Of Hostages; Yeilds to Demands of Relatives," *New York Times*, August 13, 1984.

3. Reuters, "Big Rise in Lebanon Deaths," *London Times*, January 3, 1986.

4. Mohammed Hussein Fadlallah, "To Avoid a War of Terror," *Washington Post*, April 6, 1986.

5. "Hostages in Lebanon: And Others," *The Economist*, July 5, 1986.

6. "1986 Toll in Lebanon," *Washington Post*, January 2, 1987.

7. "Raid in Lebanon took High Toll of Anti-Syrian Fundamentalists," *Washington Post*, January 13, 1987.

9. Jim Muir, "Waite and the Hostages: Why Are They Being Held?" *Middle East International*, February 6, 1987.

10. Caroline Moorehead, "Syrian Troops Accused of Massacring 200 in North Lebanon," *London Times*, March 14, 1987.

11. Associated Press, "Amnesty Accuses Syria of Abuses in Lebanon," *Washington Post,* March 14, 1987.

12. Mendel Weinbach, "David's Slingshot," *Jewish Press,* May 29, 1987.

13. "Lebanon Civil War Victims Begin Protest March," *Boston Globe,* October 13, 1987.

14. Rev. Benjamin Weir, "Seize the Present While There Is Still a Measure of Hope," *Palestine Focus,* September-October 1987.